D1765042

Public Diplomacy and
International Politics

Public Diplomacy and International Politics

THE SYMBOLIC CONSTRUCTS OF SUMMITS AND INTERNATIONAL RADIO NEWS

Robert S. Fortner

PRAEGER SERIES IN POLITICAL COMMUNICATION

Westport, Connecticut
London

Library of Congress Cataloging-in-Publication Data

Fortner, Robert S.
    Public diplomacy and international politics : the symbolic
constructs of summits and international radio news / Robert S.
Fortner.
      p.   cm. — (Praeger series in political communication, ISSN
1062–5623)
    Includes bibliographical references.
    ISBN 0–275–93594–9 (alk. paper)
    1. Radio journalism. 2. Radio broadcasting—Political aspects.
3. Summit meetings. 4. World politics. I. Title. II. Series.
PN4784.R2F67 1994
070.4'332—dc20   93–37879

British Library Cataloguing in Publication Data is available.

Library of Congress Catalog Card Number: 93–37879
ISBN: 0–275–93594–9
ISSN: 1062–5623

First published in 1994

Praeger Publishers, 88 Post Road West, Westport, CT 06881
An imprint of Greenwood Publishing Group, Inc.

Printed in the United States of America

The paper used in this book complies with the
Permanent Paper Standard issued by the National
Information Standards Organization (Z39.48–1984).

10 9 8 7 6 5 4 3 2 1

Contents

Illustrations

FIGURES

Series Foreword

Those of us from the discipline of communication studies have long believed that communication is prior to all other fields of inquiry. In several other forums, I have argued that the essence of politics is "talk" or human interaction.[1] Such interaction may be formal or informal, verbal or nonverbal, public or private, but it is always persuasive, forcing us consciously or subconsciously to interpret, to evaluate, and to act. Communication is the vehicle for human action.

From this perspective, it is not surprising that Aristotle recognized the natural kinship of politics and communication in his writings *Politics* and *Rhetoric*. In the former, he establishes that humans are "political beings [who] alone of the animals [are] furnished with the faculty of language."[2] And in the latter, he begins his systematic analysis of discourse by proclaiming that "rhetorical study, in its strict sense, is concerned with the modes of persuasion."[3] Thus, it was recognized more than twenty-three hundred years ago that politics and communication go hand in hand because they are essential parts of human nature.

Back in 1981, Dan Nimmo and Keith Sanders proclaimed that political communication was an emerging field.[4] Although its origin, as noted, dates back centuries, a "self-consciously cross-disciplinary" focus began in the late 1950s. Thousands of books and articles later, colleges and universities offer a variety of graduate and undergraduate course work in the area in such diverse departments as communication, mass communication, journalism, political science, and sociology.[5] In Nimmo and Sanders' early assessment, the "key areas of inquiry" included rhetori-

cal analysis, propaganda analysis, attitude change studies, voting studies, government and the news media, functional and systems analyses,
technological changes, media technologies, campaign techniques, and
research techniques.[6] In a survey of the state of the field in 1983, the same
authors and Lynda Kaid found additional, more specific areas of concern such as the presidency, political polls, public opinion, debates, and
advertising, to name a few.[7] Since the first study, they also noted a shift
away from the rather strict behavioral approach.

A decade later, Dan Nimmo and David Swanson argued that "political communication has developed some identity as a more or less
distinct domain of scholarly work."[8] The scope and concerns of the area
have further expanded to include critical theories and cultural studies.
While there is no precise definition, method, or disciplinary home of the
area of inquiry, its primary domain is the role, processes, and effects of
communication within the context of politics broadly defined.

In 1985, the editors of *Political Communication Yearbook: 1984* noted that
"more things are happening in the study, teaching, and practice of
political communication than can be captured within the space limitations of the relatively few publications available."[9] In addition, they
argued that the backgrounds of "those involved in the field [are] so
varied and pluralist in outlook and approach, . . . it [is] a mistake to
adhere slavishly to any set format in shaping the content."[10] And more
recently, Swanson and Nimmo called for "ways of overcoming the
unhappy consequences of fragmentation within a framework that respects, encourages, and benefits from diverse scholarly commitments,
agendas, and approaches."[11]

In agreement with these assessments of the area and with gentle
encouragement, Praeger established in 1988 the Praeger Series in
Political Communication. The series is open to all qualitative and
quantitative methodologies as well as contemporary and historical
studies. The key to characterizing the studies in the series is the focus
on communication variables or activities within a political context or
dimension. As of this writing, nearly forty volumes have been published
and numerous impressive works are forthcoming. Scholars from the
disciplines of communication, history, journalism, political science, and
sociology have participated in the series.

I am, without shame or modesty, a fan of the series. The joy of serving
as its editor is in participating in the dialogue of the field of political
communication and in reading the contributors' works. I invite you to
join me.

                                                    Robert E. Denton, Jr.

NOTES

1. See Robert E. Denton, Jr., *The Symbolic Dimensions of the American Presidency* (Prospect Heights, IL: Waveland Press, 1982); Robert E. Denton, Jr., and Gary Woodward, *Political Communication in America* (New York: Praeger, 1985; 2d ed., 1990); Robert E. Denton, Jr., and Dan Hahn, *Presidential Communication* (New York: Praeger, 1986); and Robert E. Denton, Jr., *The Primetime Presidency of Ronald Reagan* (New York: Praeger, 1988).

2. Aristotle, *The Politics of Aristotle*, trans. Ernest Barker (New York: Oxford University Press, 1970), 5.

3. Aristotle, *Rhetoric*, trans. Rhys Roberts (New York: The Modern Library, 1954), 22.

4. Dan Nimmo and Keith Sanders, "Introduction: The Emergence of Political Communication as a Field," in *Handbook of Political Communication*, ed. Dan Nimmo and Keith Sanders (Beverly Hills, CA: Sage, 1981), 11–36.

5. Ibid., 15.

6. Ibid., 17–27.

7. Keith Sanders, Lynda Kaid, and Dan Nimmo, eds., *Political Communication Yearbook: 1984* (Carbondale: Southern Illinois University, 1985), 283–308.

8. Dan Nimmo and David Swanson, "The Field of Political Communication: Beyond the Voter Persuasion Paradigm," in *New Directions in Political Communication*, ed. David Swanson and Dan Nimmo (Beverly Hills, CA: Sage, 1990), 8.

9. Sanders, Kaid, and Nimmo, xiv.

10. Ibid., xiv.

11. Nimmo and Swanson, 11.

Acknowledgments

This book developed from a suggestion made by David Paletz at the IAMCR Conference in Barcelona that I develop a book based on a paper I presented on the 1987 Washington summit. I remain grateful for his suggestion, despite the enormous task that acting on it created. Once under way, I could not have completed the task without outside help. The BBC Monitoring Service, Radio Netherlands, and the Voice of America all taped portions of the broadcasts used in the analysis when I was unable to do so because of other commitments. Ginger De Silva, Elizabeth Smith, and Sam Younger all provided useful perspectives in the early going. Jeremy Curtin helped keep me on track in assessing the changing public diplomacy environment in 1988. I am most grateful to four people who agreed—probably against their better judgment—to slog through the entire manuscript and keep me honest. Each of them caught a variety of egregious errors and thus contributed greatly to the quality of the final product. They are Stanton Burnett, Randall Bytwerk, Alan Heil, and Graham Mytton. I remain in their debt, even when I chose to disagree with them in the final product. I must therefore be held accountable for whatever errors may remain.

Calvin College deserves special mention, too, for providing a faculty research grant that allowed me to devote three months' full-time work to data coding. Kathleen Lewis-Workman, one of my students, contributed greatly to the coding process during the long summer of 1991, a time we seem to have spent with earphones on, struggling to hear through the static that seemed to bedevil essential stories.

As so many authors before me have said, my family must receive special mention. I spent too much time away from them while dutifully recording programs night after night: They undoubtedly came to rue any announcement of another summit meeting. My wife, Marcia, and son, Matthew, even bravely helped record from time to time, preventing an irrecoverable gap in the data. They rose to the occasion even when Peter and Rachael refused to acknowledge the significance of the task. I offer all of them my deepest gratitude.

Public Diplomacy and International Politics

Chapter 1

Introduction

This book began as a book about politics, aimed at addressing two questions: What (if anything) does the use of international shortwave radio by countries around the world contribute to the new world information and communication order (NWICO) debate? Were U.S. efforts to exercise "public diplomacy" through the media effective in influencing how news organizations reported news, specifically, U.S.–Soviet summit meetings?

Each of these questions implied subordinate issues as well. Concerning the NWICO debate, the principal issue was whether, given a variety of radio services reporting on a single event, it mattered which service a listener tuned in? That is, would the report of an event vary from one service to another, and would ideology play a role in determining what or how extensively services reported, what their sources of stories were, or how they would play different aspects of the event? Would it make any difference if the reporters at an event were from Western countries, socialist countries, or developing countries? Or was it the existence or absence of information that was crucial to what was reported, and how?

The second issue—the use of media as vehicles of public diplomacy—also implied subordinate concerns. Was the Voice of America (VOA) truly an independent news medium?[1] Did the existence of military and political alliances, such as NATO and the Warsaw Pact, affect the coverage of events that might influence their strategies or operations? Or were "news values" themselves—the significance of stories, the existence or absence of other important stories on any given day, the geographical proximity of events, timeliness, or availability of information—the determining factors in what news was reported, and how?

Events caught up with the research. What began as a study that concentrated on the superpowers and their allies, that assumed the existence of an Iron Curtain and irreconcilable ideologies, and that was premised on the staging of infrequent summits to iron out differences between warring ideologies found itself overrun by events. One summit ended only to have another announced. Relations between the superpowers thawed, and one of them tumbled toward collapse. The Iron Curtain crumbled. Each country tried to outdo the other in proposing deeper and deeper cuts in nuclear, and eventually conventional, arms. Old disputes—Afghanistan, Angola, Nicaragua—were no longer intractable. China became the new communist bully, quashing the democratic aspirations of its own citizens. The Soviets and some American reporters declared that the Cold War was ending.[2]

All of this required the analytic frame to shift. New questions emerged. Did the winding down of the Cold War reduce the level of propaganda by any news organization? Did the new freedoms in central and Eastern Europe loose new approaches to reporting news about the West? Did the thaw between the superpowers give Western European radio news services new boldness in asserting points of view? Would political rhetoric cool as quickly as the apparent rapprochement warmed? Or would the old shibboleths die harder? Did Gorbachev, sitting at the head of an "evil empire," really matter?[3] Would a new U.S. president make a difference, particularly one apparently more interested in foreign policy? Did the rest of the world care?

Although all of this delayed the book, I hope the events allowed it to become more interesting, even if more difficult to construct. From being just a work on politics, it also became a book of history. The basics are the same: How did the news organizations of international shortwave radio services cover superpower summits and ancillary summit meetings between the 1987 Washington Reagan–Gorbachev summit and the 1990 Washington Bush–Gorbachev summit meeting? What did these organizations say? Where did their information come from? How extensive was their coverage? What patterns can be discerned in their coverage? How did they treat the principals, their respective countries and discussions, in news programs? Whose point of view or policy perspective was paramount in the coverage—a U.S. view, a Soviet view, a European, Asian, or other view?

The summits covered by this research are as follows:

Washington, D.C.	Ronald Reagan–Mikhail Gorbachev	December 1987
Moscow, U.S.S.R.	Ronald Reagan–Mikhail Gorbachev	June 1988
Beijing, China	Mikhail Gorbachev–Deng Xiao Peng	May 1989
Brussels, Belgium	NATO Member States	May 1989
Malta	George Bush–Mikhail Gorbachev	December 1989
Washington, D.C.	George Bush–Mikhail Gorbachev	May 1990

The 1987 Washington summit marked the first visit to the United States by a Soviet general secretary since that of Leonid Brezhnev in 1973. The following year's Moscow summit was the first visit to the Soviet Union by a U.S. president since Gerald Ford's 1974 visit. Both were thus historic. Gorbachev was from a new generation of Soviet leadership: he would see the United States firsthand.[4] Reagan's acceptance of the offer to visit a land he had called an "evil empire" was equally significant: He would also see firsthand whether the portrait he had painted of the Soviet Union was true.

Gorbachev's visit to Beijing was equally significant, for two reasons. First, it marked the first visit between Soviet and Chinese heads of state since the falling out of the two communist giants nearly twenty years earlier. Second, Gorbachev's visit to Beijing and the accompanying press coverage contributed to the decision of Chinese students to occupy Tiananmen Square, seeking the same political freedoms Gorbachev had begun to introduce into the Soviet Union. While Gorbachev was in Beijing, the students protested with little interference, building a statue of the Goddess of Democracy but setting into motion the confrontation that would eventually result in the Tiananmen Square massacre, within a few days of Gorbachev's departure.

Later in the same month NATO members met in Brussels to consider what the changes in Eastern Europe and the thawing of the relations between East and West would mean to the future of the alliance. They also discussed approaches to arms control issues, including conventional force reductions in Europe, and continued the dialogue on this issue set into motion by reduction rhetoric from Moscow. At this summit, as Beschloss and Talbott put it (1993, p. 80), George Bush "scored his first major foreign-policy success of his presidency," by proposing significant conventional forces reductions in Europe and suppressing interalliance squabbles over deployment of short-range nuclear weapons.

Following George Bush's inauguration in January 1989, if the improved relations between the United States and the Soviet Union were to continue, a new round of summit talks would have to begin. Thus the Malta "get acquainted" summit (also called the "seasick summit") was arranged, occurring in neither principal country, but in neutral seas on Soviet and U.S. warships.[5]

Finally, to round out the analysis, a return to Washington. By this time the Iron Curtain was down, and the new East-West issues were the impending reunification of Germany and its involvement in NATO and the beginning of the breakup of the Soviet empire itself, with the demand for independence by the Baltic states of Estonia, Latvia, and Lithuania.

It would be impossible to listen to all the news reported by international radio stations, particularly in the multiple languages they use directed all around the globe. This book, therefore, although it offers a comprehensive examination of the treatment of a set of specific events by a variety of radio services, cannot be seen as definitive. No single effort could achieve a definitive view.

Three aspects of this book lead me to refer to it as comprehensive. First, as my study focused on summit meetings and as the participating countries usually announce the dates months in advance, I could use a defined time frame to examine each summit. This time frame began one week prior to the announced first day of summit meetings and ended one week after the last day of the summit. Most individual analytic time frames were seventeen days in duration, depending on the length of the summit itself.[6]

Second, I could identify several days in advance of the analytic time frames the most complete news broadcast available from a given radio service and could select services for each summit that would provide points of view potentially contrasting with those of the United States and the Soviet Union themselves. In addition to recording the Voice of America and Radio Moscow for each summit, I also recorded the British Broadcasting Corporation (BBC) World Service, generally acknowledged as the premier international radio news operation in the world. Beyond these three services, my priorities were to try to record at least one NATO country's radio service, one Warsaw Pact country's service, and then other services I could locate from other parts of the world. Services recorded for one or more summits were Deutsche Welle (West Germany), Radio Berlin (East Germany), Radio Netherlands, Brussels Calling (Belgium), Radio Spain, Radio Switzerland International, Radio Budapest (Hungary), Radio Bucharest (Romania), Radio Sofia (Bulgaria), Radio Prague (Czechoslovakia), Voice of Turkey, Voice of Baghdad (Iraq), Voice of Cairo (Egypt), Radio Israel, Radio South Africa, Radio Canada, Radio Havana (Cuba), All India Radio, Radio Australia, Radio Japan, Voice of Free China (Taiwan), and Radio Beijing (People's Republic of China).

Third, within each broadcast, I coded stories according to a general definition of what constituted a summit story. That is, not only did I code stories that were obviously about the summit itself, but I also coded stories about other events or containing opinions concerning topics that were under discussion at, or related to, the summit. For instance, since the question of Soviet involvement in Afghanistan was a matter of discussion at the 1987 Washington summit, I coded all stories about the conflict in that country during the time frame, even if there was no summit "hook" for the story. I adopted this procedure to assure that the services' inclusion of summit stories within a larger context that might affect interpretations of the summit itself could be examined. This procedure increased the total number of coded stories for each summit.

Despite the effort to be comprehensive, however, there are limitations. First, the exclusive use of English as the broadcast language examined obviously reduces the ability to determine whether the same approach to a story or its perceived significance changes from one language to another. It was possible to see whether the same approach was used in broadcasts to different parts of the world, however, as the broadcasts recorded across the summits included English-language services directed to North America, South America and the Caribbean, Africa, and Europe.

Second, because of propagation limitations inherent in the use of shortwave radio, I could not hear some days' reports at all, and on other days the broadcasts were subject to so much interference that I could not understand the stories. For several days during the 1987 Washington summit, Radio Japan's satellite feed to Gabon was disabled, so that the station broadcast no news—which normally was relayed from Tokyo via satellite and broadcast to North America from Africa No. 1's Gabon site.

Third, the nature of the broadcasts recorded changed over the four-year period of the recording. This occurred because the services changed the time of broadcasting a particular type of program or because they altered their approach to a given program over time.[7] They dropped some program elements and added others, as they changed their priorities or altered their strategies for attracting specific (and perhaps new) audiences. This meant that, even when the stations recorded over the entire study maintained relatively consistent schedules (as in the case of BBC, Radio Moscow, and VOA), the recorded news formats differed. The BBC reworked its news programming about halfway through the four-year period, and Radio Moscow included and excluded different elements over the period. For recordings of the Voice of America, the daily editorial sometimes followed a news program and at other times did not.

Several radio services also begin their daily news broadcasts with "headlines," followed by longer versions of the same reports. I did not code the headlines, as they were nothing more than truncated versions of the stories; and I did not want the analysis to give the impression that the services had reported more stories or spent more time on the reports than was the case. This required judgment calls, however. The BBC, for instance, often reported complete stories, using as the source a BBC correspondent in Moscow or Washington. Following a set of such stories, it would then introduce an amplifying news segment, "correspondent's reports" that would contain the original report and additional analysis or information. In these cases I coded both stories, the first as part of the BBC's "world news" and the second as part of its "news analysis." Thus, it was possible that two stories would be ranked number one for that day. This situation also pertained occasionally to other services as well.

Such approaches enhanced the effort to determine the nature of reporting by the various radio services. The point was not to pick up every single reference to a summit meeting in every news broadcast of every day. Rather it was to compare and contrast the nature of the reporting that characterized the broadcasts of the services: whether they depended on firsthand or secondhand reports of events, whether they incorporated sound bites as part of their report, and whether they stuck to the facts or attempted to impart presence, contextualize, or analyze facts for their listeners. If they moved beyond the practice of ripping wire copy and reading it over the air, did the approach they adopted explain more fully the unfolding events?

When I began work on the first summit in 1987, I was fortunate enough to be able to interview the counselor of the United States Information Agency (USIA), who was organizing the summit venue, press credentials, and other details. From him I learned that the National Security Council, an advisory group to the president on matters of national security, had adopted a set of themes, or "talking points" as Stan Burnett called them, that were to guide U.S. spokespersons' statements to the press. This approach reflected the Reagan administration's belief in the potency of what was called public diplomacy, which had been promulgated and defended by Charles Z. Wick, then director of USIA.[8]

The belief in the efficacy of public diplomacy led the Reagan administration to begin such projects as Radio and eventually Television Martí, directed to Cuba, and Worldnet Television, a global set of satellite links to U.S. embassies that could be used to set up interactive press conferences between U.S. administration officials and journalists and government functionaries in foreign countries. Worldnet also originally delivered other active and passive programming to U.S. compounds abroad. All of these were controversial initiatives, both within the Congress and among the foreign policy establishment, including professionals in USIA and VOA.

Although this belief has only indirectly been confirmed by other sources, I suspected that this talking point strategy was also partly defensive.[9] Reagan had frightened his advisors, arms control experts and foreign policy analysts as well as the U.S. diplomatic corps, at the previous summit with Gorbachev in Reykjavik. There he had seemed prepared to agree, with little prior briefing or consideration, to massive cuts in the U.S. nuclear arsenal. I saw the talking point strategy as an effort to rein Reagan in, to prevent another potentially dangerous off-the-cuff comment that might compromise U.S. security or create domestic political problems, either with arms control experts among the Democrats, such as Senator Sam Nunn, or with the conservative wing of the Republican Party itself.

Because these talking points were not classified, I was free to use them as part of the basis for examining the recorded news broadcasts. This provided the ability to answer one specific question: Did public diplomacy work? Under the Reagan administration public diplomacy was clearly focused. USIA under Wick fought for budget increases to modernize VOA, to set up new surrogate radio services, and to start up Worldnet. USIA's budget increased by 93% from 1981 to 1986. All of this was done, as Wick put it, to get the U.S. story across to a worldwide public using the "vanguard of the tidal wave of technology and information" ("Wick, Worldnet and the War of Ideas," 1986, pp. 78, 80). With the enormous effort made to get the U.S. position across to the world's press (as well as through U.S.–sponsored organizations such as the VOA and Worldnet), surely the talking points would surface in officials' comments at the summits. If not, questions about the efficacy of investing in public diplomacy would emerge.

This approach worked well for the 1987 Washington summit. What had begun as five succinctly stated talking points in 1987, however, expanded to over three pages of single-spaced type for the 1988 Moscow summit. The National Security Council (NSC) seemed more enamored than ever with the idea, although its enthusiasm made my coding using twelve talking points with various permutations an enormous undertaking. Even more disconcerting, however, were two other problems. First was the change in U.S. administrations (of course anticipated) and the NSC's decision to drop explicit guidelines for U.S. administration spokespersons. This decision reaffirmed my view of the defensive or fearful posture of the NSC under Reagan, but it made the coding process for Malta 1989 and Washington 1990 more problematic. Even more troublesome was the other set of changes: the end of the Cold War, the Velvet Revolution in eastern and central Europe, and the beginning phases of the breakup of the Soviet Union itself. As Mason (1992, p. 160) put it, "The disappearance of the communist threat . . . left the United

States in a conceptual 'vacuum.' The Cold War had always provided a framework for U.S. foreign policy and had dictated its foreign, military, and national security policies. . . . With containment of communism no longer necessary after 1989, the United States lost this conceptual framework for its foreign policy." Without such a framework, and absent explicit statements about the goals of the Bush administration for the Malta and Washington summits, was it possible to continue to assess the effectiveness of public diplomacy? Most of this type of diplomacy occurred through United States Information Service (USIS) posts in American embassies. Without specific talking points, the entire public diplomacy effort might resubmerge, at least insofar as this research was concerned, even if it were more natural for the administration to trust these well-established and proven channels.

I leave it to the reader to determine how well I was able to adapt to changing world circumstances in completing this work. Flexibility in thinking, even while remaining constant in method and perspective, was required.

The basic methodology used in this study was content analysis. I coded each story according to a schematic that was constant in some respects and in others was evolving. Once a summit was recorded, I did not return to recode it according to some different schematic that had emerged in response to world events. I did not code the first two superpower summits recorded, for instance, on the issue of whether the Cold War was ending or was over. There was little question in 1987 and 1988 that the Cold War was alive and well. This question was significant, however, by the time of the Malta summit. Some of the services claimed it was over; others, that it was ending; still others, that it continued. Treatment of the question of the Cold War thus seemed appropriate where it had not before. Likewise, during the 1987 Washington summit, the issue of disinformation as a Soviet tool of public diplomacy and of Western access to the Soviet public through the media was a live issue. By 1989, however, it was not: Gorbachev's *glasnost* initiative had taken root, and Soviet citizens were experiencing new freedom to express themselves and to seek out information.

The basic coding scheme for all summits included calculations of the number of summit stories broadcast, the placement of these stories, and their length. These measures allowed calculations of the relative importance that each service placed on the summits. It also allowed a time series analysis over each two-week period to determine whether the service was "reactive" or "contextual" in its approach to summits. The Western press tradition is a reactive tradition. When events occur, the press is there to report what happened. A reactive news organization would report about the summit or about pre- and post-summit press conferences and interviews as they occurred: I could expect that such an organization's number of stories, placement, and time would be a function of events. A contextual news organization's stories, however, would not necessarily respond quantitatively to the events themselves. The Soviet press tradition was of this sort: It sought to explain the significance of events within a predefined ideological context.

The Western tradition has the advantage of fostering independence from government. It has the disadvantage, however, of being prone to manipulation by government. Its very practices suggest the means to manipulate: Call a press conference and create what Daniel Boorstin called a "pseudo-event," one designed for a single purpose, to get media attention (Boorstin, 1964).

The Soviet tradition, however, accepted government control as legitimate. What mattered was ideological consistency. All events were understood within the doctrines and policies of the state that defined them, using the presumptions of ideology: historical materialism, the conflict with capitalist-based industrial powers, the state as the manifestation of the people's will to egalitarianism and justice, and so on. The disadvantages of such an approach for news coverage are apparent. It also had advantages, however. These include reporting "the day's events in a context which gives them meaning," to use one of the phrases from the 1947 report of the Commission on Freedom of the Press (p. 20).[10] As Mehta (1987) put it, Soviet media "conform to certain basic norms, the most important being to operate in the framework of the political system and to support the ideology on which the system is based" (p. 12; see also Siebert, Peterson & Schramm, 1956, Chapter 4, for a discussion of Soviet press theory). Another advantage from the Soviet perspective was that the reporting was not hostage to events themselves. Rather than reacting to events, reports of events would be inserted into an ongoing stream of information serving ideological certainty.[11]

The paradox of Soviet media theory is that, although it provided the basis for comprehensively contextualizing the confusing array of news stories occurring worldwide on a daily basis and thus making sense of them for audiences, it was, as an inherent function of this ability, what would be considered propagandistic in the West. In other words, its strength, to interpret and to construct meaning for its audiences based in ideological certainty, was also the means to obfuscate and twist events to force them to release their "truth." What could have been meaningful news was often what Jowett and O'Donnell (1986) have defined as propaganda: "the deliberate and systematic attempt to shape perceptions, manipulate cognitions, and direct behavior to achieve a response that furthers the desired intent of the propagandist" (p. 16; see also Ellul, 1973, p. 61, for another definition of propaganda). I wanted to be more circumspect in this analysis, however, separating if possible the process of contextualization from propaganda per se. This, I thought, would provide a more analytic precision. I didn't want to assume that all analysis and contextualization occurring in news products are by their nature propagandistic.

Also, although propaganda is a pejorative term in Western press theory, it was not so in Soviet ideological theory. The Soviets separated two concepts, propaganda and agitation, that Western theory tends to consider together. Ellul (1973), for instance, claims that "true modern propaganda seeks . . . to obtain an *orthopraxy*—an action that in itself . . . leads directly to a goal" (p. 27). In Soviet theory, propaganda is the "dissemination of political, philosophical, scientific, artistic, or other views or ideas, with the aim of instilling them in the public consciousness and encouraging mass action" (*Great Soviet Encyclopedia*, vol. 21, p. 269). The encouragement mentioned, however, is more passive than the expectation of agitation, which is defined as "a weapon in the struggle between classes and their parties. Agitation is the spreading of a certain idea or slogan that arouses the masses to action" (*Great Soviet Encyclopedia*, vol. 1, p. 137). The difference here is significant. Propaganda, by this distinction, aimed to inculcate views (hence the "war of words" with the United States, aimed at "winning the hearts and minds" of the world's peoples). Although the aim was "action," the propaganda was not aimed, in its own right, at fomenting revolution, as Ellul's notion of orthopraxy suggests. Agitation, however, was so directed. It was the repetitive use of particular phrases or slogans (e.g., "Liberté, Égalité, Fraternité!") for the express purpose of inciting action.

For the purposes of this analysis, the separation of contextualization from propaganda was operationalized as follows. The two approaches to news (reactive and contextual) were used as operational equivalents to Western and Soviet definitions of the function of the press. At one end of a continuum, then, was "value-free" reactive practice; at the other, value-laden contextual practice. Any radio service, according to the nature of its reporting, could find itself anywhere along this continuum and could find that its position had shifted from one summit to the next.

Propaganda was operationalized using a numeric technique adapted from Janis and Fadner (1949, pp. 153–169) and applied by Lindahl (1978, p. 197). This approach measured the relative significance of positive versus negative presentations of particular issues or personalities. The technique was modified to account for degrees of bias in presentation, to quantify the degree to which presentations could be judged propagandistic. A service, for instance, might be highly contextual in its approach to the news, but still be neutral in its presentation of the U.S.

and Soviet presidents, their countries' activities, or particular foreign policy positions. (This is explained in greater detail in Chapter 4.)

Another set of coded items concerned the sources for the stories reported. Were sources of information acknowledged? Was coverage live? Who was quoted? What sound bites were incorporated? The issues here concerned whether a radio service would change the nature of its coverage because of the place of origination (Washington, Moscow, Beijing, Brussels, Malta) or would strive to achieve a consistent approach to the event regardless of location. Some analysts have suggested that a major determinant of news covered is "proximity." If that were true, then I could expect the amount and type of coverage provided by, say, Voice of America would differ depending on whether the summit was held in the United States or elsewhere. Western European coverage would increase if a summit were held in Europe and decline when the site shifted to North America or Asia.[12]

Still another set of coded items concerned the focus of news reports. The summits provided a variety of possible news items. Reports might center on particular summit agenda items (which the participating countries would busily try to influence prior to the beginning of the meetings), on pseudo-events such as Reagan's speech in Helsinki on his way to Moscow or Gorbachev's interview on ABC prior to his second Washington summit, on the men themselves or their wives, on ancillary issues such as Jewish emigration from the Soviet Union, and so on. There were enough potential stories that a service, if it chose to do so, could avoid dealing with the "substance" of the summit meetings altogether.

There was also the matter of treatment of the summit "principals," including the United States and the Soviet Union in most cases, but also China during the Gorbachev–Deng summit. It also included the major actors themselves—Bush, Deng, Gorbachev, and Reagan—as well as Raisa Gorbachev and Nancy Reagan. When the women accompanied their husbands on summit trips, speculation abounded concerning their relationships with their husbands and each other. Barbara Bush, however, was never a summit principal.

This set of items concerning the treatment accorded to summit principals was designed as a litmus test largely for determining how the world's radio press was defining the relationship of the superpowers. Reagan, prior to the Washington summit, had labeled the Soviet Union an "evil empire." Yet Britain's Margaret Thatcher had endorsed Mikhail Gorbachev as a man the West could "do business with." Would the press separate Gorbachev from his empire, tar them with the same brush, or allow his acknowledged charisma to "rub off" on the Soviet Union? Would Reagan's reputation as a "shoot from the hip" president affect the treatment of the United States? In other words, did the man define the country or vice versa?

The next set of coded items was the National Security Council talking points. Were they affirmed or denied by the news organizations, by those whom they chose to quote, or by the sound bites the news organizations chose to include? Were they included at all? In other words, were the official positions that the U.S. government wanted to espouse to the world's peoples being presented by the radio press?

Finally, a potpourri of items concerned the treatment of issues that were summit-specific. These included such items as the end of the Cold War, domestic Soviet issues (e.g., the development of *glasnost* and *perestroika*), references to earlier summit meetings, treaty adherence or violations, regional conflicts, and so on. The radio services could choose how to apply a summit "hook" to a particular story; the question was whether they chose to do so and, if so, how.

The use of time series analysis with each summit period has already been discussed. I was also able to complete a second time series analysis across the six summits to determine whether the nature of coverage within a service changed over the period. This analysis had to be somewhat circumspect, because of the changes in format, inclusion and exclusion, and specific programs recorded from one summit to the next. In other words, the data from a given service over the four-year period were not always comparable. Nevertheless, some useful analysis was possible, particularly as regards Radio Moscow and the Eastern European services, whose focus and approach changed dramatically prior to the 1989 Malta summit. The Cold War mentality of the Western services, too, began to thaw prior to the 1990 Washington summit, which also could be portrayed from the data.

I have already referred to the general reasons for initiating this research. As a result of deciding to continue the effort after the first Washington summit and based on the data collected, the specific questions that this book now addresses are as follows:

- Perhaps most significant, but completely unanticipated in 1987, is the question of whether *glasnost* made a difference in the reporting of Radio Moscow and the Soviet Union's European allies, of whether the Velvet Revolution mattered?[13]

- Did it matter that a listener to international radio news selected one service or another? Were the differences in defining what was newsworthy, how to report the news, on what to concentrate, and how much attention to devote to these stories significant from one news organization to another?

- Do these services make a difference in how we should judge the debate over a new world information and communication order? Does the admitted domination of the world's wire and television services by Western countries also carry over into radio services?

- What difference, if any, did the declared end of the Cold War have on the reporting of news about the two superpowers or on their relationship with each other and the rest of the world? (There were still two superpowers when this research time frame ended.)

- Does public diplomacy work, insofar as the activities of international radio news organizations are concerned? Were the U.S. government's efforts to put across its versions of events, or its spin on them, successful in influencing how summit stories were reported? Did Washington set the agenda for the international radio press? Did the ideological commitments of individual radio stations insulate them from U.S. public diplomacy efforts or make them more likely to be sympathetic to these efforts?

- Does the conventional wisdom about decision-making by the press (which emphasizes such elements as proximity, timeliness, and geographical bias) apply to international radio services? Or are there different explanatory variables to use in understanding their behavior in selecting and reporting the news?

A limited theoretical perspective has been developed in this chapter as the basis for introducing the research. Further theoretical development will come in subsequent chapters as the results are discussed. First, however, a historical overview and discussion of the four-year period under review here is useful. News is never reported in a vacuum. News reporters function within a historical context that they do not control, although they may help to alter it. That context is framed by such factors as the ideological commitments of states and parties, the definitions and declared characteristics of adversaries and enemies that emerge from such commitments, and the symbolic and rhetorical constructs used as shorthand descriptors by the press that provide "meaning" grounded in these characteristics. Although such descriptors do not necessarily "explain" anything, they do provide the basis for the press to report news efficiently.

NOTES

1. By independent I mean free of political pressure in choosing news stories and approaches to them. Hachten (1987, p. 97) claims that

USIA and VOA have long had an identity crisis: are they objective news and cultural organizations reflecting the diversity of American life and culture or are they arms of the State Department, vigorously pushing U.S. foreign policy objectives? . . . The long-running dispute over VOA, the "government mouthpiece," vs. VOA, the "public radio," continually tests what VOA staffers know as the "charter"—Public Law 94–350, which was the result of years of feuding between VOA news editors and foreign service officers who wanted VOA controlled and censored.

To what extent, then, was VOA a mouthpiece, and to what extent was it independent in making news judgments?

2. Gennadi Gerasimov, Soviet Foreign Ministry spokesman, claimed at the conclusion of the Malta summit in 1989 that "We buried the Cold War at the bottom of the Mediterranean Sea." Gorbachev himself declared in his New Year's message to the Soviet people, aired on January 1, 1990, that the previous year had been the "year of the ending of the Cold War" (quoted by Beschloss & Talbott, 1993, pp. 165, 172).

3. Bialer, writing as late as 1988, claimed (1989, p. 412) that the "preservation of its East European empire remains among the key goals of the Soviet party-state. . . . To paraphrase Winston Churchill, Gorbachev was not elected to the position of General Secretary to preside over the dissolution of the Soviet East European empire."

4. Gorbachev was the first (and last) Soviet general secretary to be born after Stalin's death. He ascended to leadership of the party after the death of three Soviet general secretaries in four years: Leonid Brezhnev in 1982, Yuri Andropov in 1984, and Konstantin Chernenko in 1985. Gorbachev only saw Washington, D.C., "firsthand" in 1987. When he returned in 1990, he traveled by helicopter to Camp David with George Bush and "was taken aback by the extraordinary wealth of 'average' Americans" (quoted by Beschloss & Talbott, 1993, p. 225). He then flew to Minneapolis, where he saw a "typical Minnesota family farm," and then on to San Francisco to visit George Shultz at Stanford University and to meet with the South Korean president, Roh Tae Woo (see Beschloss & Talbott, 1993, pp. 228, 229).

5. As Beschloss and Talbott put it (1993, p. 128), Gorbachev would have had to make three trips in a row to the United States if the get-acquainted summit had been held on American soil. That "would flout protocol and make him look like a supplicant." He had already come in 1987 and was scheduled to return in 1990.

6. The analysis period for the NATO summit in May 1989 was an exception, as it was part of the month-long summit analysis period that encompassed both it and the Gorbachev–Deng Beijing summit. The analysis period ended just after the conclusion of the NATO summit.

7. Shortwave broadcasters have to change both frequencies and times of broadcasts to respond to changing atmospheric conditions occasioned by the change of season, amount of daylight, and the sunspot cycle.

8. Hachten (1987, p. 98) says that "there is no question that under President Reagan appointee Charles Wick as USIA director, the agency has reflected a tougher anti-Communist approach, especially in commentaries following VOA newscasts." USIA underwent a thorough transformation under Wick, Hachten says, despite Wick's "somewhat simplistic views on public diplomacy."

9. Talking points were developed for other reasons in earlier administrations, too. Even Henry Kissinger had them drawn up while he was secretary of state under President Nixon, but not to rein in either himself or the president. In Reagan's case, however, this rationale was probably paramount.

10. The commission's entire requirement (p. 20) was that reporters provide "a truthful, comprehensive, and intelligent account of the day's events in a context which

gives them meaning." The Soviet theory would not meet this entire requirement, although it would meet the latter half of it.

11. Van Oudenaren (1989, p. 125) insisted that Gorbachev remained "committed to the traditional Soviet goals of seeking both control and viability [in Eastern Europe]." He had to work within the framework of "cooperation" developed by his Soviet predecessors, even if he was more adventurous than any of them.

12. Proximity is not merely a calculation of geographical distance, so that a NATO summit in Brussels would be expected to have greater U.S. press coverage than a superpower summit in Moscow. As in both cases the United States would be a major player, proximity would be essentially equal. It would apply, however, to European coverage of superpower summits, as Europeans would not be participants, regardless of location. It would apply to the superpowers, I would argue, based on three types of locations: a U.S. site, a Soviet site, and a neutral site. This division is evident in the decisions between the superpowers about summit venues. Both Reagan's and Bush's initial meetings with Gorbachev (and Reagan's first two meetings) were on neutral soil and thus carried less political significance. Once a president visits his counterpart's country, protocol demands that the next summit occur in his own. If proximity works, then VOA would attach more significance to a Washington summit than to one in Moscow, and more to Moscow than to Malta. Similarly, the order for Radio Moscow would be Moscow, Washington, Malta. For West European services, it would be Malta, Washington, Moscow (because of the NATO alliance); and for East European services, Moscow, Malta, Washington. Outside this North American–European orbit, geography would play a larger role, tempered always by the salience of the issues being discussed.

13. The term "Velvet Revolution" refers to the bloodless transitions from communism to more democratic forms of government that occurred in Poland, Hungary, Czechoslovakia, and East Germany. Romania was not part of this revolution, nor does it include the dissolution of the Soviet Union.

Chapter 2

International Broadcasting as Public Diplomacy

More than one hundred nations are using shortwave and medium-wave radio as a means to reach the citizens of other countries. In addition, privately owned commercial companies, nonprofit religious organizations, and pirates operate dozens of radio stations designed to reach potential consumers, converts, or adherents to their cause. The available shortwave frequencies are so crowded that the United Nations organization responsible for overseeing broadcasting, the International Tele-communication Union (ITU), has increased the number of frequencies available for shortwave broadcasting, and proposals have emerged to allow a new method of radio wave propagation to be used so that still more broadcasters can go on the air.[1] What is perhaps surprising is that shortwave is a low-fidelity means of broadcasting. It does not reproduce music well and it is subject to all manner of interference from sunspots, thunderstorms, and man-made electric engines and appliances.[2] It is difficult to tune in, it often fades in and out during transmission, and sometimes reception is so poor that the broadcasts are not understandable at all.

Nevertheless, shortwave (and to a lesser extent, medium-wave, or AM) radio remains a vital means of providing information, entertainment, and perspective (whether political, economic, or religious) to millions of the world's peoples. Despite the recent rapid development of satellite television (including CNN, and World Service projects by the BBC and Deutsche Welle) shortwave and medium-wave radio remains the most important—and in many cases the only—means available to reach people irrespective of political boundaries or obstacles. In the old Soviet Union, too, shortwave was the principal means for the Communist Party to reach people throughout its multiethnic "empire." Both the BBC World Service and the Voice of America (VOA) estimate their regular weekly audiences to be in excess of 120 million people. Many of these listeners are the best educated, wealthiest, and most politically powerful people in their countries. This is especially true in the developing world. Surveys undertaken throughout the world suggest, too, that the principal attraction of most international broadcasting for citizens of other nations is news, for they often do not trust the media within their own countries.

International broadcasting has developed as an important instrument of international communication for many reasons. Radio waves cannot be confined to precise areas. Shortwaves, which bounce between the earth's surface and the ionosphere surrounding the planet, can travel entirely around the globe from a single transmitter. The world's peoples also own hundreds of millions of shortwave radio sets, making it the second most accessible technical medium of communication (after AM radios) in use across the globe. Shortwave also has a long history of use as an international communications medium, with its history stretching back to Guglielmo Marconi's experiments to provide transatlantic "beam telephone" service in the 1920s.[3]

Those countries that decided to employ shortwave for long distance communication early in radio history—including France, Germany, Great Britain, Japan, the Netherlands, the Soviet Union, and the United States—often did so to pursue specific economic, political, or military ends. This made radio a purposive means of communication: broadcasting intended to have results. When shortwave became a major international communications medium in the 1920s, most of the world's empires were still functioning, especially the British, Dutch, and French. The Germans saw shortwave as a means to avoid the British stranglehold on the world's submarine cable network; the Soviet Union saw it as a means to export revolution. U.S. commercial radio networks viewed shortwave as a means to extend their commercial hegemony, particularly into Latin America; and various European companies, especially the London-based International Broadcasting Service (IBS) saw it as a means to circumvent state broadcasting monopolies.[4] By the late 1920s the British used shortwave to export their public service broadcasting philosophy around the globe and to communicate with their own citizens throughout the British empire.

The focus of international broadcasting was dependent, of course, on the purpose it served. Some international activities focused on the elites of neighboring countries, striving to persuade them to adopt or abandon particular policies. Others focused on more general audiences, seeking to provide information not otherwise available to them, or to convince them to purchase products, or to pressure their government to adopt specific political, economic, or military policies. Still others targeted specific nonelite audiences, such as the "working class," seeking to forge pan-national solidarity in times of political fluidity or upheaval. It was always difficult, however, to determine the size of audiences attracted to such broadcasts, because of methodological difficulties, language barriers, and foreign government restrictions. These difficulties persist even today (although the methodological constraints have eased).

The lack of generalizable knowledge about the size and response of audiences also makes it difficult to assess the impact of international broadcasting. Although several international broadcasters tried to judge audience impacts (especially after the outbreak of World War II in 1939), most early efforts were confined to expert assessments based on general knowledge of a country's population or on fragmentary and possibly idiosyncratic reports. Although broadcasters have conducted more systematic research on international audiences since the 1960s, the difficulties of field research, language barriers, political restrictions, and the very immensity and expense of the task itself (five billion potential listeners worldwide) continue to limit detailed knowledge about audiences. Broadcasters do know the general characteristics of audiences in various parts of the world and can estimate audience sizes for many countries. It is unlikely, however, that broadcasters will ever be able to complete research on every country of the world within a tight enough time frame (even a decade) to allow them to construct a worldwide portrait of the international broadcasting audience. They will have to continue to extrapolate from the known to the unknown on a regional basis.

What is most crucial about international broadcasting is its effect on the monopolies of knowledge that various governments invariably construct about themselves. All countries act, in one way or another, to restrict the flow of information across their borders. Most countries of the world have national copyright restrictions; many have tariff barriers, quotas on imported technologies, or prohibitions on certain technologies that reduce people's ability to retrieve information. Even the United States, which arguably has the world's freest media, is not immune from these impediments. Americans typically have only a superficial knowledge about the world outside the United States.[5] World geography, history, political leaders, and government philosophies are not the stuff of American journalism. The commercial orientation and local bias of the U.S. press restrict American knowledge of the world. The first amendment to the U.S. Constitution (protecting freedom of speech and press) thus has the effect of protecting the provincial monopolies of knowledge constructed by U.S. newspapers and radio and television stations. Other countries suffer from monopolies of knowledge as well, although usually for different reasons.[6]

International broadcasting is a potential corrective for monopolies of knowledge constructed and maintained by governments or privately held media.[7] BBC audience research indicates, for instance, that listening to foreign radio stations is inversely related to the degree of "political constraint" used by governments to control local media (Mytton & Forrester, 1988, p. 476). When people trust local media, their attention to foreign stations diminishes; when they distrust, their listening increases. Specific instances can be seen in the audience figures for the Franco and post-Franco periods in Spain, where audiences declined as the Spanish media were freed from constraint, and among Afghan refugees in Pakistan, who listened at levels far above those in Afghanistan prior to the Soviet invasion.

The ability of international broadcasting to break down monopolies of knowledge has often led to criticisms that it is merely propaganda (a rhetorical "devil" term in the United States). This label implies that the information provided by international broadcasters is at best untrustworthy and at worst unscrupulously tainted, the worst sort of self-serving polemic. Such condemnation worked hand in glove with restrictions on domestic media to assure that countries could manage public discourse and opinion, thus achieving social control (see Robins, Webster & Pickering, 1987).

It is difficult to disentangle the term *propaganda* from its "devilishness," despite the fact that scholars have suggested that it is an "integral feature of democratic societies" (Robins, Webster & Pickering, 1987, p. 7; see also Ellul, 1973, especially Chapter 3). It is integral in democracies because people pay attention to public opinion. Thus, if public opinion is instrumental in decisions about policy and governance, then it is also important to governments that they influence public opinion. Otherwise, they will be at its mercy. The more governments can manage opinion, the better able they are to assure that it legitimizes their own policies.[8]

There is incentive, then, for all sorts of governments, whether authoritarian, totalitarian, or democratic, both to use propaganda and to prevent its taint. Totalitarian regimes seek to control the information environment of their own people; thus, they protest against external propaganda. They also seek to influence the opinion process of their adversaries (if their adversaries are democratic societies) or to crack the information monopolies of other totalitarian states. Democratic societies may likewise seek both to crack monopolies constructed by totalitarian nations and to protect their influence over the formation and maintenance of public opinion in their own societies. They object to propaganda as an illegitimate means to distort public opinion, although they attempt to manage it themselves. They may seek to provide a "corrective" to the information monopolies of totalitarian states, even while denying that what they provide is propaganda.[9]

This is not meant to equate the practices of totalitarian regimes with those of democratic societies. Totalitarian governments often resort to a variety of coercive practices beyond propaganda to enforce their will: restrictions on import or ownership of technologies, laws against communication practices (such as listening to foreign radio stations), ownership or severe censorship of the press, fines, arrests, and so on. Democratic societies, while often as interested in controlling information environments and enforcing their monopolies of knowledge, are nevertheless more constrained in their use of tools. However, they are not necessarily less interested in the use of propaganda, which, despite its devilish qualities, is a useful (even necessary) and more benign means to maintain power (political, military, or symbolic).

The rationale for involvement in international broadcasting differs from one country to another. Many countries justify such broadcasting as a means to allow their citizens to remain "tuned in" when they cross borders on business or holiday trips. Some also wish to allow nationals who are working in other countries, who have residence abroad, or who have emigrated to remain up-to-date on events "at home." This is one reason that so many countries broadcast signals toward the United States, one of the only countries in the world that continues to accept large numbers of immigrants.[10] Another reason is to provide people of other countries the opportunity to hear about the cultural traditions of the broadcaster's country, explain the official policies of its government, or report about world events using the news values of its own journalistic tradition. This is the obligation as laid out in the charter of the Voice of America (VOA), Public Law 94–350, adopted under the Ford administration in 1976. Still other countries engage in international broadcasting because they believe it to be part of the "public service" ethic that defines their domestic broadcasting system. This is the case with the BBC World Service. Others wish to retain influence in former colonial possessions or to continue cultural traditions established during colonial domination (as French broadcasting to Francophone Africa, or Germany's Deutsche Welle to East Africa). There are also "surrogate broadcasters," which purport to inform people about events happening in their own countries that go unreported by their domestic media. This has been the avowed purpose for the U.S.–sponsored broadcasters,

Radio Free Europe (RFE), Radio Liberty (RL), and Radio Free Afghanistan, and of other proposed services such as Radio Free Asia.

This list of rationales does not exhaust the reasons for international broadcasting. Most broadcasters, despite the specific examples cited here, operate international services with multiple motives, including the desire for international esteem or legitimacy.

The mix of rationales for international broadcasting affects not only the specific practices of a given broadcaster but also a country's perceptions of others' activities. Countries that centrally direct their broadcasting activities and thus use services as an official voice tend to judge the activities of other broadcasters by the same standard. In other words, they assume that broadcasts from other countries are also official voices. Countries that censor their press for defined purposes also tend to assume that other countries do as well, despite contrary evidence or specific denials. The difference in perceptions between communication philosophies and practices was the cause of complaints, for instance, about the practices of both the BBC and the VOA by Arab countries during the Persian Gulf conflict (see Fortner, 1991, pp. 3–8).

Another significant element in perception is the history of international broadcasting itself. Arguably its most remarkable period was the "radio war" of the 1930s following the turning of international radio to propaganda by the Italian Fascist and Germany Nazi governments. World War II saw a massive outpouring of international propaganda delivered by radio, along with clandestine broadcasting, use of turncoats (such as Lord Haw-Haw, an Irishman who broadcast for the Nazis and was executed for treason at the end of the war, and Ezra Pound, an American poet who broadcast for the Italians), and extensive use of radio signals to gather intelligence useful in planning military campaigns. After the war, international radio quickly became a significant tool in the Cold War, with the United States clandestinely funding Radio Liberty, broadcasting into the Soviet Union, and Radio Free Europe, broadcasting into what were called the "captive" nations of central and eastern Europe.

It is therefore difficult to disentangle the truth about what international broadcasting is today. Is it merely a means to increase useful information flow between countries, a flow that may reduce tensions by increasing international understanding? This is the avowed focus of the BBC, for instance, whose historical motto is "Nation shall speak peace unto nation." Is international broadcasting intrinsically propaganda? This was the claim of some during the 1930s, when the BBC considered the question of whether to begin broadcasting in foreign languages. For an English-speaking nation to broadcast in Arabic, Italian, or German was ipso facto propaganda (see Mansell, 1982, Chapter 3). More recently, has international broadcasting become a means to practice "public diplomacy"?[11] This was the assumption that underlay the U.S. Smith–Mundt Act, which finally put American international broadcasting on a permanent basis following its partial collapse after the end of World War II and in response to the Cold War.[12]

The claim that international broadcasting is (or should be seen as) nothing more than a means to transfer information may seem naive. Information is powerful. Decisions about what information to transfer and how to transfer it (in what format, using what production values, and in what language or dialect) affect the power of information. VOA's budget-driven decision to cease shortwave broadcasting in Thai in favor of placing its programs on local Thai radio stations resulted in protests that this was an indication that the United States no longer considered Thailand an important nation. Burma questioned whether citizens could serve as government employees who thought it a "good idea" to listen to foreign radio broadcasts such as the BBC or VOA.

Nevertheless, there are suggestions in the operating principles of international broadcasters that do suggest that at least some programs are fundamentally the transfer of information. The BBC *Guidelines for factual programmes* (n.d., Section 21), for instance, say that "Impartiality lies at the heart of BBC programme making. . . . Viewers and listeners should not be able to gauge from impartial BBC programmes the personal views of presenters and reporters." Its *Producers Guidelines* (n.d., Section 3) state, "The facts are sacred, comment is free. The BBC's reputation depends upon the accuracy of its reporting and the public's perception of whether its programmes seek to reflect the truth. Producers in all areas must be prepared to check, cross-check and seek advice, to assure that this reputation is not diminished."

The VOA's Charter (Public Law 94–350, July 12, 1976) also invokes similar considerations. It notes, "To be effective, the Voice of America must win the attention and respect of listeners." To that end VOA's broadcasts are to be governed by three principles:

1. VOA news is to be reliable and authoritative. "VOA news will be accurate, objective, and comprehensive."
2. VOA is to present "a balanced and comprehensive projection of significant American thought and institutions."
3. VOA is also obliged to present the policies of the U.S. government "clearly and effectively" and to provide "responsible discussion and opinion on these policies."

These requirements for VOA mean that it broadcasts editorials "reflecting the official policy of the United States government" and that it clearly separates these editorials (using both a signature tune and an announcement) from its news broadcasts. Editorials are not aired during scheduled news broadcasts.

However, neither VOA's policy nor that of the BBC (which carries no editorials, as it is independent of the British government) solves all the problems of differentiating information from propaganda. Although the BBC's guidelines apply to all its programming, it does carry a press review during one of its major news programs that reports the major stories in British newspapers for each day. British newspapers are significantly more partisan in their news coverage than either U.S. newspapers or the BBC news itself. Carrying such reports, then, could make a listener wonder whether the selection of material allows the BBC to include "editorial" material while claiming not to do so. Other services, such as Germany's Deutsche Welle, the Voice of Turkey, and Belgium's Brussels Calling, likewise carry such reviews. The BBC also invites commentators to interpret and evaluate events, thus providing perspectives that differ little from labeled editorials on other radio services.

Differentiating the content of international radio, then, is not an easy task. Some stations merely summarize major news stories from their studios, using a "rip and read" method that relies on wire services for their feeds. They may define major news of interest as being principally that which occurs in their own country or region. Radio South Africa (now Channel Africa) was such a station. Other stations carry such summaries along with correspondents' reports from the field or commentary, analysis, and press reviews. A variety of international broadcasters, including the BBC, Radio Netherlands, and Middle Eastern stations, follow one of these approaches. Some do features or recast their news programs in response to predictable newsworthy events, such as summit meetings. The BBC, VOA, and Radio Moscow all follow such strategies.

Examining the content of newscasts from different broadcasters, then, is a study in both news judgment and news philosophy. Differences in the coverage of major predictable international events thus allow scholars to make judgments about the nature of international news flow, the significance of so many countries reporting on the same events, and the role of differences in news philosophy on the level of understanding a conscientious audience might achieve by listening to multiple news sources.

As already stated, international radio broadcasting is a focused, purposive activity whose impacts cannot be readily ascertained and whose audience cannot be totally and precisely known. This activity, however, has an impact on the functioning of monopolies of knowledge within countries, either maintaining or challenging them.

Some international radio broadcasting is explicit propaganda. It has discernible repetitive themes and relies on catch words, sloganeering, or stock interpretations to focus on particular aspects of events as they occur. It often relies more on emotion (or pathos) than rational or objective, dispassionate analysis (logos) to report events. It tends to paint the world in contrasts, black versus white, rather than in the subtle hues that characterize the interaction of peoples and nations. Such broadcasting seeks reaffirmation of its own *Weltanschauung* (or world-view) rather than the reporting and analysis of events that might challenge it. It intentionally attempts to manipulate.[13]

Hawthorn (1987, p. x) has correctly argued that the underlying rationale of persuasion is the desire to control information, achieved both by what is said and what is left unsaid. People who depend on others for their information (as inevitably all people do) are thus subject to both interpretation and misinterpretation, to representation and misrepresentation. Essentially, he argues (p. xiii), the effort to persuade is an exercise in power.[14] Thus, the choice of words, interpretative frameworks for words, the geopolitical realities that lead to these frameworks, and the underlying ideologies (both political and journalistic philosophies) that instruct their application must be understood if persuasion is to be correctly analyzed. Rhetoric, once the "art" of persuasion, has become, as Nevitt (1982, p. 26) put it, "propaganda—a total culture in action." The question is, he says, "how the resonant interplay of a medium and its program achieves an intended *effect* with its 'public.' " Propaganda, as Ellul puts it (1973, p. 9), must be total, using every technical means available to saturate a culture to make its effect inescapable. Otherwise it loses its power: it becomes avoidable.[15]

Propaganda is a specific form of persuasion (see Fortner, 1978). The end result of persuasion, as Pratkanis and Aronson (1991, p. 9) put it, is "education for both the audience and the speakers," while propaganda (p. 14) aims at "securing our compliance." Understanding propaganda requires, as Robins, Webster, and Pickering (1987, p. 5) suggest, that it be located "within the wider context of political phenomena and theory: legitimation, democracy, bureaucracy, social administration, public opinion, social control, the nation-state." Although their concern is propaganda within the state and the control of information within an "information society," their analysis is equally applicable to the flow of information across borders: the global information society. The activities of any single international broadcaster must be understood within this framework. International broadcasting thus appears, on its face, to call for judgments about possible propagandistic uses or characteristics.

International broadcasters contribute to the global information society: some by summarization (itself requiring news judgments based in ideological commitments), some by interpretation, some by contextualization, some by a combination of these activities. If the activities of broadcasters are examined alongside one another, the degree to which any single broadcaster adopts a specific news philosophy or engages in propaganda can be more readily determined than when the activities of any single broadcaster are analyzed independently. In other words, the larger context of information control provides the basis for concluding that an international broadcaster is reactive or contextual or is using propaganda than does measuring its practices against abstract definitions.

For instance, Jowett and O'Donnell (1986, p. 16) define propaganda as "the deliberate and systematic attempt to shape perceptions, manipulate cognitions, and direct behavior to achieve a response that furthers the desired intent of the propagandist." This is a perfectly adequate abstract definition of propaganda. Using such a definition requires, however, that the *intentions* of any information manager be known or assumed a priori. This is easy to do when those in charge of information activities avowedly declare their intentions, as a variety of Nazi apologists (including Hitler, Joseph Goebbels, and Eugen Hadamovsky) did in defending the *Propagandaministerium* of the Third Reich. It is less satisfactory, however, when a nation declares that it eschews propaganda (as does the United States) or that its propaganda is based in truth, while that of other countries (all of whom are declared to use it) is based on manipulation and lies (as the Soviet Union claimed about itself in contrast to its Western adversaries).

Further complicating the application of abstract definitions to specific information activities are the relations between political elites who define the policies of governments and news elites who are called upon to carry them out. The political legitimacy of the government bureaucracies charged with forming and executing policy and of the journalistic bureaucracies charged with representing that policy affects the control of information. During the Reagan administration, for instance, concerns that the president was engaging in ad hoc arms policy negotiations in Reykjavik with General Secretary Gorbachev led to efforts to control what he said, both in private negotiations and in his public pronouncements.[16] By the time of the 1987 Washington summit, the National Security Council (NSC) had produced a set of "talking points" that were ostensibly to control all official statements made concerning U.S. policy on arms control, bilateral relations with the Soviet Union, human rights, and the intermediate-range nuclear forces (INF) treaty. These points, however, not only restricted the president's public statements (as well as those of Marlin Fitzwater, George Shultz, and other spokespersons) but also necessarily governed the negotiating sessions with the Soviets.

This step was necessitated by the new context of U.S.–Soviet relations.[17] The INF treaty was a watershed in that it was the first treaty to eliminate a class of nuclear weapons. It was also widely perceived, principally because of its on-site verification requirements, as an archetype for subsequent U.S.–Soviet negotiations on reducing nuclear arms. It spawned one of Reagan's favorite aphorisms, "Trust but verify," and raised the possibility that the two countries would successfully negotiate a strategic arms reduction treaty (START) cutting arsenals by up to 50% before Reagan left office.[18] At the 1988 Moscow summit, both countries spoke of the possibility of a fifth summit to sign such a treaty.

The problem was that, of all the postwar presidents, Reagan had used the most strident anti-Soviet rhetoric. His ardent anticommunism was credited as a major element in his electoral popularity. How could he step back from that posture without compromising the Republican Party? His own rhetoric ran the risk of delegitimizing any arms control agreement he might sign with the "evil empire," regardless of the extent of verification. This was, in fact, the posture taken by more conservative critics of the INF treaty, such as Jesse Helms, who nearly succeeded in delaying Senate ratification of this treaty until after the Moscow summit. Reagan and Gorbachev wanted ratification before Moscow, however, because the summit lacked a centerpiece as a result of unexpectedly slow and difficult negotiations on strategic weapons reduction (unexpected because of White House optimism that such a treaty could easily be patterned after the INF treaty). Reagan needed the support of the Republican Party's conservative wing (as did George Bush as well, since he was running for president by the time of the Moscow summit). How Reagan negotiated with the Soviets and, more to the point, how he explained those negotiations and publicly defended American interests mattered too much to leave anything to chance.

The governments of all countries face similar difficulties in one way or another. They formulate and execute policy, but they must also explain and defend both the policies and their execution. These explanations and defenses, however, usually occur using the media as the means to link with different publics. The media may be controlled by the state, which facilitates this linkage. Where the media are independent, however, their news philosophy, selection of news to report, and methods of reporting can significantly affect the strength of this linkage and the perceived legitimacy of leaders and policies.

On international issues, however, the situation is even more difficult. First of all, different political administrations are seeking legitimacy, influence, and linkage with publics. Both the U.S. and the Soviet governments sought to influence the focus of news about arms control, their bilateral relations, human rights, and regional conflict issues. Both sought to influence their own constituencies' perceptions of their relations for domestic political reasons; they sought to influence each other's citizens' perceptions; and they sought to influence the public opinion of their own and their adversary's allies, as well as the world's citizens at large. In addition, their own allies had similar, although distinct, interests that they pursued using the same linking media. Finally, each political administration had differing degrees of access to the international media: Each had not only to influence its own domestic outlets but to satisfy media reporting from differing ideological perspectives, using differing sets of journalistic philosophies, and making news judgments and using different reporting methods.

The publics whom they sought to influence (various national publics, or the collective world public opinion) were also active, choosing from the available news sources to follow the events and explanations provided. Some publics would attend to single sources they trusted; others would seek out multiple reports. The mix of attention, however, was unpredictable. The political actors could not afford to take anything for granted if they wished to exercise political authority, achieve legitimacy for their policies, or control information flow.

Models of such complex relationships inevitably oversimplify them. It is useful, however, to sketch them out to capture the essential elements. Governments draw on ideologies when they respond to domestic political situations and to their international political and military relations to formulate policies and the strategies for implementing those policies. They also weave symbolic constructs to explain and justify their policies and activities. These constructs are the basis of their rhetorical efforts, which consist of their characterizations of their own, their allies', and their adversaries' activities; their declared commitments to defensible values (such as human rights or negotiated resolution of conflicts); and their justifications or condemnations of political or military actions.

For several reasons, organizations reporting the news do not merely report the events, their justifications, and the declared intentions of governments. First, during diplomatic negotiations, journalists are allowed no firsthand observations. All they have to work with are official statements from official spokespersons about those negotiations (or leaks and speculation). This differs from most other types of news that reporters cover: wars, riots, demonstrations, parliamentary debates, and so on. Second, in interpreting such accounts, they make choices based on a particular philosophy of news, judging what news should be reported and using techniques for reporting it. These filters mean that only some events are reported and that those events are reported in certain ways. Reporters select some statements made in the context of longer speeches to disseminate; they discard the remainder. They report some events; they ignore others.

Two types of international news organizations report on such matters. International news organizations based in a specific country (such as the U.S.–based Associated Press [AP]) report on events, and others based in different countries (such as the Paris–based Agence France Presse [AFP]) report the same events. The "domestic" international news organization (e.g., AP) shares at least some of the ideological commitments of its country's government, either because of state control or censorship or because of shared national values. Outside international news organizations (e.g., AFP) may have different values and thus may report the same events from another perspective.

Audiences attend to these reports, but selectively. Some reports will not be available to them. They will select only some of those that are available and will pay differing levels of attention to them. Some they will attend to because they trust the reports, others by happenstance, still others because they are seeking differing points of view. These audiences collectively make up the international publics that governments seek to influence by their policies, strategies, and rhetorical declarations.

The specific context of the U.S.–Soviet struggle to control information flow should influence any conclusions drawn about their use of persuasive strategies, or propaganda. For instance, since the end of World War II the United States Information Agency (USIA) has tried off and on to distinguish between propaganda and what it now calls "public diplomacy." By this latter term USIA has meant, in terminology first used in the 1980s, "civilized persuasion," appeals based on fact, logic, and understanding rather than emotion.[19] USIA was content to allow the Soviet Union and its ideological partners to practice "propaganda." The difference was not merely that USIA eschewed emotion and the Soviets did not. It would be unrealistic to expect that all constructed messages would avoid emotionally charged appeals or images. The difference, as defined by USIA, was premised on the assumption that its audience had the capacity to reason and that this was the only characteristic to which a legitimate appeal could be made. Reason, not emotion, was to drive the appeals. It thus condemned propaganda as based in emotionally laden or manipulative lies, while communist states affirmed it as a technique for establishing and maintaining essential truths.

Whatever the model of communication followed, however, states are dependent to a large extent on the use of public media that are not always in their control. Even when they own and operate an international radio operation, the information they provide is filtered by their intended audiences (assuming they pay attention to it at all) according to certain assumptions about how news gathering and distribution are practiced. These assumptions differ from one interpreter to another. Because the goal of using such media is to influence what is often called international public opinion, a good beginning is to ask how such public opinion may be formed. Figure 2.1 collapses a complex process into a simplified (but understandable) flow. From the top, the model presents the intangible basis of government international communication practice: its ideology, the nature of its domestic politics, and its international political and military relations. Working within this context, government communication organizations form strategies for communication, establish policies to implement these strategies, and couch their communication rhetorically, to make it believable and suasive. From that point on, however, other factors come into play: The model must be read from the bottom up. The international publics that governments wish to reach have certain media available to them. They select from that available pool and pay differing levels of attention to it. Gatekeepers, such as wire services, newspaper editors, TV network news producers, or international radio service news editors, manage (some would say "massage") what is available, standing between the government and its intended audience. Both top and bottom are dependent on the media standing between. These media report on government activities and pronouncements using a particular philosophy of news and established reporting methods, making judgments along the way about the significance of the stories available to include in each day's menu. Both domestically based and other international news media make such judgments and may choose what to report or how to report, using different criteria.

Between 1987 and 1990 the relations between the United States and the Soviet Union underwent a crucial change. The 1987 Washington summit was the first one that the Soviet Union chose to approach using Western-style public relations techniques. General Secretary Gorbachev made himself available for an extensive and wide-ranging pre-summit interview with Tom Brokaw and demonstrated more spontaneity, humor, and preparation than had previous Soviet leaders. He was surrounded by an entirely new phalanx of spokespersons, military and arms control experts, and journalists, who appeared to be operating by radically different guidelines than the Soviets had used before. Some of the spokespersons were decidedly Western in style and engagement with reporters, although they frequently reverted to more normal Soviet behaviors when pressed. They weren't entirely comfortable, it seemed, in their newly adopted roles. Gorbachev himself seemed genuinely interested in learning about the United States and met with U.S. journalists, intellectuals, and business leaders to hear their perspectives and

Figure 2.1
A Model of News Flow in International Broadcasting

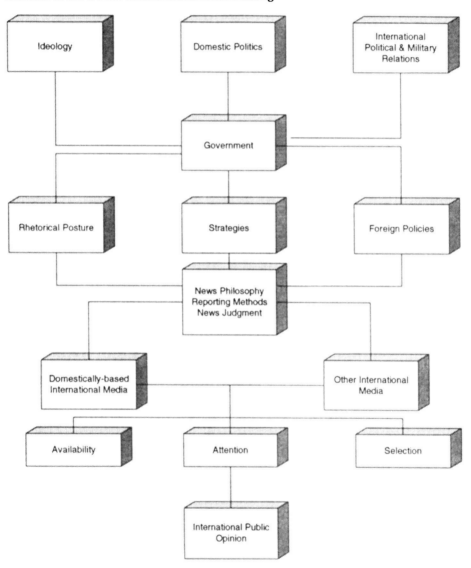

explain his own. Following the summit he held a Western-style news conference. Such acts suggested that *glasnost* had been applied to Soviet external relations and communication practices. They changed the rhetorical posture of the Soviet Union vis-à-vis the media, and argued for new understandings of Soviet political and media strategies.[20]

The 1988 Moscow summit was a similar watershed for Ronald Reagan. Although the basic U.S. approach to summitry did not change as dramatically as the Soviets' had prior to Washington, the Reagan administration felt confident enough in the changing nature of superpower relations to press delicate points such as Jewish emigration, human rights, and freedom of speech in public pronouncements and private discussions alike. It was in Moscow, too, that Reagan recanted his "evil empire" description of the Soviet Union and affirmed Gorbachev's reform efforts in that country (see Goodnight, 1992, p. 49).

Such changes should result in perceptible alterations in the news products of international radio services, particularly in Radio Moscow and VOA, for two reasons. First, both countries did attempt to massage the press generally to provide news that followed their specific agendas. Both countries had foreign policy agendas that they wanted the world to accept. They needed the legitimation of a neutral observer (the press) for these policies to succeed, and they took every opportunity to define for the press what their policies were, what justified them, and why they were beneficial to people generally. At each superpower summit there were press materials prepared by the host country, press pools, a variety of communication links, regularly scheduled briefings by spokespersons from both countries, and printed updated material ready for distribution each day during the summit. The Soviets even prepared a new press center prior to the Moscow summit to replace a dilapidated and antiquated one.

Both countries also attempted to articulate their foreign policy objectives and justifications as clearly as possible. On the U.S. side, as already noted, the National Security Council prepared a set of talking points to direct the statements of American spokespersons. The basic five-point outline prepared for Washington was significantly elaborated for Moscow, although its thrust remained consistent.

The second reason that perceptible alterations should be expected is that the wider context for the summits was changing. To generalize, the intensity of the Cold War between East and West was gradually diminishing. Moscow had accepted Reagan administration arms control proposals, which the administration apparently never expected to have the Soviet Union take seriously (see Ignatius, 1988). Serious negotiations were under way in Geneva on reducing conventional forces in Europe, a number of regional disputes seemed on the verge of resolution, and by the time of the Washington summit there seemed to be areas where the United States and the Soviet Union found their interests beginning to coincide.

These newly cordial relations required moderation in the rhetoric used to describe the former adversary. The result for international radio news, particularly for the services that made extensive use of sound bites and/or on-site correspondents, should have been fewer rhetorically charged treatments of the principal actors and their respective countries in news reports. As the descriptions of adversaries from the actors themselves became more subdued, the news reports would likewise become more bland. The greatest change should be expected in the reports of VOA and Radio Moscow. Lesser change should occur in more politically distant news operations such as the BBC and Radio Netherlands, or in stations dependent on studio staff readers such as the Middle Eastern services or "Brussels Calling," or in geographically distant (i.e., remote from Europe) stations such as Radio Australia, Radio Japan, and Radio South Africa.

Political change introduces tension within international radio news organizations. There is potential conflict between how they may define or portray themselves to audiences and the nature of the news they report. This conflict emerges for a variety of reasons.

First, services that define their role as providing comprehensive and objective factual news are potential hostages to rhetorical excess. This excess may emerge from newsmakers themselves (such as Reagan or Gorbachev) or from press narratives that they may carry as part of their news packages. Their declared unbiased posture may seem compromised by the rhetorical excess they carry from either source, unless stories are carefully crafted. When such immoderation diminishes, however, whatever the reason, their news product may seem insipid and uninteresting. This is a primary difficulty for Western-style news: It is "reactionary," that is, its focus and intensity ebb and flow with the nature of events, personalities, and rhetorical strategies that are its subjects. It usually reacts, rather than contextualizes.

Second, in the radio services that serve the interests of the state, such as Radio Moscow, Radio Prague, Radio Bucharest, Radio Budapest, Radio Sofia, and Radio Berlin, the changing relations between the superpowers can create dissonance in their reporting. Their interpretations of U.S. motives, for instance, long explained to their listeners using one set of definitions and explanations, can suddenly appear dated, or even false, as the rhetorical approach of their countries alters and formerly unthinkable policies are accepted as valid.

In either case, a potential crisis exists. It is useful, therefore, in explaining the news process and its role in information transfer, propaganda, or public diplomacy to consider this possible crisis and the response of different services to it. That response can be discerned in the ways that the news products and their treatments of individuals and countries alter in response to changing circumstances.

NOTES

1. The proposal calls for the use of single-sideband broadcasting, which would theoretically double the number of stations that could be accommodated in the existing frequencies. Because of the expense of converting to this transmission method, however, it does not appear that it will be adopted by ITU members.

2. For a discussion of the technical characteristics and difficulties of shortwave broadcasting, see Fortner (1993), pp. 58–69.

3. The early history of shortwave broadcasting can be seen in Fortner (1993), Chapters 4 and 5.

4. IBS set up transmitters on the European mainland, primarily in France, to broadcast back to the United Kingdom. The stations were forced off the air by the sweep of the German armies through the north of France at the beginning of World War II.

5. I use the term "American" here advisedly. All the peoples of the Americas are Americans. Citizens of the United States, however, are generally known around the globe as Americans, and it is this usage that I will use in this book.

6. The extent of communication freedom can be seen in the work of Article 19 (1988) and Sussman (1988). Difficulties created by the nature of U.S. news reporting and control can be seen in such works as Fishman (1980), Gans (1979), Iyengar & Kinder (1987), and Merrill (1991).

7. Morgenthau (1985, p. 283) correctly points out, however, that modern technology also gave totalitarian governments the ability to restrict access to information. The result is, of course, a tit-for-tat technology conflict between those who seek access to people and those who seek to deny it.

8. This is a matter of significant dispute among historians and political scientists. Morgenthau (1985, p. 164) argues, for instance, that any government "must secure the approval of its own people for its foreign politics and the domestic ones designed to mobilize the elements of national power in support of them." Gergen (1991, p. 49) says, however, "For most of U.S. history, diplomats have been guided by their own judgments and only later have worried about public reaction." His point is reinforced by Paterson (1992, pp. 150, 151), discussing the approach of Harry Truman in shaping public opinion.

9. Not all democratic societies would object to propaganda per se. Some would rather object to manipulation through lies or distortion, without using the term propaganda, which the society sees as a legitimate process of educating or otherwise planting a perspective or worldview. This is the view in Italy, for instance, where the Catholic Church, the source of the word propaganda itself, is crucial and where the word is used to describe propagating the faith.

10. Over a third of the United States' population growth in the 1980s was the result of immigration. The number of immigrants entering the United States during the 1980s was the largest total for a single decade since 1910.

11. The practice of public diplomacy, or using media to promote a country's policies or point of view directly to the people of another country, precedes its application in

broadcasting or in nationally directed radio services. Any effort to influence press accounts of events, personalities, or agreements on behalf of a nation-state is public diplomacy.

12. There is an extensive body of historical literature about international radio broadcasting. Good examples, in addition to Mansell (1982), include Alexandre (1988), Barrington (n.d.), Cole (1964), Fejes (1986), Frederick (1986), Green (1988), Hale (1975), Lewin (1982), Rolo (1942), Short (1983), Short (1986), Shulman (1990), Soley (1989), West (1986), and Winterbotham (1974).

13. Often this manipulation takes the form of the seven propaganda devices: name calling, glittering generality, transfer, testimonial, plain folks, card stacking, and bandwagon. These devices were first outlined in Lee and Lee (1939).

14. This is not a point unique to Hawthorn. Goldfarb (1989, p. 35) discusses the relationship between reason and power in public discourse, which is related to Ellul's concern for culture and Michel Foucault's interplay of politics and culture, specifically, the "intimate connection among the culture of modern tyranny, totalization, and subjection."

15. A complementary perspective is provided by Pratkanis and Aronson (1991, p. 9):

Propaganda was originally defined as the dissemination of biased ideas and opinions, often through the use of lies and deception. However, as scholars began to study the topic in more detail, many came to realize that propaganda was not the sole property of "evil" and totalitarian regimes and that it often consists of more than just clever deceptions. The word *propaganda* has since evolved to mean mass "suggestion" or influence through the manipulation of symbols and the psychology of the individual. Propaganda is the communication of a point of view with the ultimate goal of having the recipient of the appeal come to "voluntarily" accept this position as if it were his own.

16. Gaddis (1992, p. 129), while largely sympathetic to Reagan's foreign policy approach, concludes that "The sweeping agreements contemplated at Reykjavik grew out of hasty improvisation and high-level posturing, not careful thought."

17. Talking points had been used before, although with more maneuvering room for those who used them. Their construction is the result of the political and the bureaucratic styles of those who most influence preparations for summit meetings within an administration.

18. Beschloss and Talbott (1993, p. 18) say that Gorbachev took Reagan's repetition of this proverb as an insult.

19. There is some question about whether or not the U.S. foreign policy establishment, particularly the diplomatic corps, has adhered to this distinction. President Reagan's administration clearly attempted to politicize the foreign service, and many of his appointees—arguably including Charles Z. Wick—were not comfortable with the idea of "civilized persuasion." Their attitude was expressed in several VOA editorials in the period 1982–84.

20. It is important to recognize that, even if the rhetorical and media strategies adopted by the Soviets under Gorbachev changed fundamentally, questions continued about how representative the changes were of real change in the Soviet Union itself. As Goldfarb (1989, p. 187) argued, "If Gorbachev is for real (not at all a certainty), he will face the entrenched power of the status quo, especially from high-level bureaucrats in the *nomenkultura*, who derive their benefits from the inefficiency of the present system, enforce their interests through totalitarian culture, and explain their interests as the common good, using Newspeak. . . . Realistic variants of this theme start with the distance between Gorbachev's rhetoric and reality."

Chapter 3

Symbolic Constructs in International Broadcasting

The main tool of either propaganda or public diplomacy is language. One might argue the point, suggesting that it is images or ideologies that are more basic, but all these suggestions at root share a common characteristic: They identify symbolic constructs. Images are a function of language, for language allows us to "conjure up" images. We think in language, create images, and then recreate them in response to either stimuli or evocative thinking. Ideologies, too, are a function of language and of images, each providing tools for the abstraction (or explanation and analysis) that is the basis of ideology. Eagleton (1991, p. xiii) provocatively defines ideology as "what persuades men and women to mistake each other from time to time for gods or vermin." Clearly language, abstraction, and metaphor are the basis of ideology.[1]

Countries have used radio since its early days as a vehicle to influence both allies and adversaries. In World War I, when radio was still the "wireless telephone," governments attempted to provide information to the foreign press that would subsequently be published in newspapers. In 1918, with World War I bogged down in trench warfare, the United States "broadcast" President Woodrow Wilson's "Fourteen Points," a plan to end the war and assure that the bloody battles would constitute "the war to end wars."[2] The warring powers eventually accepted Wilson's Fourteen Points as the basis for a peace settlement and the establishment of the League of Nations, but both the league and the peace foundered in the 1930s for a variety of reasons, not the least of which was the rise of Fascism and Nazism in Italy and Germany.

The 1930s saw the rise of a "radio war" in Europe, with active participation from Italy, Germany, and Japan on one side and from France, the Soviet Union, and the United Kingdom on the other. After the United States joined World War II in 1941, it added its voice to the airwaves, creating the Voice of America (1942). Throughout the war, these stations and others carried on a propaganda and antipropaganda war, appealing largely to citizens and soldiers fighting against their respective countries. Even at the end of the war, because of the rapid transformation of the world into a bipolar stalemate, radio continued to be a weapon aimed at the populations of foreign lands (see Fortner, 1993, Chapters 6 and 7).

The early use of radio as an ideological and military tool resulted in protracted struggles in political and regulatory arenas, primarily in the United Nations General Assembly, the International Telecommunication Union, and UNESCO. Particularly after World War II, West and East, led by the United States and the Soviet Union, battled over freedom of information, the right to communicate, and national sovereignty issues as they applied to communication. Such struggles, as well as the broader ideological struggle that underlay them, led these countries to characterize each other in demonic terms that also infected broadcast content. Words often took the place of bullets, but they were aimed to wound, nonetheless. The two superpowers, seeing themselves engaged in a titanic struggle to win the hearts and minds of the world's peoples, used symbolic structures as one means to achieve their objectives (see Morgenthau, 1985, pp. 352–353).

The significance of this struggle over symbols is perhaps difficult to grasp in a country where relatively few people pay attention to news produced by those outside their own domestic reporting apparatus. This is particularly true in an age that has come to believe in the myth of a global village, fostered by CNN. Regardless of the breadth or timing of coverage by network or twenty-four-hour cable news stations, however, the domestic media of any country operate using a similar—or even identical—set of assumptions about the world, definition of news, presentational styles, and appropriate technologies to enhance the news product.

U.S. news, for instance, is reactive, technology-driven, and personal in orientation. Reactive news coverage responds to events. When summit meetings occur, U.S. troops are sent to the Persian Gulf, or natural disasters strike, the U.S. news media send reporters, camera crews, network anchorpersons, and their accompanying paraphernalia to the site and then send back streams of words and images to waiting audiences. People and equipment then move on to the next event. Reactive news is event-driven. It is short on context and analysis.

U.S. news is also technology-driven. When news crews land on foreign shores, they immediately link themselves via satellites with their domestic news centers. They carry the latest in microphones, cameras, recording equipment, and satellite up-link and microwave technologies. They concentrate on the production of sound bites or visuals to accompany their reports. They produce many reports live, standing before the scenes of disaster or even sticking cameras out of hotel room windows to record the bombing of cities, as CNN's Peter Arnett did in Baghdad in 1991.

The personal orientation of U.S. news products is well known. Reporters personalize war or disaster by concentrating on victims. They interview the relatives of victims. They emphasize personal tragedy and material damage (particularly that which can be attached personally to an individual, such as the loss of a home or treasured belongings in a fire or hurricane or bombing). They provide background stories on personal relationships between people, such as the developing relationship between Reagan and Gorbachev from the Geneva get-acquainted meeting in 1986 through the 1988 Moscow summit or that between the two presidents' wives, Nancy and Raisa.

This, then, is the sort of news that Americans are used to.[3] Most other countries' media organizations, however, have different news values: They emphasize different aspects of events, and they are often more contextual and less dependent on technology. Thus they create symbolic constructs distinct from those of U.S.-based media. Because, as Edelman argues (1964, p. 6), "every symbol stands for something other than itself, and . . . evokes an attitude, a set of impressions, or a pattern of events associated through time, through space, through logic, or through imagination with the symbol," different symbols connote different "somethings," evoking different attitudes, impressions, or patterns of events and making often dissimilar connections through space, logic, or imagination.

Recognition of these dissimilarities and their significance has led to efforts to control information flow and to objections to the hegemony of Western news services over the flow of global information. For instance, developing countries have complained since the early 1970s about the unequal flow of information between North and South and about the dominance of Western news agencies over what people hear of their countries and peoples (see Fortner, 1993, Chapter 7; MacBride, 1984, pp. 111–121; Masmoudi, 1981, pp. 77–96). One exception to this hegemony has been international radio, a technology now used by many developing countries to reach across their borders and by their citizens to seek out alternative information.[4]

Because the peoples of developing countries are much better equipped with radio receivers than with any other type of communications equipment, the symbolic constructs provided by international radio services are crucial to their understanding of the world (see, for instance, Manet, 1988, pp. 11–12). Of all information technologies, radio has been, and remains, the one most likely to provide the people of developing countries with the ability to receive alternative points of view. With more than a hundred countries using shortwave and medium-wave radio to reach across international borders and with most of these stations run directly by governments or subsidized by governments, commercialized interests have not been able to dominate this technology. Also, as governments have exercised differing degrees of control over these operations and function with differing political and information ideologies, opportunities have been increased for hearing varying points of view and differing symbolic constructs through radio.

Edelman argued (1964, p. 16) that two symbolic forms that have dominated U.S. political institutions are "rite and myth." His conclusion also applies to superpower summits as they developed in the postwar period. Although the "first" modern summit, a 1941 secret meeting between Franklin D. Roosevelt and Winston Churchill at Placentia Bay, Newfoundland, was carried out entirely outside the purview of the press, subsequent summits, including the famous 1945 Yalta conference that included Roosevelt, Churchill, and Stalin, occurred publicly (see Wilson, 1969, pp. 1–8, on Placentia Bay; on Yalta, see Wilhelm, 1990, pp. 21–23; and Thompson, 1981, pp. 83, 94–105).[5]

Over time, summit meetings between the superpowers took on certain ritual characteristics. They occurred usually in three places—the two national capitals and "neutral" sites. The venue for meetings was itself largely symbolic. The superpowers often selected neutral sites to allow new leaders to "get acquainted" or to meet without seeming to certify the legitimacy of the adversary by visiting a "hostile" capital. By the time of the Reagan–Gorbachev 1987 Washington summit, following the 1985 get-acquainted Geneva summit and the 1986 Reykjavik "presummit," the press was able to make much of the fact that Gorbachev was the first Soviet leader since Leonid Brezhnev (1973) to visit Washington.[6] Likewise, Reagan became the first U.S. president since Richard Nixon (1974) to visit Moscow.[7]

When the two countries' respective leaders did visit the host's capital city, the rituals were elaborate. Welcoming ceremonies, artillery salutes, state dinners, joint communiques, and eventually joint press conferences became part of the pomp and circumstance of the meetings. Often the very act of meeting in the hostile capital itself was more significant than agreements reached or treaties signed (see, for instance, Time's report [Church, 1990, pp. 12–13] on the 1990 Washington summit). This was particularly true of Reagan's 1988 meeting with Gorbachev in

Moscow, following his earlier pronouncement to the National Association of Evangelicals that the Soviet Union was "the focus of evil in the modern world." This speech had translated "domestic and foreign policy debates into an apocalyptic Christian parable" (Erickson, 1985, pp. 76; see also pp. 79–80).[8] It was true, too, for the two Washington summits, where previously agreed-to treaties were formally signed, as public relations gestures. In 1987 the intermediate-range nuclear forces (INF) treaty was the centerpiece, while in 1990 new agreements on verification of nuclear tests, cutting chemical stockpiles, and bilateral trade were central, along with thirteen other accords. Even in Moscow in 1988, where no new agreements were predicted (and thus no "centerpiece"), a last-minute ratification of the INF treaty by the U.S. Senate allowed "instruments of ratification" to be exchanged. Such ritual acts, with their mutually agreed-upon meaning of progress toward a peaceful world and mutual respect between the superpowers, became much of the substance of the summit meetings.

"Each summit," as Armitage (1987, p. 51) suggests, "is very powerfully influenced by the time and circumstances and by the issues and dispositions of the two sides." Reagan's disposition, given his focus on the significance of communication, was on public relations. Reagan wanted to achieve "symbolic victories, without risking American lives" (see Ignatius, 1988, p. 175). He understood that "the central battle in a political conflict is often 'the struggle over whose symbolic definition of a situation will prevail' " (Hinckley, 1990, p. 1, quoting Elder & Cobb, 1983, p. 129).[9] During his presidency,

> the dramatic tension in Reagan's epic narrative [thus resolved] into a "battle for men's minds," fought not so much with guns and bombs as with symbols, language, and propaganda. As [Reagan] said in his speech of July 19, 1982, marking Captive Nations Week, "Two visions of the world remain locked in dispute." When using rhetoric to defend his American vision, Mr. Reagan wages war with imagery that conjures up sublime and terrible scenes, transforming the physical world into an allegorical battleground between good and evil. (Erickson, 1985, p. 69)

Despite Reagan's reputation with the American public as the "great communicator," Mikhail Gorbachev was, in many ways, his match—he also knew the necessity of symbol construction.[10] His innovation was to adopt Western-style public relations and thus to provide a fundamentally changed presentational style, compared to that of his predecessors. Soviet diplomats came to the 1987 Washington summit practicing this new style. The entourage was greatly enlarged, and its practices more adept in meeting the expectations of the Western press. It was able to make effective use of the electronic media, and its emerging leaders were "better trained and better informed than their predecessors" (Laird, 1989, p. 7). As Bell put it, "President Reagan had obviously at last met someone in his own league as a 'PR' man" (Bell, 1989, pp. 53–54). Gorbachev had managed, during his tenure as leader of the Soviet Union, to regain the initiative from the United States. He had "won a new respectability, confidence, and authority for the Soviet Union, by largely dismantling the enemy image that other nations and peoples held of his country" (van Borcke, 1989, p. 33).

The symbolic structures employed by Reagan and Gorbachev increased the stakes for diplomacy—particularly for diplomacy practiced through public media. These structures fundamentally changed the nature of U.S.–Soviet relations, which had been defined since 1946 by the notion of an "iron curtain" irreconcilably separating two power blocks (see LaFeber, 1985, pp. 37–49, and Thompson, 1981, pp. 126–130, concerning Churchill's speech in Fulton, Missouri).[11] The actual relationship between the two countries, however, remained adversarial, although on a less confrontational plane, until the Berlin Wall began to come down, revolutions erupted across Eastern Europe, and the Soviet Union began to dissolve. Nevertheless, the symbolic alteration that preceded the material one was historically significant in its own right. As Hinckley puts it (1990, p. 5), "Symbols evoke ideas the society wants to be true. The term *symbolic*, then, should not be opposed to *real*. Symbols have reality, clearly, as a projected self is seen and perceived by others and as patriotic slogans can move an entire crowd to action." As a function of the rhetorical changes—implicit statements that suggested that the United States wanted to see the Soviet Union differently—Mikhail Gorbachev (1990, p. 266) was willing to tell the Soviet people via a television interview on December 3, 1989, that "the world is ceasing the Cold War and entering (as we believe and hope) a long period of peaceful development. . . . I would like to say that the Cold War is over. This is correct in principle. But much from that period still remains in the approaches and foreign-policy of some states."

The Cold War did not end, however, with Reagan's presidency. George Bush's arrival at the White House marked not only a change in administrations, but also a change of style in dealing with foreign policy. The role of the National Security Council in outlining summit talking points and clearly using public diplomacy to make the American case was downgraded by Bush's more personal style.[12] Rather than depending on public pronouncements, sometimes apocalyptic rhetoric, and his own skill (or lack of it) as a communicator, Bush depended on one-on-one discussions with world leaders. As Duffy and Goodgame (1992, p.

53) put it, "Privacy was a big part of Bush's courtship" of world leaders. He practiced what they call "Rolodex diplomacy." To make it work, Bush had "White House communications officers . . . install direct secure telephone lines to London, Bonn, and Paris and upgraded the 'hot line' to Moscow from a noisy Teletype to a direct high-speed data link" (p. 54; see also Berman & Jentleson, 1991, p. 112).

Bush also had the difficulty of trying to keep up with a rapidly changing global landscape. Continuing Reagan's well-planned public diplomacy strategies—in the face of arms control initiatives from the Soviet Union, the dismantling of the Berlin Wall and rapid movement toward a unified Germany, the collapse of communism in Eastern Europe, the breakaway of the Baltic republics from the Soviet Union, and the Soviet Union's inability to control its own breakup—was probably impossible. As Rockman (1991, p. 15) puts it, "Given the momentous events occurring in the world, especially during the last part of 1989 and most of 1990, almost any grand strategy would have been rapidly outdated. Events outpaced any serious capacity for long-term thinking. While the world shook, it veritably can be said that Washington stood still." This was true both of policy and of statements about policy, that is, of public diplomacy (see also Berman & Jentleson, 1991, pp. 93, 95).

At both the beginning and the end of the Cold War, the changes in the presentation of ideas preceded actual change (see Laird, 1989, p. 8). In the Soviet case, the change in rhetorical strategy was more evident, as it proceeded from one leader's making a change in policy: Stalin at the beginning and Gorbachev at the end. In the American case, however, particularly at the conclusion of the Cold War, the changes are more difficult to pin down, as the change in administrations brought with it presentational changes based on personal abilities and preferences. Nonetheless, the changes of 1987 to 1990 allowed the Cold Warring powers to alter their images of one another and thus to begin the process of withdrawing from the military stalemate that had characterized the postwar period. Since the Cold War had begun with rhetorical condemnations, it was appropriate (and arguably necessary) that changing rhetorical constructs begin the process of ending it as well.

Groundwork was laid in Geneva and Reykjavik for the rhetorical turn required to end the Cold War. Geneva had not led to any breakthroughs, however, on the issue of arms control; and Reykjavik had found Reagan and Gorbachev at odds on the issue of the strategic defense initiative (SDI). Although important as precursors to the symbolic restructuring to come, neither summit led to an actual change in rhetorical strategy. The two superpowers each seemed to be waiting for their adversary to make the first move. After two summits on "neutral soil," however, it was clear that, if any progress were to be made to reduce tensions, it would be necessary to hold a third summit in one of the capitals. As a U.S. president had been to Moscow last (Richard Nixon in 1974), it was Washington's turn to host the next summit. But Gorbachev had to agree to come.

For this reason the U.S.–Soviet summit held in Washington, D.C., in December 1987 was widely seen as being historic. Not only had the two superpowers signed an intermediate-range nuclear forces (INF) treaty that for the first time actually reduced the number of nuclear weapons by mutual agreement and inaugurated stringent on-site verification procedures on foreign soil, but Ronald Reagan, whom some considered the archetypical Cold War warrior, had successfully negotiated it.[13] The decision to visit Washington by Gorbachev—the first Soviet general secretary to do so since Brezhnev—also seemed to signal a warmer turn in superpower relations. Some observers even anticipated that the INF treaty might lead to substantial progress on an agreement to reduce strategic nuclear arsenals and might serve as a model for negotiating reductions in conventional forces in Europe. They thought that a fourth summit might be scheduled in Moscow (allowing Reagan to legitimize his Soviet counterpart's visit) to continue the expected momentum of the Washington talks.

All of this was known in advance of Gorbachev's arrival at Andrews Air Force Base on the afternoon of December 7, 1987. The world's press could therefore anticipate enough significant news to show up in force, which they did. Nearly 7,000 sets of press credentials were processed by the United States Information Agency (USIA) for the summit, 3,000 of them for foreign journalists. The ballrooms of the Washington Marriott Hotel were converted into a press center, press pools were created to allow live coverage of several staged events (such as the INF treaty signing, Reagan's official welcome and departure ceremonies, meetings at the Soviet embassy, and the like), hundreds of telephone lines and instruments were installed on short notice, and dozens of volunteers were assigned duties as runners, guides, and escorts. When Reagan visited Moscow a few months later, Soviet recognition of the role of the press was also apparent. Gone was the ramshackle press facility that journalists had cursed for decades. In its place—although barely complete—was a new and elaborate facility built specifically for such occasions.

The press cannot prepare for many of the stories it reports: Events are unanticipated and must be reported as they unfold with the resources available near the scene. But summits are different. Their dates are set several months in advance; their agendas are established; photo opportunities, press briefings, and news conferences are scheduled; and their press pools determined. By 1987 Reagan and Gorbachev had also established the ground rules of their relationship in two previous meetings. All of this allowed the press to anticipate its coverage, to assign reporters appropriately, to schedule equipment, to arrange satellite up-links or telephone connections, to prepare for interviews and generally to rationalize its coverage.

The Washington summit and the summits to follow were pseudo-events, staged largely for the purpose of getting press coverage. They were also political events, series of "pictures" creating "a moving panorama taking place in a world the mass public never quite touches . . . a passing parade of abstract symbols" (Edelman, 1964, p. 5). But this panorama was not left to chance. Both the United States and the Soviet Union attempted to orchestrate events, including interviews, press conferences, speeches, and press releases, to ensure that their version of the summit and its significance would lead journalists in a particular direction.

The symbolic problem confronting government-directed radio services, as well as "independent" journalists, over the period from 1987 to 1990 was the fragmentation of the accustomed symbolic portrayals. This fragmentation can be seen in the differences in statements at the beginning and the end of this analysis period. After the conclusion of the 1987 Washington summit, the Voice of Free China (Taiwan) aired two lengthy post-summit commentaries. One commentary wondered whether Reagan's "terrific act of faith in Gorbachev" would pay off and reminded listeners that Stalin had "manhandled" the United States at the end of World War II, that the West had "trusted Mao with China's future," an "almost unforgivable" act, and that, after SALT I, "detente was just another word for a massive military build-up" in the Soviet Union. The commentary concluded, "Now we are hearing that Gorbachev is a different type of Communist. We've heard that before. . . . The record of trusting Communist leaders holding up olive branches is tragic. We can only hope that Gorbachev is the real thing and not like his predecessors."

The second commentary was titled "Odd Man Out." It suggested that the leaders in the People's Republic of China were full of "sour grapes" about the positive results of the summit. "Now that things seem to be hunky-dory between Washington and Moscow," the service opined, "Peking is getting nervous that a balance in the Washington-Moscow-Peking tri-axis is slipping away from Peking, leaving them out." It asserted that both Peking and Moscow had been the "odd man out" at certain periods following World War II and ended with the question: "Is it possible that Washington, leader of the free world, can avoid being the odd man out?"

Although there was some recognition in these commentaries that the world was changing, the radio commentaries continued to examine the results of the summit largely from the perspective of East-West confrontation. Could the Soviets be trusted? Was the United States likely to lose out if Peking and Moscow could patch up their differences? In other words, was the United States a naive superpower?

Contrast these remarks with those of Radio Moscow (1989) and VOA (1990). By then the Voice of Free China's black-and-white symbolic categories for making sense of the world were nearly nonsensical. A Radio Moscow commentary aired four days after the Malta summit's conclusion explained the difficulties of making the transition to a post–Cold War symbolic structure:

> One year ago Mikhail Gorbachev made his widely known speech at the United Nations. Victor Glasinov comments: Although a new idea takes some time to catch on, Gorbachev's address to the United Nations last year was at once and universally recognized as an essentially new vision of the world. The Soviet leader suggested freeing the globe of war and violence and ending confrontation and assuring that humanity's future will be decided on the basis of humanitarian interests, viewed as superior to ideological, political, ethnic, and other interests. He called in no uncertain terms to abandon the old practice of regarding world developments in the light of the struggle between two systems: capitalism and socialism, in which one must necessarily defeat the other. For decades the Soviet Union's calls for peaceful competition had been disregarded, and this country had been viewed as the grave-digger of capitalism. In the early 1960s Chancellor Konrad Adenauer described the USSR as a deadly enemy of the West. And as recently as the early 1980s the Soviet Union was referred to as the evil empire. Hence the position-of-strength policy and the calls for wiping of the USSR out from the world map. Such were the Cold War realities. Mikhail Gorbachev's address to the United Nations came as a political signal for ending the Cold War and stepping into an era of peace. The year that has passed since then has shown that achieving peace, free disarmament, and cooperation is more than a beautiful dream. The past twelve months have been marked by dramatic change the world over. The socialist countries have launched a vigorous drive toward renewal, making the capitalist world take a fresh look at the world of socialism. The unseemly intensive dialogue between East and West has yielded the first signs of consensus on problems that are indeed of vital importance to humanity. The Malta summit between the Soviet and American presidents has given reasons to speak of the Cold War as a reality of the past. Personally, however, I wouldn't go as far as that, writes Victor Glasinov. The Malta

summit did mark a breakthrough towards new heights. But that was only a conceptual breakthrough, which is yet to be met by practical action. What needs to be done is completing next year the treaty for 50% cuts in strategic and chemical stockpiles. Only when all of the barriers to East-West cooperation have been removed will one be justified in saying that the Cold War is over. So far, however, humanity is only halfway to that goal.

The day before the start of the 1990 Washington summit the Voice of America also tried to make sense of the "new world order." The lead of the story concerned the ritual before all U.S.–Soviet summits: the round of briefings by experts in Washington's "so-called think tanks. Everyone has an opinion." VOA then included paraphrases and sound bites of some of Washington's experts.

[Sound bite: Michael Mandelbaum]: "This summit is taking on a curious air. What we have is a whole series of issues left over from the Cold War, like arms control, issues that were terribly important when the United States and the Soviet Union were bitter adversaries, but at the same time we have a series of new issues that arise from the ending of the Cold War and the two sets of issues are kind of jamming together and they may produce a kind of traffic jam." A conservative skeptic, Kenneth Adelman, thinks the summit can be a success. The shift from conventional forces to nuclear ones over the past eighteen months is a mistake. Secretary of State Baker disagrees. [Sound bite: James Baker]: "Nuclear force reductions are bilateral; conventional forces reductions are not. The U.S. will not agree to a CSCE [Conference on Security and Cooperation in Europe] summit without a treaty on conventional arms." [Sound bite: Spurgeon Kenney, Arms Control Association]: "The summit is going to be a major success; it will be an arms control summit." [Sound bite: James Baker]: "Disagreements still remain; we must continue to engage our Soviet counterparts."[14]

The changes that seemed to be occurring in the world and that journalists, commentators, and radio services attempted to capture were creating new symbolic realities in preparation for new geopolitical arrangements. The symbolic structures had to come first for the arrangements that followed to seem sensible. A complete reorientation of symbolic structures was required. A new drama was unfolding, one that had no prepared script but already had critics waiting in the wings. This unfolding drama was itself a significant set of acts, one that attracted star actors to play significant roles—even to improvise during the performance. What unfolded in this impromptu drama thus deserves attention if the resulting new world order, and its significance for the world, is to be understood adequately.

Analyzing this unfolding drama required that questions other than those originally prompting the research be addressed. The principal difficulty was to identify the symbolic structures employed by radio services in covering summit meetings and to track changes over the three years studied to determine whether the means employed to explain these events were changing. Defining the symbolic structures required a comprehensive examination of summit-related broadcasts over a significant time frame.

This research examined summit news beginning with the 1987 Washington Gorbachev–Reagan summit and including the 1988 Moscow Gorbachev–Reagan summit, the 1989 Beijing Gorbachev–Deng summit, the 1989 Brussels NATO conference, the 1989 Malta Gorbachev–Bush summit, and the 1990 Washington Gorbachev–Bush summit. The analytic periods for these summits are listed in Table 3.1.

One major evening news broadcast for each service was used as the analytic frame. All stories about the summit were used for analysis. The broadcasts for all services were taped; they were coded according to a classification and coding system devised, revised, and verified by pretesting and retesting. The principal unit of analysis was the individual news item, although some coding required that individual assertions be examined, particularly as they related to treatment of summit principals (Reagan, Bush, Gorbachev, and Deng) and NSC themes. Individual items were identified during a playback session, and notes on content were taken; items were then counted, timed, and coded. Data were aggregated at various levels to draw conclusions on particular aspects of the study or to serve as the basis for additional analysis. Coding allowed for aggregations to be made by date, radio service, geographical location, story focus, thematic content, treatment of principals, or source of story. All statements made individually and collectively within stories served as the basis for coding, because the nature of radio news leads does not allow them to be used as the primary vehicle for understanding story focus or content.[15]

International radio news coverage differs from the typical news examined in content analysis research in three important respects. First, it originates with government-operated or financed services, not with "independent" news organizations.[16] Although one cannot assume that a news report on such services indicates an official government point of view (as it clearly does in some cases but not in others), the reports are at least reflective of a national or "public" perspective. Second, international radio services are typically not subject to pressure from advertisers, which

Table 3.1
Time Frames for Summit Analyses

Summit Venue	Summit Dates	Analysis Dates
Washington, D.C.	December 7–10, 1987	November 30–December 13, 1987
Moscow, U.S.S.R.	May 29–June 2, 1988	May 22–June 7, 1988
Beijing, P.R.C.	May 15–18, 1989	May 1–31, 1989
Brussels, Belgium	May 29, 30, 1989	May 1–31, 1989
Warships off Malta	December 2–3, 1989	November 27–December 10, 1989
Washington, D.C.	May 30–June 2, 1990	May 23–June 8, 1990

may affect news judgments in some cases (see Hulteng, 1979). Third, although such services typically adhere to established program patterns, they may violate these patterns if events are significantly important to warrant it. News coverage on international radio, then, is not subject to the "zero sum" equation typical of domestic services, which suggests that time given to one story must be taken from another because the amount of time available for a news broadcast is finite (see Harrison, 1986, p. 414). It was not unusual, then, to find that news services would extend or reorder their reports during the summit or provide additional commentary as the summit proceeded. This was particularly true of Radio Moscow and the Voice of America and, to a lesser extent, of Deutsche Welle, Radio Netherlands, and the BBC.[17]

Another contextual consideration in analyzing international radio is the issue of propaganda. Was it possible to code news stories with sufficient precision so that one could tell the difference between manipulation and civilized persuasion? Would the contextualizing focus of some services be sufficiently different from the reactive focus of others to allow contrasts to be drawn? Was contextualizing more likely to contain manipulation? Ellul (1965, p. 126), for instance, had suggested that, because of the inability of democratic governments to depend on public opinion, "opinion must follow the government" (see also pp. 124–125). What values shaped news reports emanating from democratic countries with free media that sought to influence the opinion of citizens in other countries? Did they treat public opinion abroad as though it differed from public opinion at home? Did VOA propagandize in efforts to influence, despite the prohibition against doing so? Was contextualization sufficiently distinct from propaganda that the two concepts could be adequately separated?

Other governments are interested, too, in influencing American public opinion, because they understand the significance of that opinion to the formation and pursuit of U.S. government policies. This understanding seemed to lead Radio Moscow to saturation coverage of the 1987 Washington summit, even to broadcasting—on a slightly delayed basis—Mikhail Gorbachev's interview with Tom Brokaw, although Americans could watch the interview live on television.[18] The understanding also affected the Voice of Free China (VFC), which chose to ignore the 1987 summit almost entirely while reporting about American-Taiwanese trade relations. Only at the conclusion of the summit did VFC spend time commenting on the results of the summit, particularly on U.S.–People's Republic of China relations. Although VFC may have understood the nature of U.S. media coverage of the summit—possibly making its own coverage seem unnecessary—it also saw an opportunity to put a "spin" on the summit that could affect American thinking (public opinion) on issues significant to its own relationship with the United States. This phenomenon seemed to lessen, however, as the research continued over time, although it is possible that changing the services analyzed resulted in missing such continuing activity.[19]

Little significant research has been done on the content of international radio service newscasts. What has been done is also narrow in focus, concentrating typically on only two services at any given time.[20] "Almost completely lacking," as Hur has put it (1984, p. 7), "is research on news flow between and among developed nations, such as the Soviet Union vs. the U.S. or advanced European nations vs. the U.S., or among other developed nations." This study is a beginning in the effort to redress that situation.

NOTES

1. Eagleton continues (1991, p. xiii) on a somewhat less poetic note. "One can understand well enough how human beings may struggle and murder for good material reasons—reasons connected, for instance, with their physical survival. It is much harder to grasp how they may come to do so in the name of something as apparently abstract as ideas. Yet ideas are what men and women live by, and will occasionally die for."

2. The word "broadcast" is in quotation marks here because the United States used the wireless telegraph to transmit Wilson's proposal to the Europeans and depended on the press to disseminate it.

3. This is the term of choice in describing Soviet-American relations. The Russian word for U.S. citizens is "Amerikan" or "Amerikanski." For better or worse, that term came to be the one applied in superpower relations.

4. While many countries operate international radio services, the countries of Europe and the United States dominate these airwaves, judging by the amount of total frequency space they occupy worldwide.

5. Wilhelm argues, too (1990, p. 26), that Yalta and the events leading up to it "largely ushered in the Cold War." A convenient definition of the Cold War is that suggested

by John W. Spanier: " 'The conflict between the Communist nations led by the Soviet Union and the Western nations led by the United States, fought by all means—ideological, economic, political, and limited military action—short of total war.' Because of the advent of nuclear weapons, it no longer seemed feasible to engage in total war, and both sides therefore resorted to the foregoing 'cold' means of conflict." There is an immense literature concerning the beginnings of the Cold War. Some of the more famous explanations include those of Acheson (1969), Fontaine (1970), Gaddis (1972), Gardner, Schlesinger & Morgenthau (1970), Kennan (1947, 1967), and Paterson (1990). Other accounts are those of Donnelly (1965), Seabury (1976), and Thompson (1981), among many others. Winston Churchill's memoirs include his account of Yalta and the origins of the Cold War, and recently released Soviet archival material has prompted new assessments (see Churchill, 1953, pp. 603–606; Jensen, 1991).

6. Haslam (1990, p. 158) said that, although the Geneva summit was the most important event of 1985, "Nothing was resolved with respect to space weapons—still the chief focus of Soviet concerns—and in this respect the summit was a failure." While the U.S. side basically attempted to avoid discussing SDI, the Soviets were equally insistent on "linkage" in reductions in offensive missiles and limitations on SDI. Despite the failure to achieve such a linkage, however, Geneva was significant, at least to the Soviets, as Burlatsky wrote (1987, p. 6). Reykjavik was "billed in the US as a 'pre-summit' rather than the authentic article" (Bell, 1989, p. 68). Nevertheless, Reykjavik altered the pessimism "about the probability of any substantial agreement in [arms control] between Moscow and Washington during the Reagan years" (Bell, 1989, p. 67). The agreement that the Soviets sought at Reykjavik on SDI again caused the talks to founder, much to the relief of many U.S. arms control experts, as well as America's western European allies (see Haslam, 1990, pp. 166–167).

7. After the 1974 Moscow summit, summits were held in neutral locations by President Gerald Ford and General Secretary Brezhnev (Vladivostok, November 23–24, 1974, and Helsinki, July 30 and August 2, 1975), President Jimmy Carter and General Secretary Brezhnev (Vienna, June 15–18, 1979), and President Ronald Reagan and General Secretary Mikhail Gorbachev (Geneva, November 19–21, 1985, and Reykjavik, October 10–12, 1986). See "Gist: US-Soviet Relations," 1991, pp. 608–609).

8. Reagan delivered his "evil empire" speech in 1983. He did not repudiate this apocalyptic rhetoric, although he recognized that his statement had caused a "critical furor" (see Gaddis, 1992, p. 125). But, he asked in a speech at the Hudson Institute in 1991, "Why all the fuss about a simple truth known to every person forcibly subjected to that empire's domination, a simple truth known to every person forced to endure the extraordinary evil of systematic denial of human freedom?" ("Evil Empire," 1991). Reagan's characterization was not without precedent, however. As Paterson (1992, p. 170) writes, "One Soviet historian has found an 'amazing similarity of the images' that the Soviets held of Americans and that Americans held of Soviets. These images were one-dimensional (black and white), categorical (truth not to be doubted), stereotypical (substituting for an informed view), asynchronous (looking too much at past behavior rather than at present reality), demonized (the enemy as absolute evil), uncompromising (a duel to the death with the devil), and ideologized (made rigid by ideology)." Morgenthau (1985, pp. 8–9) discusses the "demonological approach" to foreign policy that focuses evil in the person, thus making its exorcism possible.

9. Hinckley is quoting C. Elder & R. Cobb (1983), p. 129.

10. Lenin was also acutely aware of the necessity to influence symbolic constructs. His government used radio within the Soviet Union as "an all-penetrating instrument of 'civil training' and propaganda." Although it pursued its foreign policy less consis-

tently, it did "intervene" in the affairs of other states from time to time, including revolutionary appeals and "theoretical debates" (see Whitton & Herz, 1942, pp. 4–5). What Gorbachev broke free of, as Kaiser (1991, p. 162) put it, was the "Stalinist mythology" that had "successfully defined reality for millions of Soviet citizens, including many who considered themselves free-thinking and cynical but who still could not escape the world view inculcated by official propaganda from kindergarten onward. The myths became a kind of political and intellectual straitjacket, limiting the freedom of movement of several generations of Soviet leaders. Gorbachev broke out of the straitjacket." Goldfarb (1989, pp. 18–19) has described the "historical darkness" of that mythology. The superpower summits in the Gorbachev era, Sharlet (1989, p. 159) has written, influenced human rights performance in the Soviet Union. "The imperatives of *perestroika* combined with the impetus of the summits has significantly accelerated the emergence of civic alternatives to official reality in the USSR."

11. LaFeber (1985, pp. 38, 39, 49) traces the beginnings of the Cold War to Joseph Stalin's election speech of February 9, 1946; to Winston Churchill's Fulton, Missouri, speech, on March 5, 1946, that included the famous "iron curtain" phrase; and to President Harry Truman's presentation of the "Truman Doctrine" to Congress on March 12, 1947.

12. While this is certainly true, it is equally the case that Bush's presidency seemed paralyzed at first insofar as relations with the Soviet Union were concerned. "At the White House [in February 1989], a reporter asked Bush about Sheverdnadze's Middle East trip and the 'widespread impression' that the U.S. president had 'no foreign policy' " (Beschloss & Talbott, 1993, p. 31). In March, Secretary of State Baker "was in the awkward position [in Vienna] of having to explain why the United States was still refusing to reciprocate Gorbachev's initiatives" (Beschloss & Talbott, 1993, p. 39). In mid-April, "Ronald Reagan was telling friends of his 'uneasy' feeling about Bush's 'foreign-policy indecisiveness' " (Beschloss & Talbott, 1993, p. 50). Bush did not ask to meet with Gorbachev until mid-July.

13. Gaddis (1992, pp. 130, 131) wrote, "There is no question that the President and his advisors came into office with an ideological view of the world that appeared to allow for no compromise with the Russians." Thus it was ironic that "it fell to Ronald Reagan to preside over the belated but decisive success of the strategy of containment George F. Kennan had first proposed more than four decades earlier."

14. Mike Feinsilber wrote (1991) for the Associated Press about the possible symbolic confusion created by the end of the Cold War. He began:

> It was a boast of breathtaking impudence. And a historic miscalculation, though no one knew it then.
> "Whether you like it or not, history is on our side. We will bury you," a strutting Kremlin boss Nikita Khrushchev said three decades ago during a confrontation with his Cold War adversary, the United States of America.
> But the burial this New Year's Eve, in the Kremlin, will be of communism. They'll haul down the hammer and sickle.
> Everyone knows where that leaves the losers, the ex-Soviet people, struggling for bread and order.
> But where does that leave the winners?
> According to the Census Bureau, 171,097,033 Americans—more than half the population—were born during the Cold War. They've lived with both the unnerving threat of cataclysm and the unifying purposefulness it offered.
> So what happens now?
> Have Americans—who gave up 110,000 lives in Korea and Vietnam and $4 trillion in taxes fighting the Cold War—been so affected by the prospect of universal destruction

that they're hooked on anxiety?
Does the country need an enemy to have a purpose?
Who will take the Soviet Union's place?
Questions to ask the people who used to think about the unthinkable.

15. Using story leads or introductory paragraphs as the basis for coding news is typical within newspaper content analysis, which is better suited to such an approach (see, for instance, Schillinger & Jenswold, 1987, pp. 826–833).

16. The BBC World Service—and the BBC more generally—prides itself for its independence from government control. This generalization is not meant to disparage this independence, which certainly exists, but to indicate that most international radio—the commercially sponsored services aside—is associated officially either directly with governments or at least with particular nation-states.

17. VOA commentaries were included in the analysis for some summits, depending on their availability in the particular service analyzed. They were also included for other services, notably Radio Moscow, Deutsche Welle, Eastern European services, and the Voice of Free China, because they are a part of those services' news programming. Radio Netherlands's "news analysis" is not precisely the same length each evening. BBC and Deutsche Welle news programs included press reports from domestic newspapers—both front-page stories and editorials—and their coverage of the summit was thus sometimes extended by the focus of the print media on the event.

18. Radio Moscow used a different translator than did NBC. The result of the delay was that Gorbachev's normal hesitations in speech as he tried to answer Brokaw's questions could be eliminated. This made him seem more in control, and more decisive, on radio than he appeared on television, where the two men interacted more "equally" in a dialogue.

19. It was necessary to change the services used for each summit for three reasons. First, the nature of shortwave propagation is such that it was not possible to obtain detectable and sufficiently clear signals from the same services each time a summit occurred. Second, the changes in Eastern Europe reduced the quantity of service and often the broadcast signal quality available from stations located there. It became more difficult to locate them or to record them over the period of analysis. Some had to be dropped midway through a summit period because of a deteriorating signal. Third, some of the recording was completed in the United States and some in the United Kingdom, either by myself or the British Broadcasting Corporation. Different signals are available in different parts of the world.

20. Two recent studies are those of McLeod, Viswanath & Yoon, 1987; and Frederick, 1986.

Chapter 4

The 1987 Washington
Superpower Summit

In 1987 Mikhail Gorbachev came to Washington, D.C., to meet with President Ronald Reagan. The two leaders had met twice before, in Geneva in 1985 and in Reykjavik in 1986, and had established a personal relationship despite their deep ideological differences. Gorbachev remained committed to communism and the Communist Party in the Soviet Union, although he had initiated two policies, *perestroika* (restructuring) and *glasnost* (openness or publicity), designed to revitalize his country's economy and to gain support from its intellectual and journalistic establishment by opening up new possibilities for expression. This meeting took place four years after Reagan's characterization of the Soviet Union as the "evil empire."

Despite his personal liking for Gorbachev, Reagan remained skeptical about fundamental changes occurring within the Soviet Union. His famous warning, taken he said from a Russian proverb, was "Trust but verify." This statement seemed to apply to more than just the INF treaty, however. Reagan continued to press for increased emigration of Soviet Jews, the end to Soviet and Eastern European jamming of Western radio signals directed into their countries, Soviet withdrawal from Afghanistan, and reduction of aid to Nicaragua and other "hot spots."

In preparation for the summit, the U.S. National Security Council established five "themes" that were to guide all official statements concerning the summit. These themes were to keep the summit "on track," make sure that all perceived Soviet deficiencies were addressed, and influence press coverage. They were, in essence, pre-summit "spin control," in that they set out the parameters by which the U.S. participants would participate in and comment on the summit agenda and discussions. They dealt with such matters as arms control, regional conflict, human rights, and freedom of communication. These themes instructed everyone, from principals directly involved in the summit—the president; his press secretary, Marlin Fitzwater; Secretary of State George Shultz; members of the Joint Chiefs of Staff; and so on—down to other officials who might be asked to provide specialized commentary, explanations, or information to the press on summit agenda items. These themes were also implied in the briefing materials distributed to the press and in the press briefing papers periodically distributed during the summit. They were the marching orders for public diplomacy.

The summit occurred between December 7 and December 10. Gorbachev completed a televised interview with Tom Brokaw prior to the summit (providing his own version of pre-summit spin control), and both Reagan and he gave post-summit press conferences. Between November 30 and December 13 the eight international radio services, including VOA, Radio Moscow, the BBC, Deutsche Welle, Radio Netherlands, Radio Japan, Radio Spain, and the Voice of Free China, provided a total of 265 news stories, analyses, commentaries, and press reports, using a total of 819.71 minutes of air time during the broadcasts analyzed.[1] The number, length, and frequency of these stories, by radio service, are shown in Table 4.1. Some services do not broadcast news on Sunday, some were unintelligible, one BBC program inadvertently went untaped, Deutsche Welle was taped beginning on December 4, and Radio Japan lost its satellite link for two days.

VOA VERSUS RADIO MOSCOW COVERAGE

Based on quantitative measures alone, there seemed to be few differences in VOA's and Radio Moscow's summit coverage (see Table 4.2). The differences that do exist, however, are easily explainable by reference to the stories themselves. No VOA editorials were included in the analysis, as they were not part of the VOA news reports used. Radio Moscow's news program, however, contained several extensive commentaries, as well as the complete NBC–Gorbachev interview that preceded the beginning of the summit. Slight adjustments based on such factors would provide nearly identical quantitative measurements for the two services. But examining the percentage of available news time for the two services (one hour per program for VOA; forty minutes per program for Radio Moscow) reveals a significant difference. VOA devoted 30.5% of its "news hole" to the summit, Radio

Table 4.1
Basic Quantitative Comparisons of Summit Coverage by International Radio
Services

Service	Stories	Minutes	Days
VOA	75	256.26	14
Radio Moscow	71	297.10	14
BBC	46	98.90	13
Deutsche Welle	23	49.82	7
Radio Netherlands	22	64.33	11
Radio Japan	13	28.02	11
Radio Spain	12	14.00	14
Voice of Free China	3	11.28	14
TOTAL	265	819.71	

Moscow 53.05%. The bulk of this difference is explained by the longer
format of the VOA news program. Also, Radio Moscow did actually
exceed its forty-minute news hole twice, once on December 9 by
providing extensive commentary on the INF treaty and again on the
last day of coverage analyzed when it was still contextualizing the
summit's meaning for its listeners.

   More interesting than these aggregate comparisons, however, is an
examination of the day-to-day coverage of the two services. Both VOA
and Radio Moscow consistently filed about the same number of stories
over the period, but in both cases the amount and percentage of time
devoted varied widely. VOA's coverage peaked on December 8, Radio
Moscow's on December 9. VOA reported no stories on the summit on
December 13 (the last day of the analysis and three days after the end
of the summit); Radio Moscow—whose coverage had fallen between
the 9th and the 12th—devoted considerably more time to the summit
on that day (see Table 4.3).

   Examination of the relationship between the number of stories filed per
day and the total time devoted to the summit also revealed a significant
difference. VOA's correlation was .953, a nearly perfect correlation. VOA's
lengths were tightly controlled: the more stories reported, the more time
devoted to coverage. Radio Moscow's correlation, however, was only
.256, indicating a lack of relationship between number of stories reported
and amount of time devoted to the summit. VOA's reporting format was
thus more consistent and controlled than Radio Moscow's. The difference,
again, was largely due to the number of extensive commentaries and
interviews completed by Radio Moscow on the summit, with relatively
less attention being given simply to reporting the news.[2] The same
conclusion is apparent, too, in the comparison of the average length of

Table 4.2
VOA versus Radio Moscow, Stories Filed and Time Used, Washington Summit
1987

Service	Stories	Minutes	Average Story Length (minutes)
VOA	75	256.26	3.417
Radio Moscow	71	297.10	4.185

stories (mean length) and the standard deviation from this mean of the stories reported. VOA's standard deviation (2.8) is less than its mean (3.42), whereas Radio Moscow's is significantly greater (mean of 4.18 and s.d. of 6.2). This suggests either clear differences in broadcast news styles between the two services or a more volatile news product and less control of the news process by Radio Moscow than by VOA.

In terms of reacting to the events of the summit itself, there was little difference between the two services. If the total time used to report the summit and the percentage of each day's newscast used for summit reports are compared, it appears that both concentrated on reporting or commenting on the summit's actual business. VOA's coverage peaked on December 7 and 8, when the INF treaty was the major topic, and on December 10 and 11, the last day of and the day after the summit. Radio Moscow's major peaks occurred on December 8, 9, 10, and 13; if the difference in time zones is taken into account, the patterns are nearly identical.[3] Radio Moscow did consistently devote more of its available daily news hole to the summit prior to its beginning than did VOA, although in number of stories reported each day there was little difference. This seems to reflect the Soviet concern for promoting the summit itself and thus the Soviet Union's own significance in the world.

As previously mentioned, the National Security Council (NSC) adopted five talking points that were to inform American commentary on the summit and summit issues. These talking points were also an effort to set the agenda for press coverage of the summit, as both the United States and the Soviet Union recognized its significant "public diplomacy" potential. Dr. Stanton Burnett, U.S. coordinator of the summit, suggested that this was the principal justification for the summit, as ongoing negotiations were occurring on substantive arms control issues, regional conflicts, and media access, and the INF treaty had already been successfully negotiated.[4] The first talking point claimed that the INF treaty was a solid foundation for a safer world, while the fifth was a broader statement, to the effect that arms control strengthens security and ensures peace. The point was not restricted, however, to nuclear arms control; it also included the imbalance of conventional forces in Europe, the global elimination of

Table 4.3

Number of Stories Filed and Percentage of Time Devoted to Summit Stories by VOA and Radio Moscow, by Date, Washington Summit 1987

Date	VOA		Radio Moscow	
	Stories	Percent	Stories	Percent
November 30	3	12.3	2	9.4
December 1	4	19.9	3	36.1
December 2	7	32.4	6	19.3
December 3	6	27.7	6	47.4
December 4	6	28.2	7	44.0
December 5	1	14.2	9	41.9
December 6	2	3.7	2	18.0
December 7	11	62.3	3	36.0
December 8	13	85.7	4	92.1
December 9	2	21.3	8	117.3
December 10	9	45.8	8	88.8
December 11	7	49.7	4	45.8
December 12	4	23.8	7	39.9
December 13	0	0	2	106.8

chemical weapons, and acknowledgment of the 4:1 ratio in Soviet to American reductions in intermediate-range nuclear weapons in Europe.

The first talking point was easier to code, because of its succinctness, than the fifth. All stories were examined to determine whether services included these talking points in their reports and how they treated them. On both of these talking points, Radio Moscow followed the NSC design more closely than did VOA. It included both in more stories and included them more directly than did VOA.

All the talking points were evaluated using adaptations of a coefficient formula developed to determine bias in communication. The original formula, developed by Janis and Fadner (1949, pp. 153–169), concentrated on determining the "average presentation of relevant content" (p. 169). It required that negatively biased statements be subtracted from positively biased ones and that the result be divided by the total number of relevant statements. Their formula is:

$$(f - u)/r$$

Lindahl (1978, p. 197) refers to this as the Im coefficient.[5] The coefficient could vary in this formula between +1 (perfectly positive) and -1 (perfectly negative).

The adaptation of this coefficient required that all statements be weighted. Statements were coded to account for a variety of approaches that services might take to reporting about a person, issue, or event. For instance, when including Mikhail Gorbachev in a report, a station could simply mention him (a relevant but unbiased occurrence), quote him (affirming his statement or person), comment favorably about or praise him (doubly affirming him), comment both favorably and unfavorably about him in the same report (considered a negation), or comment only unfavorably about or criticize him (doubly negating). The formula used was thus:

$$Im^1 = ((2f + 1f) - (2u + 1u))/r$$

The coefficients could vary between +2 (perfectly positive) and -2 (perfectly negative). This formula was used to determine the nature of treatment accorded to the NSC talking points, summit principals, and other subjects.

On talking point 5 the two superpower radio services were nearly identical in their treatment, with a positive Im^1 coefficient of nearly +1.5. Given the more general nature of this talking point, however, that is not surprising. On talking point 1, however, Radio Moscow's coefficient (nearly +1.5) was significantly higher than VOA's (nearly +1). This result is interesting, too, because VOA knew the themes prior to the summit and thus could have couched its reports to take account of them, while Radio Moscow could not.[6]

This situation indicates the independence of VOA news from national direction, a conclusion that the organization would probably embrace. If one views the NSC themes as providing the basis for propaganda, too, VOA's stance clearly suggested that news value was more important than propaganda points. If the themes were significantly represented in official statements about the summit, however, then arguably VOA missed the story. Putting it more pointedly, if the themes were apparent, some might even accuse VOA of being perverse in its treatment.[7]

Talking points 2 through 4 were more problematic as a basis for comparing VOA and Radio Moscow. All three talking points portrayed the Soviet Union negatively, making it unlikely that the services' coverage would support them. More likely, they would be ignored or denied. Talking point 2 claimed that respect for human rights was as important as arms control, point 3 that Soviet conduct in regional conflicts impeded improvement in U.S.–Soviet relations, and point 4 that Soviet espionage, disinformation campaigns, and lack of reciprocity in media access undermined trust between the superpowers.[8]

As expected, Radio Moscow did not include these three themes often in its reports. Sixty percent or more of all stories it reported on the summit failed to include them. This was also true of VOA, however, which matched Radio Moscow in avoiding talking point 2, included point 3 slightly more frequently, and point 4 slightly less frequently. On this measure, then, there was almost no difference between the two services. On human rights Radio Moscow actually directly stated the point more often than VOA, although VOA implied it more often. VOA also affirmed talking points 3 and 4 more frequently and carried no negative statements about them, which Radio Moscow did (see Appendix 1). The one talking point that Radio Moscow did have a negative coefficient for was number 4, which condemned Soviet disinformation campaigns and efforts to control its citizens' access to information.

Although there were differences between the two services, there was no consistent pattern that would allow conclusions concerning ideological bias to be made. This observation is true, too, across all services examined. Dividing the eight services into five groups, based on possible political bias, and performing multiple regression analysis yielded no significant correlation coefficients at the .10 level (see Table 4.4). Therefore, no predictions about coverage could reasonably be made on the basis of previous patterns. (Such analysis was dropped for subsequent summits, as the two superpowers had begun to move toward political accommodation.)

The qualitative dimensions of the summit coverage, like the thematic analysis, were difficult to measure. The coding instrument was designed to determine, for instance, whether the descriptions of Reagan and Gorbachev, the United States and the Soviet Union, were positive, negative, or neutral. It also required that the *primary* source of every story be determined, even in cases where multiple sources such as actualities, on-site correspondent reports, man-on-the-street interviews, and staff reports might be mixed into a single story, with each source providing a perspective on a topic—either to provide "objective" reports, to gauge world reaction to the summit or the INF treaty, or to demonstrate the wisdom of the negotiation/compromise made. Finally, the possible foci of all stories were collapsed into five larger categories for analysis: (1) hard news—news about the summit itself or actions taken by allies (such as signing the instruments allowing for on-site inspections on their territory); (2) short-range problems—human rights, arms control violations, regional conflicts; (3) long-range problems—to-

Table 4.4
Results of Multiple Regression Analysis on Thematic Content, Using Radio
Service Bias

Independent Variable	Dependent Variable	Correlation Coefficient	T-Value
Bias	Talking Point 1	5.718	.3442
	Talking Point 2	-0.2665	.7012
	Talking Point 3	-1.258	.4903
	Talking Point 4	-0.175	.9377
	Talking Point 5	4.577	.3508
Stories filed	Talking Point 1	-0.188	.6465
	Talking Point 2	.270	.1083
	Talking Point 3	.566	.1198
	Talking Point 4	.055	.7859
	Talking Point 5	.472	.8904
Minutes of	Talking Point 1	.219	.2183
summit coverage	Talking Point 2	-0.0196	.3496
	Talking Point 3	-0.134	.1305
	Talking Point 4	.007	.8904
	Talking Point 5	.067	.4856

Bias was operationalized in five categories: VOA, Radio Moscow, BBC, other European services, and Asian services.

tal armaments, achieving peace, treaty adherence; (4) political issues—U.S.–NATO relations, Soviet–Warsaw Pact relations, U.S.–Soviet relations; and (5) personality news—about Reagan, Gorbachev, Nancy, Raisa, and so on.

There were thirteen possible source classifications for each summit story. Several of these were unused or were used only insignificantly by the radio services. Those used as primary sources included staff reporters or anchors, commentators, actualities (on-site recordings of the events as they occurred), on-site correspondents' descriptions, interviews, other media (such as newspapers), and official spokespersons (either domestic or foreign).

There were significant differences between VOA and Radio Moscow in their use of these sources. VOA stories came from three main sources: staff reporters, either in VOA studios or at the summit press center; on-site correspondents who reported from remote sites such as the White House and Andrews Air Force Base; and actualities, which were the actual tapings or live feeds of speeches as they occurred. Radio Moscow, in contrast, was more varied in the sources for its stories: It relied on staff reporters and actualities to a lesser extent than VOA and used relatively few on-site correspondents' reports, but it included more interviews, official spokespersons, commentaries, and reports carried in other media—notably TASS—in its reports.

VOA's reporting strategy made better use of the radio medium than did Radio Moscow's. Its effort to carry statements by summit principals, in particular, provided a more "trustworthy" account of the summit, in that its reports would have seemed less prone to manipulation, particularly when carried live. But Radio Moscow's strategy provided a more varied account of the summit and possibly could have been judged more "interesting" to attend to. Radio Moscow's strategy also allowed it to construct its reports in such a way that particular points could be made, thus providing more opportunity to "score propaganda points." This may help explain why Radio Moscow's reports often seemed to be more responsive to the NSC themes than did VOA's. Radio Moscow based some stories on panels of experts who were called into its studios to comment on issues that arose during the summit, particularly arms control issues. As the general positions of such experts were known in advance, they could be selected on the basis of their opinions; questions could be addressed to them that would allow particular points of view to be articulated for Radio Moscow listeners. The station also provided similar spins by using man-in-the-street interviews that allowed it to select appropriate comments to make its point.

The focus of stories reported by the two services also differed. Although both services spent significant time reporting on the summit itself, particularly about the INF treaty signing, its implications for Europe, its acceptance by the respective alliances, and its possible ratification by the legislative assemblies of each country, on other stories they differed significantly. VOA carried stories about the strategic defense initiative (SDI), NATO, and the defense of Western Europe not touched by Radio Moscow and spent more time than its counterpart in covering Gorbachev and Raisa, human rights, Afghanistan, and the relationship of the Soviet Union to its Eastern bloc allies. Radio Moscow, for its part, was more interested in reporting on such issues as U.S.–Soviet relations, strategic and conventional weapons reductions, adherence to treaties, and the means to achieve peace in the world.[9]

When all possible story focus items were aggregated into categories, few surprises emerged. The VOA reported more personality-based stories than Radio Moscow and paid somewhat more attention to short-term problems, while Radio Moscow reported many more stories on political issues (because of its commentaries and interviews with academics, Soviet experts, and people on the street, which were lacking on VOA). Both services, however, reported more summit-related stories than any other type. Of VOA's stories, 49.2% dealt with the summit itself or the INF treaty, as did 45.7% of Radio Moscow's.

Finally on this issue, when the story focus of the two services was compared during the three phases of summit research (pre-summit, summit, and post-summit), clear differences emerged. On summit-related stories, for instance, VOA's focus occurred *during* the summit period itself (December 7–10), while Radio Moscow's focus occurred *prior to* the summit, suggesting an attempt to set up cognitive screens in advance that could affect how an unpredictable event would be interpreted by audiences. This conclusion is reinforced by the fact that Radio Moscow also reported several pre-summit stories on political issues— such as U.S.–Soviet relations, which were continued through the summit and then dropped. VOA reported on both short-term and long-term issues prior to the summit in equal measure but then concentrated slightly more effort on reporting short-term problems, while Radio Moscow concentrated more effort on long-term problems from the start.

Portrayals of the two summit protagonists (Reagan and Gorbachev) and their respective nations differed significantly in the reports of the two services. Both carried mostly positive descriptions of Reagan, for instance, but Radio Moscow offset these portrayals to some extent by carrying both negative and "neutral" descriptions. VOA did not portray Reagan negatively in any story, and Radio Moscow likewise carried only positive and neutral descriptions of Gorbachev. Also, VOA carried no negative portrayals of the United States but included several negative statements about the Soviet Union. Radio Moscow was the reverse. In descriptions of both Gorbachev and the Soviet Union, Radio Moscow was moderately positive in its portrayals (with Im^1 coefficients of nearly .7 and over .8 respectively), but it was also positive in treatments of Reagan and the United States, although at lower levels. VOA was less positive in its portrayals of Gorbachev than was Radio Moscow (with an Im^1 coefficient of under .4), while its treatment of Reagan reached an Im^1 level of over .8. It was also far more positive in its treatment of the United States than of the Soviet Union, where it had an Im^1 coefficient of -0.3 (see Appendix 2).

The Im^1 coefficients illustrate two points. First, VOA's reports separated General Secretary Gorbachev from the Soviet state much more strongly than Radio Moscow separated President Reagan from the United States, although both services were more positive in portrayals of the opposing leaders than of their countries. Neither service, however, separated its own leader from his state as readily. In VOA's case, as in the United States more generally, there seemed to be a genuine willingness to see Gorbachev as a new type of Soviet leader, one who was not necessarily tarred with the past actions of the Soviet Union. The nature of the Soviet state, however, was still open for condemnation. Radio Moscow was given ample fuel for negative portrayals of the United States by the vociferous anti-INF posture taken by many conservative critics, which—along with Reagan's willingness to accept Gorbachev—also allowed Radio Moscow to separate Reagan clearly from the United States.

The data do suggest that Radio Moscow and VOA approached the task of reporting the Washington summit differently. Although on some dimensions there were similarities, on others, such as the type of coverage—as measured by sources used—the focus of stories, and the timing of story focus, the reports were sufficiently different to conclude that the means of gathering and reporting the news differed in the two countries.

OTHER RADIO SERVICES' COVERAGE

The most obvious difference in coverage of the summit by other radio services—compared to superpower coverage—lay in the sheer number of stories filed and the total time devoted to summit coverage (see Table 4.1 again). Beyond that, however, other significant differences also emerged. Staff reporters overwhelmingly provided the sources for summit stories of the various services; in some cases, no other sources were used. Also, no actuality-based reports were carried, and there was more reliance on both commentary and other media (particularly press reports from each country's domestic press) as sources for stories.

All services did not, however, approach the task of summit coverage identically. The BBC, for instance, relied more heavily on on-site correspondents' reports and other media than other services did, while other European services relied overwhelmingly on staff reporters. Asian services carried no reports from other media, official spokespersons, or interviews, all of which were used by European services.

Treatment of NSC talking points also differed significantly from that of the superpower radio services. Talking points 1 and 5 were of interest to the services, but little interest was shown in points 2, 3, and 4. These services apparently saw the summit as one nearly exclusively focused on the issues associated with arms control—issues particularly of concern in Western Europe.

Most other services carried so few stories, and relied so significantly on staff reporters—who themselves probably received their information exclusively from wire services—that analyzing their treatment of summit principals adds little. But in two cases enough information exists to allow conclusions to be drawn: the BBC World Service and Radio Netherlands.

The BBC's reports about both Reagan and Gorbachev were more positive than those of Radio Netherlands, but neither station's were as positive as VOA or Radio Moscow (see Appendix 2). Both services' treatment of the summit nations, however, was equivocal. The Im[1] coefficient of coverage for the BBC was positive concerning the United States, but Radio Netherlands's Im[1] coefficient was slightly negative. Both services' Im[1] coefficients of coverage for the Soviet Union were negative. Although the bulk of the BBC's reports on the United States were neutral, it carried more negative portrayals of the Soviet Union than either positive or neutral descriptions. Radio Netherlands carried more negative than positive descriptions of both countries (see Appendix 2).

Based on this analysis, Radio Netherlands seems to have been conservative in its coverage, avoiding excessively positive treatment of any summit participant and maintaining a more skeptical posture on the summit than other services. One report perhaps best captures Radio Netherlands's approach. On December 11 it carried a report on the results of the summit for human rights. In Geneva, the report said, the U.N. Human Rights Commission viewed the results "with dismay." The summit had yielded "no results whatsoever as far as human rights are concerned." The report went on to remind listeners that the United States had never ratified U.N. human rights instruments, claiming that the Constitution adequately guaranteed human rights. But, the report continued, the Constitution "is no match for dozens of detailed and legally binding documents." The Soviet Union had ratified these documents, Radio Netherlands said, but had "not joined complaint procedures for individual citizens which are part of these treaties." So, it concluded, Soviet ratification of the instruments remained "somewhat of an empty gesture." Neither superpower was allowed to escape criticism.

On one measure, coverage by the BBC was similar to that of the superpower services: the pattern of its coverage over the period analyzed. The number of stories remained fairly high over the thirteen-day period (BBC World Service news was inadvertently left unrecorded on December 13), while the total time it devoted to the summit gradually rose after December 5, peaking on December 9. As a percentage of available time, peak BBC coverage was also provided on December 9, with another, slightly lesser peak on December 11.

Radio Netherlands's coverage was more erratic than the BBC's. The number of stories reported peaked before the summit on December 1 and 4, then dropped to zero on December 6, the day before the summit. Coverage then rose through the summit period, peaking on December 10, and then rapidly fell off to zero again by December 12. The percentage of its broadcast devoted to the summit followed the same pattern (see Table 4.5). In sum, Radio Netherlands's coverage, while quite comprehensive at some points, was not as consistent over the period as was that of the BBC, VOA, or Radio Moscow.

Table 4.5
Number of Stories Filed and Percentage of Time Devoted to Summit Stories by
the BBC and Radio Netherlands, by Date, Washington Summit 1987

	BBC		Radio Netherlands	
Date	Stories	Percent	Stories	Percent
November 30	1	4.1	1	3.6
December 1	2	7.2	3	55.3
December 2	5	13.4	1	4.3
December 3	4	6.0	1	15.4
December 4	3	7.6	2	16.2
December 5	2	2.0	1	65.4
December 6	5	14.5	0	NA
December 7	4	25.2	2	20.4
December 8	4	32.6	2	20.5
December 9	5	37.5	2	24.0
December 10	3	18.7	4	55.2
December 11	3	32.1	3	41.5
December 12	4	18.9	0	NA
December 13	NA	NA	0	NA

Coverage patterns for the other European services and Asian services differed again. Aggregating European services provided peaks in the number of stories filed on December 1, 4, 8, and 10, while Asian services peaked on December 11, largely the result of Voice of Free China providing post-summit commentary on an event which it had otherwise ignored. The same general pattern also existed for the total time devoted to summit coverage by the various services.

In terms of the control of summit stories (calculations of mean length and standard deviations), the BBC, Radio Netherlands, and Radio Japan all demonstrated similar levels of control as that of VOA, with Radio Spain slightly lower. Deutsche Welle, however, like Radio Moscow, had a standard deviation greater than its mean, while Voice of Free China had a mean of nearly 4.0 compared with its standard deviation of less than .5, as it had reported no stories, but only provided two extensive (and largely negative) commentaries on the summit after its conclusion.

COMPARATIVE SUMMIT APPROACHES

These data suggest that the superpower services' approach to the summit differed significantly from that of other services, with the exception of the BBC on some dimensions of coverage. On nearly every criterion, quantitative and qualitative, there were enough differences to suggest that the services outside the summit countries approached their task of reporting differently—perhaps because they were less involved and had less need to engage in the "propaganda battle" over whose interpretation of the summit would prevail.

There were also significant differences in the ways the various radio services used radio as a medium to report the summit. Some services apparently relied exclusively on wire service copy to construct their reports about the summit. This was true, for instance, of Radio Spain and Radio Japan.

The BBC relied primarily on two sources for its reports: on-site correspondents and domestic press commentary. In the context of this study, use of the domestic press stood out, particularly given the BBC's keen desire to have its news reports seen as fair, objective, and trustworthy around the world. But including the press reports (as Deutsche Welle also did) clearly provided an opportunity to provide commentary within the news program by allowing someone else to do it. Although there is no evidence that this necessarily slanted the reports themselves, using the press accounts could certainly allow listeners to see the reports in this way, as their context was partially molded by press headlines and editorials.

The on-site correspondent reports (BBC) and commentaries (Radio Netherlands) both did make good use of radio by providing material from distant sites to listeners. None of the nonsuperpower radio services used the medium as well as VOA and Radio Moscow, however. VOA's reports stood out in their use of actuality coverage; Radio Moscow's by its varied source material and breadth of stories carried. Both provided more variety in their use of radio than other services, thus creating a more interesting news product for the listener.[10]

There were questions raised, too, about whether those involved in the summit had adequate opportunity to be heard. A marketplace of ideas may have been created by the variety of approaches taken to the summit by these radio services, but this marketplace was clearly under the control of the stations, not those who were active summit participants. It was a marketplace largely consisting of secondhand observations. The Voice of Free China did not reflect the summit events at all and commented on it only after its conclusion. Other services carried reports about the summit but relied on their own staffs (either in their studios or the field) to select aspects of the summit to report or to comment on the progress (or lack of progress) of the summit. Some allowed domestic newspapers to speak; others searched for responses from world leaders, people on the street, or experts who could be interviewed.

One method devised to get at this issue was to look at the treatment of NSC talking points over the total analysis period. Doing so shows rather erratic coverage patterns by various services.

Throughout the period, VOA, for instance, paid more attention to points 2 through 4 (particularly 2 and 3) than to the arms control points (excepting two days, December 10 and 11) and actually dropped talking point 1 twice (December 5–6 and December 9), before ending coverage altogether on December 13. Radio Moscow, on the other hand, emphasized talking points 1 and 5 to a far greater extent than others, clearly seeing the summit as a place to pursue arms control issues and hoping to put a "spin" on the summit that would play to the Soviet Union's strong suit: Gorbachev's ability to suggest that dramatic progress was possible on this important issue.[11] European services' coverage followed a different approach, tending to emphasize talking point 5 over point 1 (the long-range arms control issues over the short-term one—the INF treaty) and dealing with other matters (such as human rights and regional conflicts) as concerns that deserved only sporadic treatment (on December 4 and December 8–10). The BBC shifted its emphasis over the analysis period, emphasizing point 5 at the beginning and end of the period, point 1 twice (on December 4 and 9), and points 2 through 4 between December 6 and 9. The most dramatic pattern for the BBC coverage applied to talking point 1, concerning the INF treaty's contribution to a safer world.

Another approach taken to this question was to examine the extent to which various services relied on actualities and on-site correspondents, as both imply a commitment of resources that presumably would be used. The VOA, of course, had an advantage in its coverage, because it was operating locally. Therefore, as might be expected, it used actualities and on-site reports most often of all services. Two other services, however, that had significant resources devoted to on-site coverage were Radio Moscow and the BBC. But neither of these services relied on these two possible sources for reports to the extent that VOA did. VOA's dependence on such reporting made it the most "reactive" of the services examined, as it had tied its coverage most closely to the technology necessary to provide these reports.

A third method of determining whether or not the services approached the summit in the same fashion was to look for correlations among several appropriate variables. Variables used included the bias of the service (United States, Soviet Union, Western European, BBC, Asian); total number of stories filed, total minutes devoted to summit coverage; total positive and negative portrayals of Reagan, Gorbachev, the United States, the Soviet Union, and the summit itself. Using a cutoff of .670, positive correlations existed across a broad range of these variables. However, no statistically significant positive correlations existed between the bias of the service and any other variable. Bias itself, then, does not explain treatment of summit principals, countries involved, or evaluation of the summit itself.

Significant correlations did exist between total number of stories filed and various portrayals. The same was true of the total minutes of time used to cover the summit (see Table 4.6). The fact that negative portrayals lacked high positive correlations with these quantitative measures suggests that these radio services' reportage was not emphasizing the negative aspects of the summit and its participants. It is also true, however, that the reporting practices of both VOA and Radio Moscow affected the outcome of these correlations, as it did in all subsequent cases.

Positive descriptions of both summit principals were also highly correlated with positive descriptions of their respective countries. Negative descriptions of Ronald Reagan were also highly correlated with negative descriptions of the United States, but negative descriptions of Mikhail Gorbachev were not significantly positively correlated with negative descriptions of the Soviet Union. Both positive and negative descriptions of the United States, however, were correlated with positive descriptions of Mikhail Gorbachev (see Table 4.7).

In general, too, positive statements about the Soviet Union and Gorbachev were more highly correlated with positive descriptions of the summit than were positive statements about the United States or Reagan (see Table 4.8).

Positive descriptions of the summit were also correlated highly with *negative* descriptions of the United States (.830), at a level even slightly higher than they were with positive descriptions of the United States.

In general, listeners' choice of radio service did matter. Selecting VOA meant extensive actuality coverage, no commentary, and pursuit of focused stories not necessarily confirming the legitimacy of the agenda setting attempted by the NSC. Selecting Radio Moscow meant a wider range of issues addressed and more sources of information, but information filtered largely through staff reporters, with little reliance on real-time reports of summit events. While this was also an agenda-setting approach to the summit, as most clearly seen in Radio Moscow human rights stories that emphasized quite different rights than did U.S. reports, in many respects the agenda set by the service more closely mirrored the NSC talking points than did the reports of VOA. Selecting any other of the international services examined meant far less coverage, fewer stories, and dependence on staff reporters and domestic press headlines and editorials—with the exception of the BBC, with its exten-

Table 4.6
Correlations between Stories Filed and Reporting Time versus Portrayals of
Summit Principals, Countries, and Success of the Summit

	Reagan+	Gorbachev+	U.S.+	U.S.S.R.+	Summit+
Total stories	.720	.678	.810		.741
Total minutes	.760	.843	.910	.680	.850

Table 4.7
Correlations of Descriptions of Summit Principals and Summit Countries

	U.S.+	U.S.-	U.S.S.R.+
Reagan+	.952		
Reagan-		.806	
Gorbachev+	.860	.751	.888

Table 4.8
Correlations of Descriptions of the Summit and Summit Countries and Principals

	Reagan+	Gorbachev+	U.S.+	U.S.S.R.+
Summit+	.738	.977	.800	.903

sive cadre of on-site correspondents. However, it also meant hearing a less politically involved service, which resulted in a more skeptical approach to the summit by some and more attention paid to nonsuperpower reaction in most.

Propaganda was also present, although subtle, in the reports. VOA, even when carrying actuality reports, tended to use American statements first; Radio Moscow followed the opposite tack. Both services usually were selective, too, in the amount of any statement carried, which allowed them to pick and choose among statements made. Radio Moscow actually repeated portions of prior programs on subsequent occasions, providing a measure of repetition of message to listeners or the chance to reach new listeners with the same message. Both superpower services portrayed their own countries and leaders more positively than their opposites, though VOA was somewhat harsher on the Soviet Union than was Radio Moscow on the United States.

In some respects VOA operated at a disadvantage compared to Radio Moscow, even though VOA was operating on its own territory. VOA's news service operates using the same principles for news gathering and reporting traditionally adopted by the American press. But the summit provided little grist for the event-oriented news operation, because of limited briefings on the status or progress of negotiations, leaving VOA to report only ceremonial events. Also, because the event occurred in Washington and no Soviet leader had visited the United States since Brezhnev, there was great curiosity about Mikhail Gorbachev. The Soviet leader exploited his opening well, beginning with the NBC interview, stopping over to see Margaret Thatcher; scheduling meetings with American business and industry leaders, editors and publishers, and members of Congress; holding an American-style press conference; and then returning to Europe to brief Warsaw Pact allies. Few of these activities were realistic options for Ronald Reagan. The result was an "exposure gap": Reagan in the Rose Garden and Gorbachev on the stump.

Perhaps the principal fallout from the difference was the perception, at least as indicated by international radio coverage, that descriptions of the success of the summit were more highly correlated with positive portrayals of the Soviets than of the Americans. Although this may be an ephemeral perception, it indicates that the conventional wisdom about the positive results of hosting an important foreign leader may be overstated. When, as the United States Advisory Commission on Public Diplomacy put it (1988, p. 5), "Foreign attitudes directly affect America's ability to achieve its national security goals and indeed become a substantive part of the policy process," relying on incorrect conventional wisdom may result in quite unexpected results.

Every service emphasized different portions of the summit, spent varying amounts of time reporting on those elements selected, and shifted emphasis over the course of the two-week period—all of which is probably intuitively to be expected. Each service, too, spent time reporting elements that were important to its domestic constituency. Voice of Free China saw the summit in terms of the relationship of the superpowers to Beijing. Western European services saw it in terms of their own security concerns, with Deutsche Welle concerned about possible further nuclear arsenal cuts without deep cuts in conventional arms imbalances, Radio Netherlands with a more internationalist perspective, bringing in commentary from U.N. agencies, and the BBC with Margaret Thatcher's role in preparing Reagan and pressing Gorbachev on his U.K. stopover to make progress at the summit.

One recurring problem in news flow is the issue of bias, whether it be an ideological or political bias, a northern industrialized country bias, or a cultural bias.[12] Larson (1982, p. 20) has noted the frustration of journalists, researchers, and politicians from developing countries at the "event orientation" of news, which largely ignores process. Events themselves are not always perceived identically: The media can influence perceptions by choosing how much attention to devote to a story, how to report it, and what to focus on in the reports.[13]

Of all services, the VOA was the most "event-oriented." It was tied both to the American journalistic standard of objectivity and to the technology that seemed best able to make that objectivity a reality. Hence it relied on actuality and on-site correspondent reports. Other services provided various contexts for the summit of one sort or another. Radio Moscow had the most opportunity to provide context, as it spent the most time and covered the most subjects. But other services also set up contexts, either by their own commentaries (as in the case of Radio Netherlands or Voice of Free China), by use of domestic press opinion (as did the BBC and Deutsche Welle), and by relying exclusively on read wire service copy (as Radio Spain and Radio Japan did). In general, however, the criticism would hold: Clearly, there was an event orientation. The summit, of course, was the major event. Other important activities included Gorbachev's NBC interview, his stopover in Britain to talk to Margaret Thatcher on his way to Washington, his return stop in Berlin to brief members of the Warsaw Pact, Reagan's post-summit address to the American people, and George Shultz's trip to Brussels to brief NATO allies. Other less obvious events included statements made by major figures such as NATO's Lord Carrington, West German Chancellor Helmut Kohl, and even members of the U.S. Senate.

Each service provided, then, what Dahlgren and Chakrapani (1982) have called "ways of seeing" the world. They distinguish two major ways of seeing, the mythic and the historical. "Mythic modes," they suggest (p. 61), "provide meaning to events and affairs by stressing the eternal and recurring features of the human condition. . . . Mythic ways of seeing explain reality by an appeal to ontological properties." There are differences, of course, between the mythic ways of seeing practiced by journalists and those of audiences. So it is dangerous to suggest, as they do, that news accounts provide meaning: Audiences also actively interpret and make news accounts meaningful. They interpret news within their own contexts.

It is fair to say, however, that the different services attempted to provide different ways of seeing the summit and its component parts, even while retaining their event orientation. No service saw or reported the summit absolutely objectively or with perfect balance. They treated summit principals and their countries from particular points of view. Given the nature of the services examined, this meant that the United States and President Reagan received, on balance, more positive ratings than did the Soviets. However, that would not necessarily translate into perceptions of Americans as more interested in, say, peace than the Soviets. Every country's citizens will filter information about the summit, the INF treaty, and human rights through "terministic screens" constructed on the basis of historical experience with the two superpowers and with ongoing relations with the world community on such issues.[14] Neither superpower should expect, then, to have world opinion on its behavior hinge on only its relations with the other or on summitry. Every country has myths about its place in the world, through which it interprets the actions of others.

NOTES

1. All time calculations in the research are based on minutes, calculated to two decimal places. Numbers following the decimal points, therefore, are not seconds, but hundredths of minutes.

2. Correlations were calculated using simple regression analysis. The correlation coefficient for VOA was .95, with a standard error of 4.4, and for Radio Moscow .26, with a standard error of 13.7.

3. December 5 was obviously a day of "agenda setting" for the summit by Radio Moscow. The service carried stories about the historic nature of the summit, man-on-the-street interviews with Muscovites, a denial of Soviet violations of the antiballistic missile (ABM) treaty of 1972, a story on a "peace march" in Moscow, and others. The 9th included extensive commentary on the significance of the INF treaty and meetings between Gorbachev and U.S. delegations, while the 10th had stories both about the official White House departure ceremony and also Gorbachev's press conference, his meeting with U.S. editors and publishers, and "human rights day" observations in the Soviet Union. The 13th included a nearly forty-one-minute summary of the summit.

4. Burnett was at that time counselor of the agency at USIA. This information came from an interview prior to the summit, on December 3.

5. A second formula is similar but adds positively and negatively biased perspectives, with the result divided by the total number of relevant statements. The formula is $(f + u/)r$ (see Lindahl, 1978, p. 197). Lindahl refers to this as the L coefficient.

6. It should be noted here that most of the NSC's strategy using such points was directed at influencing the coverage provided by foreign domestic media to the summit, not primarily U.S. domestic media or VOA. Burnett said he imagined that point 1 would be difficult for U.S.–based media to report as the administration wished.

7. The VOA newsroom itself never received the talking points from the NSC or USIA. The judgments made about what to cover and how to cover it during the summit were thus decisions based on what they considered would be news to their audience.

8. Such themes perhaps indicate the difficulties posed for coding. The Soviet Union does address issues of human rights, but it defines such rights quite differently than does the United States. Also, even when human rights are discussed—by any party—statements tend not to suggest that they are as important as arms control. Coding on such themes has to be done with less precision; what is important, then, about the coding is that it be done across all services in the same manner.

9. The issue of adherence to treaties was raised by the question of U.S. adherence to the antiballistic missile (ABM) treaty of 1972, part of the debate over the strategic defense initiative (SDI).

10. Radio Moscow's coverage was a change from its earlier staid (and boring) programming strategies, which were mired in ideological terminology and aimed principally at people who already agreed with communist political reality (see Browne, 1982, pp. 235, 236; and Wasburn, 1992, pp. 33, 34). The change in Radio Moscow's coverage is probably the result of its response to Mikhail Gorbachev, who took over as chairman of the Communist Party in 1985. His mission, as Sheehy put it (1990, pp. 192, 193), "was to save the socialist system by changing it." To that end his tactics were "surprise, compromise, improvise." Gorbachev himself claimed, during his interview with Tom Brokaw shortly before the 1987 Washington summit, "We have built up a new atmosphere in the country, an atmosphere of *glasnost*, openness, and we have plans to move forward with the process of democratization and *glasnost*" (Gorbachev, 1990, p. 14). This atmosphere also affected the activities of Radio Moscow.

11. Gorbachev (1990, p. 61) referred to the INF treaty signed in Washington as a "major event, what I would call a history-making event. . . . [It had signaled entry into] a new phase in the process of real nuclear disarmament by agreeing to eliminate two classes of missiles."

12. See, for instance, Morales, 1982, pp. 79–113.

13. See E. F. Einsiedel, quoted by Paraschos & Rutherford, 1985, p. 458.

14. This term comes from Burke, 1966, Chapter 3.

Chapter 5

The 1988 Moscow
Superpower Summit

In 1988 Ronald Reagan traveled to Moscow to meet with Mikhail Gorbachev. His visit, the first by an American president since 1974 (when Gerald Ford met Leonid Brezhnev in Vladivostok during the period of U.S.–Soviet detente), also was significant for making superpower summits almost routine. The Moscow summit marked the fourth meeting between Reagan and Gorbachev since 1984; the two men had met more frequently than any president and general secretary since the end of World War II. The summit also followed the Washington summit by only six months, indicating the increasing frequency of meetings between the two countries and the desire to capitalize on the good relations between Reagan and Gorbachev. In Moscow there was even talk of a fifth summit meeting should the difficulties on strategic weapons reduction be resolved prior to Reagan's leaving the presidency in January 1989.

The analysis on this summit was based on the reportage of sixteen radio services, concentrating on services in North America (Radio Canada and the Voice of America), the Soviet Union (Radio Moscow), Europe (Radio Berlin from the German Democratic Republic [East] and Radio Prague from Czechoslovakia in the socialist bloc, and the BBC from Great Britain, Brussels Calling from Belgium, Deutsche Welle from the Federal Republic of Germany [West], and Radio Netherlands), and the Middle East (Radio Baghdad from Iraq, Radio Cairo from Egypt, and the Voice of Turkey). Also included from the socialist bloc was Radio Havana from Cuba. From areas more remote from Europe were Radio

Australia, Radio Japan, and Radio South Africa. Altogether these services provided over 500 stories to code on the summit in the period between May 22 and June 8. The summit itself occurred between May 29 and June 1.

The most prolific services over the entire period were Radio Moscow, VOA, the BBC, and Radio Prague. The fewest stories were broadcast by Radio Havana, Radio Japan, Radio Baghdad, Radio South Africa, and Radio Cairo (see Table 5.1). Grouping the stories by region indicates that, for this analysis, the preponderance of stories were broadcast by the two superpowers and European services on both sides of the Iron Curtain.[1] Of the 527 stories coded, 23.5% were broadcast by Radio Moscow, 21.4% by VOA, 25.6% by Western European radio services, and 18.6% by Eastern European services, for a total of 89.2% of the stories broadcast by all services analyzed.

This analysis examined the main evening news program(s) broadcast in English each day. Focusing on these programs, while not inclusive of the entire coverage of the summit—for instance, live coverage of speeches or news conferences outside the news programs—is an indication of the choices made by editorial staffs concerning the most significant stories to report each day. Since each international radio organization also draws from the same news sources for its stories across its language services, focusing on one language also gives a basic indication of what is reported in other languages.[2]

The number of stories reported by the different services is not necessarily indicative of the importance each placed on the summit. This can be determined more accurately by looking at the number of times that the summit was used to lead off the various segments of each news program and at the percentage of available broadcast time over the period devoted to the summit. Before reporting these statistics, however, it would be useful to indicate the general characteristics of each country's news broadcast, as the services used were somewhat different than those of the Washington summit and as some services' news programs changed between the summits.

Radio Australia. Radio Australia's news program consisted of a summary of world news read from the studio. It lasted between ten and twelve minutes each day and contained neither field reports nor actualities.

Radio Baghdad. Radio Baghdad, like Radio Australia, provided only studio summaries of the day's events. The program lasted ten minutes daily. Radio Baghdad used no field reports or actualities.

Radio Berlin. Radio Berlin aired a fifteen-minute news program each day consisting of a summary of world news. It was always read from the studio without field reports or actualities.

Table 5.1
Basic Quantitative Comparisons of Summit Coverage by International Radio
Services

Service	Stories	Minutes	Days
VOA	116	250.34	17
Radio Moscow	127	420.68	18
BBC	80	113.47	17
Brussels Calling	15	5.66	13
Radio Netherlands	30	37.89	17
Deutsche Welle	38	41.88	15
Radio Berlin	38	23.29	17
Radio Prague	66	91.57	17
Voice of Turkey	23	13.57	15
Radio Cairo	5	1.59	6
Radio Baghdad	11	1.22	10
Radio South Africa	17	2.91	17
Radio Canada	26	17.26	15
Radio Australia	15	9.64	14
Radio Japan	3	5.57	2

BBC. BBC, during the 1988 summit period, actually broadcast two major evening news programs to North America, both of which were coded in the analysis. These programs were "Newsdesk" and "Radio Newsreel," each of which was thirty minutes in length. These two programs consisted of a number of different elements, including bulletins of world news, correspondents' reports, press reviews, and commentaries. Quite often a story carried in the bulletin of world news would paraphrase a correspondent's report that would follow later in the program. These were coded as two separate stories, however.

Brussels Calling. Belgium's Flemish community aired Brussels Calling each day. The fifteen-minute program included both studio summaries of world news and a review of major newspaper stories from the Belgian press. Brussels Calling used no field reports or actualities.

Radio Cairo. Egypt's international radio service, like Radio Baghdad, consisted only of a summary of the day's news. The program lasted ten minutes and did not include actualities or field reports.

Radio Canada. Canada provided a daily ten-minute summary of world news but included no actualities or field reports.

Deutsche Welle. West Germany's international radio service included both a bulletin of world news and a review of the stories carried by the West German press. The newscast was twenty minutes long. Deutsche Welle used no actualities or field reports.

Radio Havana. Cuba's international service carried a summary of world news but showed no interest in the summit, carrying only one story during the period. Its daily bulletin, including only studio-read stories, lasted ten minutes.

Radio Japan. Like Radio Havana, Radio Japan had little interest in the summit. Its newscast consisted of a fifteen-minute summary of world news, without actualities or field reports.

Radio Moscow. Radio Moscow's basic thirty-minute news program often ran to forty-five minutes, particularly after it began airing special summit reports and added other program elements to provide additional coverage. It also sometimes included a "Moscow Summit Report," a lengthy feature segment entitled "Home in the USSR," commentaries or discussions often led by Vladimir Posner (sometimes called "Top Priority"), and Joe Adamov's venerable "Moscow Mailbag." It is difficult to determine, when listening to Radio Moscow, what is news and what is something else. The content of the basic news program often varied, with different bits included from day to day. Radio Moscow did use actualities and sound bites, with correspondents on the street to talk with Soviet citizens or reporting from summit activities.

Radio Netherlands. Radio Netherlands's news program consisted of two parts: a bulletin of world news, and "Newsline," in-depth stories introduced in the studio and then reported by a correspondent in the field. Actualities or sound bites were often part of the "Newsline" coverage, and the stories could often be quite lengthy, providing some of the most in-depth coverage of any of the services. Both segments together ran thirty minutes.

Radio Prague. Czechoslovakia's international radio service provided a variety of program segments during its twenty minutes. These included a bulletin of world news, "The Week in Czechoslovakia," editorials, "Newsview" (a news commentary segment), and some features. The content varied from day to day. No actualities or field reports were used, however, although extensive paraphrases of speeches or remarks often were.

Radio South Africa. Radio South Africa's news program consisted of a ten-minute bulletin of news, usually concentrating heavily on Africa. No actualities or field reports were used.

Voice of America. VOA's "World Report" was a thirty-minute news program, including a world news bulletin and correspondents' reports from the field. It also aired a thirty-minute "Newsline" program, which usually included extensive field reports and sound bites, and also a daily editorial reflecting the views of the U.S. government, which lasted between three and four minutes.

Voice of Turkey. Turkey's international service lasted between ten and thirteen minutes each day. It consisted of a bulletin of world news read from the studio and a review of the Turkish press. It included no actualities or field reports.

To indicate how much importance these various services attached to the summit, two different measures were used. First, each service's total news broadcast time was compared to the time it devoted to summit stories (see Table 5.2).[3]

The second measure determined how often each service used a summit story to lead off its news programming. As some services divided their broadcasts into several different types of news-oriented segments, they could have multiple lead stories each day. The two superpower services opted to lead with summit stories most frequently, followed by the BBC. VOA, of course, used Reagan's Helsinki appearances to lead off several broadcasts (and news segments), which Radio Moscow did not. The provocative nature of Reagan's visit to Moscow (including his meeting with dissidents, a speech to students, and his visit to a monastery)—all before the Soviet Union's final liberalization prior to its collapse—guaranteed ample opportunity for news leads. Clearly the NSC intended to direct press attention forcefully by planning the visit to make it difficult for radio and other media to avoid giving coverage. VOA, too, was to some extent unable to resist such provocations, given its adoption of the American "reactive" news philosophy.

The most troubling aspect of coding these stories was determining whether they were actually summit-related. This had not been a problem with the 1987 Washington summit. Several stories broadcast by various radio services in 1988, however, began with clauses such as, "While President Reagan and General Secretary Gorbachev meet in Moscow . . . " or "The major international story carried in the press continues to be the Moscow summit, but. . . . " In these cases, the summit was used principally as a marker or transition into another subject. Such stories are not considered here as summit-related. Conversely, some stories were clearly summit-related, although they never actually mentioned the summit. The best examples were stories focusing on human rights, regional conflicts, and NATO discussions about the future in the post-INF treaty period. As each of these topics was a

Table 5.2
Summit Story Time Compared with Total Time Available, by Service

Service	Total Time (minutes)	Summit Time (minutes)	Summit Time as a Percentage of Total Time
Radio Australia	204	11.40	5.59
Radio Baghdad	130	2.03	1.56
BBC	960	127.16	13.25
Radio Berlin	210	30.83	14.68
Brussels Calling	240	7.42	3.09
Radio Cairo	150	1.99	1.33
Radio Canada	180	22.11	12.28
Deutsche Welle	320	48.46	15.14
Radio Havana	180	0	0
Radio Japan	270	5.95	2.20
Radio Moscow	1,080	445.12	41.21
Radio Netherlands	480	43.15	8.99
Radio Prague	340	102.64	30.19
Radio South Africa	130	3.52	2.71
VOA	1,070	273.32	25.54
Voice of Turkey	208	15.94	7.66

major focus of the summit and as such stories were often included in special reports devoted to the summit, they were coded.

The greatest difficulty in judging summit-relatedness occurred on the subject of regional conflicts. Various services reported stories on several regional conflicts, including the Soviet withdrawal from Afghanistan, the Vietnamese decision to reduce its forces in Kampuchea (now Cambodia), and an extension of talks between the Sandinista government and the contras in Nicaragua. Judgments about whether to consider such stories summit-related hinged on two criteria. The first was the context of the story: where it was reported in the newscast in relation to other summit stories and which service was doing the reporting. The second was the actual focus of the story: whether the United States and/or the Soviet Union was included as part of the emphasis of the story. Using these criteria, most stories on Afghanistan were coded as summit-related and so were several on Kampuchea, but only a few on Nicaragua were so coded. Afghanistan stories usually focused on whether the Soviet Union would adhere to its announced timetable for withdrawal or on the role of Pakistan (sometimes called a "U.S. surrogate") in supplying the mujahedeen forces in violation of U.N.–sponsored accords. On Kampuchea, some stories focused on the Soviet welcome of the Vietnamese withdrawal announcement; on Nicaragua, usually neither superpower was mentioned.

Another aspect the stories emphasized was the lack of focus of the summit itself. The 1987 Washington summit had a centerpiece: the signing of the intermediate-range nuclear forces (INF) treaty. The Moscow summit was supposed to have an even more significant focus: the signing of a treaty substantially reducing (by 50%) strategic nuclear arsenals. That treaty was not ready (and would not be until the Moscow summit of 1991). A secondary centerpiece, the exchange of the instruments of ratification of the INF treaty, was not predictable either. The Soviet Parliament, no doubt mindful of the U.S. Senate's refusal to ratify the SALT II treaty, postponed ratification until the U.S. Senate had acted. In the Senate, Republican senators led by Jesse Helms adopted a series of delaying tactics once it became apparent that the treaty, if voted on, would be ratified. No one could be sure that the treaty would be ready for the summit.

The question of a centerpiece and the eventual ratification of the INF treaty by the Senate on the eve of the summit had at least two significant results for news coverage. First, it resulted in an increased number of stories about the treaty with summit overtones. This both increased the total number of summit stories and resulted in a higher number of summit-related stories prior to its occurrence. Second, the lateness of the ratification meant that other issues could vie for prominence. This allowed both the United States and the Soviet Union to seek to define the issues of the summit to suit their own interests and might have resulted in more friction between them had the ratification been delayed even longer.

By the time of the ratification, Reagan had made a major address on human rights in Helsinki on his way to Moscow, and this issue became a prime focus of the summit. Human rights had already been on the summit agenda, of course, and the National Security Council had highlighted it as a talking point. It is merely speculation, then, to suggest that it achieved more prominence as a result of the Senate's delay in ratification.[4] There would still have been a vacuum to fill, as the exchange of ratification instruments was largely ceremonial and anticlimactic. Yet it is significant that the lateness of the ratification and the failure to achieve agreement on a strategic arms treaty meant that arms control, long the focal point of U.S.–Soviet relations, might be preempted. Human rights might take its place, at least temporarily, if the right approach could be taken.

Reagan clearly had planned to focus on human rights in his public pronouncements in Moscow. His pre-summit speech in Helsinki set the tone: approval of Soviet actions to improve human rights but admonishment that they were not enough. He continued his campaign by meeting with Soviet dissidents and refuseniks and by speaking in a recently reopened Russian Orthodox church and to students at Moscow University. He continued his rhetorical contrast: praise and prodding. He challenged Gorbachev to "institutionalize" human rights guarantees while praising him for *glasnost* and contrasting him favorably with "other" Soviet leaders he had known.[5]

The Soviets knew what Reagan would do in Moscow. Some stories suggested that Reagan could not afford to be "upstaged" as he had been in Washington when Gorbachev had unexpectedly stepped from his limousine to greet Americans on the street, had met with U.S. business leaders, and had appeared on U.S. television screens just prior to the summit in an interview with Tom Brokaw. They knew Reagan would try to recapture the initiative.

There were parallels in the two visits. Gorbachev's trip to the United States made him the first Soviet leader since Leonid Brezhnev to travel to the United States for such a meeting. Reagan's visit to the Soviet Union was the first since Gerald Ford's 1974 visit with Brezhnev. In the eyes of the press, this made both visits "historic." There was a parallel, too, between Gorbachev setting the stage for his visit by the pre-summit appearance with Brokaw and Reagan's speech in Helsinki to commemorate the human rights accords signed there. Both were obviously publicity-seeking efforts. Reagan also attempted to duplicate Gorbachev's spontaneous "pressing the flesh" in Washington by a stroll with him down the Arbot, Moscow's main pedestrian-only shopping street, just one block from Spaso House (the U.S. ambassador's residence). That humanized Reagan for Soviet citizens as Gorbachev had been humanized for Americans. As Gorbachev had met with U.S. business leaders in the Soviet embassy in Washington, Reagan met with Soviet dissidents in Spaso House in Moscow.

The Soviets responded to the expected U.S. human rights offensive in several ways. First, they objected to the prominence given to dissidents who were unrepresentative of the Soviet people, although they allowed the meeting to take place as planned. Second, they invited American Indians to Moscow to present the ugly side of the U.S. human rights situation. Third, Gorbachev publicly chastised Reagan for coming to Moscow to "preach." Fourth, the Soviets took every opportunity to highlight the new freedom of their people, including allowing Reagan to appear on Soviet TV and to meet ordinary Soviets in the street during his walk with Gorbachev.

All of these decisions, speeches, and acts contributed to making Moscow a human rights summit. After reports on the progress of the summit itself, reports about human rights took second place of all stories filed by Western radio services. Among all radio services coded, it was the summit itself, of course, that received the most coverage (32.5% of all stories), followed by U.S.–Soviet relations second (13%), human rights third (9.8%), and regional conflicts fourth (8.5%). In the buildup to the summit there were reports on the agenda; it was to deal with arms control, human rights, regional conflicts, and bilateral relations. There were also reports on the progress in INF ratification, Reagan's Helsinki stopover, Afghanistan, and Vietnam/Kampuchea. During the summit there were reports on each day's meetings and other activities. After the summit there were assessments of its significance.

According to the reports, the Moscow summit began to move the superpowers toward a less volatile and more normal relationship. Not only did it mark the fourth meeting between Reagan and Gorbachev but, because of the lack of a significant arms control centerpiece, it also seemed to mark a trend toward routine meetings that served to smooth U.S.–Soviet differences on a variety of fronts, rather than continue the history of spectacle and rhetorical one-upmanship. It was, then, a transitional summit. As stated before, Reagan hoped to regain the public relations primacy that many thought he had lost six months earlier in Washington, and Moscow wanted to blunt that thrust if at all possible. Nonetheless, the summit did provide a measure of routinization to superpower relations, as became more obvious in the first Bush-Gorbachev meeting in Malta the following year. The Malta meeting lacked substantive purpose altogether; it merely allowed the new president to "get acquainted" with his Soviet counterpart.

The total number of stories filed about the Moscow summit peaked during the summit itself (on June 1). Over 10% of the total number of stories filed over the eighteen-day period of analysis were filed on that day. The percentage of stories filed on a day-to-day basis, however, was surprisingly consistent between May 25 and June 3. Between 6% and 8% of all summit stories were reported each of these days, except for the 10% peak on June 1. This consistency indicates a sustained interest in the summit generally as well as the superpowers' success in pressing their agendas on international radio services and the suspense created by the question of INF ratification in the U.S. Senate.

The stories filed about the summit were dominated by in-studio staff reports or summaries. Nearly 70% of all stories were reported by in-studio staff. In-house analysts and commentators provided nearly 10% of the stories. Clearly, reports produced off-site, based on information provided by others, provided most of the information to those who depended on international radio services to hear news about the summit. By contrast, only 12% of all stories reported were reported from Moscow by correspondents on-site.

The primary sources of information used in the news reports were foreign spokespersons (nearly 25%), domestic spokespersons (about 12%), and actualities and sound bites (about 8%). "Other" sources provided more than 10% of information. Over 20% of stories reported, however, had no declared or obvious source of information. It is likely that such stories were based on wire copy provided by services such as Reuters, Associated Press (AP), or TASS. As these were not cited, however, this deduction cannot be conclusive. It is apparent, however, that services reporting news without obvious sources assume that they are credible to their listeners.

Of the eight services providing the largest number of stories, those providing the fewest obvious sources were Radio Canada, Radio Prague, Radio Berlin, Deutsche Welle, and Radio Netherlands. The most used primary sources, by service, were the following (see also Table 5.3):

- VOA: the sound bite
- Radio Moscow: Soviet spokespersons
- BBC, Radio Netherlands, Deutsche Welle, Radio Berlin, Radio Prague, and Radio Canada: foreign spokespersons (spokespersons from countries other than that of the service)

A number of points are notable about these results. Besides the large percentage of stories carrying no stated source, the services made little use of press briefings at the summit. Apparently journalists were finding their own sources to report the summit as they chose. They were not allowing official spokespersons at official briefings to determine their slants on the summit. With the exception of the superpower services, they did rely heavily on foreign spokespersons. This suggests that, though they were unwilling to accept the briefings, they were willing to seek out their actors for independent stories. Only the VOA did "official" editorials. But the percentages of "other media" as sources indicate the dependence on press reviews within news programs. Many of these reports did carry editorial commentary, although not necessarily the service's official point of view.

Most of these stories were reported by studio anchors or newsreaders. Only the VOA and the BBC had significant percentages of reports coming from correspondents on-site in Moscow, with 35.4% of VOA's

Table 5.3
Most Used Primary Sources for Stories, by Service, Moscow Summit 1988

Service	No Source	Press Brief	Sound Bite	Domest. Spokes.	Foreign Spokes.	Interview	Editorial	Other Media	Multi-Source
VOA	14.2	1.8	20.4	17.7	10.6	0	7.1	5.3	10.6
Radio Moscow	13.5	4.8	6.3	22.2	13.5	4.0	0	6.3	19.0
BBC	12.7	0	11.3	7.0	28.2	4.5	0	28.2	1.4
Radio Neth.	27.3	0	0	13.6	27.3	4.5	0	9.1	4.5
Deutsche Welle	28.6	0	2.9	5.7	34.3	0	0	17.1	5.7
Radio Berlin	32.4	0	2.9	5.9	47.1	0	0	5.9	5.9
Radio Prague	34.4	0	0	7.8	32.8	1.6	0	6.3	9.4
Radio Canada	34.8	0	0	0	43.5	4.3	0	4.3	0

reports and 15.5% of the BBC's originating from such reporters. Only 4.8% of Radio Moscow's reports originated in the field, despite the fact that the summit occurred in its own capital city. Commentators provided significant percentages of stories for VOA (9.7%), Radio Moscow (8.7%), the BBC (7%), and Radio Prague (15.6%).

The mix of reports about the Moscow summit was comprised of both those that were obviously news (including staff reports and on-site reporters' stories) and those that were "non-news" or "other" (editorials, commentaries and analyses, interview and discussion programs, and press reviews). News stories dominated the coverage, providing from two to five times as many reports per day as non-news stories (see Table 5.4).

Although they provided a relatively small number of total stories filed, five international radio services provided only news reports of the summit. These were Radio Baghdad, Radio Japan, Radio Australia, Radio South Africa, and Radio Cairo. The Voice of Turkey, Radio Berlin, and Radio Canada also relied heavily on news reports, with less than 5% of their reports categorized as "other." Services relying significantly on non-news accounts of the summit were Deutsche Welle, Radio Moscow, Brussels Calling, Radio Prague, the BBC, and the Voice of America, each of which had at least 15% of their total stories in the non-news category.

This distinction between news and non-news is not significant per se. The treatment afforded to summit participants by the two forms of reporting, however, notably differed. While the treatment these services

Table 5.4
News versus Non-News Stories, by Day and Service, Moscow Summit 1988,
Percentages of Stories Filed Each Day

	VOA		BBC		Radio Moscow		Radio Prague	
Date	News	Non-News	News	Non-News	News	Non-News	News	Non-News
May 22	NA	NA	NA	NA	100.0	00.0	NA	NA
May 23	66.7	33.3	50.0	50.0	64.3	35.7	NA	NA
May 24	100.0	00.0	100.0	00.0	100.0	00.0	75.0	25.0
May 25	85.7	14.3	100.0	00.0	37.5	62.5	50.0	50.0
May 26	83.3	16.7	60.0	40.0	62.5	35.7	50.0	50.0
May 27	87.5	12.5	00.0	100.0	66.7	33.3	50.0	50.0
May 28	100.0	00.0	77.8	22.2	50.0	50.0	83.3	26.7
May 29	70.0	30.0	80.0	20.0	75.0	25.0	100.0	00.0
May 30	80.0	20.0	75.0	25.0	100.0	00.0	100.0	00.0
May 31	91.7	8.3	100.0	00.0	72.7	27.3	NA	NA
June 1	90.0	10.0	60.0	40.0	66.7	33.3	66.7	33.3
June 2	85.7	14.3	72.7	27.3	80.0	20.0	83.3	26.7
June 3	90.9	9.1	90.0	10.0	100.0	00.0	100.0	00.0
June 4	80.0	20.0	100.0	00.0	100.0	00.0	100.0	00.0
June 5	NA	NA	50.0	50.0	33.3	67.7	100.0	00.0
June 6	75.0	25.0	NA	NA	90.0	10.0	100.0	00.0
June 7	100.0	00.0	NA	NA	100.0	00.0	100.0	00.0
June 8	50.0	50.0	100.0	00.0	50.0	50.0	100.0	00.0

accorded to U.S. and Soviet actions was similar, that accorded to Reagan and Gorbachev was not. Both men were quoted or mentioned or had neutral portrayals provided of them in about equal measure by the two forms of reporting. Thirty percent of positive portrayals of Gorbachev, however, were provided in non-news stories, and no negative portrayals were included there. In contrast, over 40% of the positive portrayals and 45% of the negative portrayals of Reagan were included in non-news stories.

The news stories reported about the Moscow summit were shorter and more "reactive" in character than the non-news stories. (This is true of news stories generally as well.) The negative portrayals of Gorbachev, then, as they occurred largely within news stories, were the result of his own actions or statements. Both the positive and negative portrayals of Reagan, however, came more significantly from the longer, softer, and more opinionated non-news material provided. They were the result of reaction not to Reagan's specific summit actions or words, but to his persona and history, cultivated over time.

There are at least two inferences possible from these differences. First, they may indicate that the radio services were generally more sympathetic (or empathetic) to the Soviet leader (or his position and/or difficulties) than to Reagan. Second, they may indicate that the Reagan administration's effort to retake the initiative in U.S.–Soviet relations at least partly failed. Whether this was the result of an actual failure or of an effort by various radio services to fulfill "prophecies" set up earlier cannot be determined from the available evidence. Whatever the reason, a variety of "soft" summit-related stories were filed that clearly sympathized with or criticized the American president, a reality that Gorbachev did not face during this period.

There were also differences in the sources of information used in news stories versus non-news material. These differences may also be the source of at least some of the differential treatment accorded to the two leaders. All the information reported about opinion surveys, press releases, and "other" information came in news stories. Also, over 80% of stories depending on multiple sources, foreign and domestic spokespersons, actualities and sound bites, press briefings, and no stated sources were news stories. Non-news reports, however, used over 40% of total "other media" sources and about the same percentage of nongovernmental sources and personal observation. These reports also used 70% of the man-in-the-street interviews and nearly the same percentage of editorial comments included in all reported stories.

In other words, the sources used in the two different forms of reports were notably different. Non-news stories depended more significantly on "soft" sources of information and were constructed to feature nongovernmental or alternative points of view. When this difference is noted alongside the portrayal differences it suggests that Gorbachev, during this summit period at least, enjoyed a more positive nonofficial opinion than did Reagan. This conclusion, in turn, implies that Gorbachev was winning the battle for "hearts and minds" (an avowed purpose of public diplomacy). As far as the international radio press was concerned, Gorbachev retained the public relations initiative captured in Washington. He was, as Reagan himself said, a different kind of Soviet leader. Even the criticism leveled at the Soviet Union for its human rights record apparently did not taint Gorbachev. This is not a surprise, however, since the American delegation to Moscow, including Reagan, assiduously avoided criticizing Gorbachev personally, choosing to critique the state rather than its leader.

The pattern of coverage provided by various classes of service over the eighteen-day analysis period differed substantially.[6] Western services (excluding VOA) filed the most summit-related stories between May 25 and 28 and between June 1 and 3. This first period was prior to the summit but during Reagan's visit to and speechmaking in Helsinki. The second period included the stories filed about the summit itself. The trough between these peaks represented the days of Reagan's arrival in Moscow, but before any substantive reportable business had occurred. This pattern of coverage is typical of Western news services, which respond to events but provide little process-oriented news.

Socialist services (excluding Radio Moscow) filed the most stories on May 29 and June 1, with lesser peaks on May 24 and 27, June 2–4, and May 26 and 28. While June 1 was during the summit, and May 28 and 29 during or immediately following Reagan's Helsinki visit, the other peaks were either before or after the obvious news events associated with the summit. This pattern is similar to the one found for the Washington summit, indicating a greater desire to contextualize the summit on the part of socialist services. However, this "bias" of the socialist services was less pronounced for the Moscow summit than for Washington, probably signifying the influence of *glasnost* on socialist radio services. They seemed to be evolving into services that were more reactive than contextual (i.e., more on the Western news model). There were still aspects of the older model operating, however, as can be seen when the percentage of time devoted each day to the summit is compared across the analysis period. Radio Moscow was still devoting a significant percentage of time to summit issues prior to its actual opening (over 100% in some cases, when it ran outside the normal news hole), whereas VOA only reached 50% once prior to the actual summit period. Radio Moscow had its highest peak in number of stories filed on May 23, a lesser peak during the summit on June 1, and another lesser peak on June 6, again indicating a concern for contextualizing the summit or reaffirming the Soviet Union's place in the world. Socialist radio services, too, peaked before the summit as well as on its final day, based on percentage of time devoted to summit stories. Western services moved more gradually toward a peak in coverage on June 2, while the percentage of time devoted to the summit by other services was actually more significant after the summit than before or during it (see Table 5.5).

In numbers of stories reported on the Western side, the BBC peaked on May 28 and June 2, 3, and 4. Deutsche Welle's main peaks occurred on May 29 and June 2 and 3; and those of Radio Netherlands occurred on May 24 and June 2. On the socialist side, Radio Berlin peaked on May 27, with lesser peaks on May 24 and June 4, while Radio Prague had major peaks on May 27, 28, and 29 and June 1, 2, 3, and 7. Most of these peaks for all services coincided with significant summit-related events, including Reagan's Helsinki appearances, but those prior to May 29 and after June 3 were more contextual in nature.

Other services (such as the Middle Eastern services, Radio South Africa, and Radio Japan), while providing lower-key coverage of the summit and thus a flatter pattern of coverage, did provide minor peaks on May 22 and 23, May 30 to June 1, June 3, and June 6. These peaks can be explained by various issues: the U.S. Senate debate on the INF treaty, wire service reports of Reagan's Helsinki visit, the summit itself, and then newspaper reaction (and press reviews) to the summit itself.

The large number of stories filed about the summit, the superpowers, and their respective leaders provided ample opportunity for the international radio services to portray both Reagan and Gorbachev as well as American and Soviet actions. Both leaders and their countries were mentioned frequently by all radio services. American and Soviet citizens, however, were relatively unimportant to the radio services, despite the superpowers' emphasis on public diplomacy. The reaction of ordinary citizens to summit events, in other words, was of little import.

Both Reagan and Gorbachev were quoted or paraphrased frequently, and some services provided extensive actualities or sound bites from their public pronouncements. A variety of both positive and negative portrayals of these leaders and the actions of their respective countries were also provided. As the Soviet Union was withdrawing troops from Afghanistan and hosting the summit, it was engaged in a variety of actions that were reportable. U.S. actions included the ratification of the INF treaty and alleged continuing weapons shipments to Afghanistan. These issues, along with less frequently reported disagreements over such issues as Angola, disengagement of conventional forces, and continuing defense of Europe, provided the opportunities to report on superpower actions.

Western services quoted Reagan in about three times as many stories as Gorbachev. Socialist services, however, quoted the two leaders about equally, and other services quoted Gorbachev over Reagan by a five-to-three margin. Western services mentioned Gorbachev more frequently than Reagan, however, by a seven-to-five margin, while both socialist and other services mentioned Reagan slightly more often than Gorbachev. Overall, then, on these two measures, the two men received equivalent treatment across all services.

There were significant differences, however, in the positive versus negative portrayals of the two leaders across the three classes of services. Using the Im^1 coefficient for measuring the intensity of propaganda reveals a mixed reaction to the two presidents: Some NATO countries (including VOA) and socialist services were more positive in their

Table 5.5
Number of Stories Filed and Percentage of News Hole Devoted to
Summit-Related Stories, by Day: VOA, Radio Moscow, NATO
(excluding Turkey), and Socialist Services, Moscow Summit 1988

	VOA		Radio Moscow		NATO		Socialist Services	
Date	No.	%	No.	%	No.	%	No.	%
May 22	NA	NA	3	3.6	NA	NA	2	2.4
May 23	3	12.1	14	96.8	3	0.8	2	1.8
May 24	7	49.7	1	0.8	3	1.8	8	17.2
May 25	7	57.0	8	66.3	14	5.4	5	13.6
May 26	6	24.4	8	41.8	11	6.6	7	27.5
May 27	8	49.0	3	108.2	12	12.6	9	32.1
May 28	3	31.7	4	68.0	14	11.8	6	20.1
May 29	10	39.8	8	79.0	9	9.8	12	39.3
May 30	6	52.8	9	50.4	13	14.9	4	15.4
May 31	12	109.6	11	62.4	10	7.5	3	9.1
June 1	19	95.4	13	122.1	14	18.3	11	51.3
June 2	8	46.9	5	12.6	20	35.2	7	33.3
June 3	10	70.5	9	30.1	17	18.6	8	21.5
June 4	5	41.9	6	23.8	8	8.0	6	16.8
June 5	NA	NA	6	78.8	3	3.3	2	4.5
June 6	4	21.5	10	52.3	2	0.7	2	3.7
June 7	2	7.4	5	15.8	2	0.7	4	12.5
June 8	4	26.7	4	22.0	6	4.0	1	6.1

portrayals of Gorbachev than Reagan, others the reverse. Still others treated the two presidents about equally, with nearly identical Im^1 coefficients. This was generally true of other services as well. Radio Moscow's treatment of the two men coincided with expectations: It preferred Gorbachev to Reagan (see Appendix 2).

The different classes of services treated the actions of the countries represented by the two leaders still differently. NATO country services treated the activities of the United States either with a tepid endorsement or slightly negatively. Radio Prague and Radio Moscow were both negative in reflecting U.S. actions, while Radio Berlin was slightly positive. Socialist services were all positive in their treatment of the Soviet Union's actions, but Western services were more unpredictable, with more being slightly negative. There was no indication of unease on the part of socialist radio services about either Soviet actions or Gorbachev's leadership, despite the changes that would shortly affect

Eastern Europe. The less partisan services were also mixed in their treatments, and several of them had nothing to say about American actions. The Voice of America and Radio Moscow both treated their own country's actions positively and those of the "adversary country" somewhat negatively. Radio Moscow was slightly more positive about the Soviet Union, however, than VOA was about the United States, although VOA was slightly more negative about the Soviet Union than Radio Moscow was about the United States (see Appendix 2).

Most services carried no reports that directly described American or Soviet citizens. Those that did were uniformly positive about Americans, while Soviets did not fare as well.

Although some of these results might have been expected, they are actually a complicated mixture. VOA's negativism about the Soviet Union was more than offset by its positive treatment of Mikhail Gorbachev. Western services' generally positive treatment of Reagan was not mirrored in their evaluations of the actions of the country he headed and whose foreign policy he directed. Radio Moscow's treatment of Reagan was only slightly less positive than that accorded to Gorbachev, and its negative portrayal of U.S. actions was relatively minor. Clearly, however, if either country wished to be portrayed by international radio services as a "white knight" with its adversary in the role of villain, its wish was not fulfilled. This may have been the result of the personalities of the two leaders themselves, both of whom, in their own ways, seemed to be moving toward accommodation and truly peaceful coexistence.

The stories that the various classes of radio services chose to report about the summit also differed. Although the summit meeting itself received the most coverage across all classes, Western radio services focused second most frequently on human rights issues, socialist services on the INF treaty, and other services on U.S.–Soviet relations.

Such choices reflected (at least to a degree) the priorities of the various countries sponsoring these services. Western services saw the exchange of documents on the INF treaty as anticlimactic; with Reagan's emphasis on human rights and their predilection to reactive journalism, human rights emerged as the single most significant topic for reporting. Socialist services, however, still following the cue of the Soviet Union, which needed a focal point for the Moscow summit, elevated the INF treaty to second place, followed by U.S.–Soviet relations, disarmament, and achieving peace. Human rights stories were in seventh place as a focus. Other services, whose world had been shaped in the postwar period by the Cold War and U.S.–Soviet rivalry, concentrated on U.S.–Soviet relations, regional conflicts, and the INF treaty. The relative lack of human rights focus there may also have resulted from either lack of concern for this issue, or some of their own poor human rights records.

Based on these different foci, it is apparent that efforts to steer the press (at least the international radio press) toward specific agendas for their reporting were not very successful. The emphases selected were more the result of long-standing reporting methods and the particular interests of the reporting services than they were of the orchestrated campaigns of the public relations apparatus of the two superpowers. In any case, because Western services were predisposed to report on human rights and attached relatively greater significance to the Helsinki Accords than countries in other regions, Reagan's comments were successful in attracting their attention. Socialist services, in contrast, emphasized those stories that were peculiarly interesting to their own political situation vis-à-vis the Soviet Union. The INF treaty would affect the positioning of Soviet missiles on their territories, and the condition of U.S.–Soviet relations would affect their own relations with both the West and the Soviet state. They emphasized those issues and steered away from human rights, where they might be vulnerable, particularly on the issue of freedom of movement. Other services, as already indicated, had similar vulnerabilities on the human rights issue and were anxious to see what the changing nature of U.S.–Soviet relations might mean for their own well-being.

Regardless of the political orientation of the nonsuperpower radio services, they used the same types of information to report their stories. Most significant to all three classes were foreign government spokespersons, which is not surprising given the fact that the event was a superpower summit where their countries had no direct representation. Western services provided no source in 18% of their stories, while socialist services provided none in 32.3% and other services in 30.8% of stories. In third place as sources of information were other media for Western and other services (because of the large number of press reviews provided) and domestic spokespersons for socialist services. Western services carried actualities as prime sources of information in only 4.4% of stories reported, with socialist services relying on them in only one story (1%), and other services did not use them at all.

In all three classes of services the majority of stories were reported by studio staff. Of Western news stories, 58% originated in studios, with 9.3% reported on-site and 8.33% consisting of press reviews, while 3.9% were provided by commentators. For socialist services 86.5% of all stories originated in studios, with an additional 10.4% provided by commentators, and 3.1% by studio interviews. Of stories carried by other services, 92.3% originated in the studio, with 3.8% provided each by commentators and press reviews.

This general analysis indicates that audiences for such services largely received secondhand news. Most of the stories reported apparently came from wire services that were unacknowledged as sources. This conclusion, however, is not entirely fair. As suggested earlier, if the reports of specific Western news services, especially the BBC, are examined more closely, differences do emerge in their reports of the summit. Both Radio Netherlands (17.4%) and Deutsche Welle (8.82%) also provided on-site reports about the summit. Radio Canada provided one on-site news feed. All other Western services, all socialist services, and all other services provided no on-site reports. The mix in the news of the BBC, Radio Netherlands, and Deutsche Welle, then, provided more firsthand reports than those of the other services examined. Many of the BBC's studio-originated news stories, too, were summaries of correspondents' reports that were carried later in the same or different news programs.

As already indicated, Reagan's National Security Council (NSC) attempted to steer the news coverage of the summit toward an American perspective by creating a set of talking points to direct the statements of the U.S. delegation to Moscow. These points merely elaborated the set that had been adopted prior to the Washington summit. If the reports carried by the various radio services affirmed the points as articulated by the NSC, it would be fair to suggest that the United States was successful in this effort at public diplomacy: Its story would have been the one that was replicated in news reports.

Generally speaking, all eleven of the NSC talking points were affirmed directly or indirectly more often than they were denied. That would seem to indicate success for U.S. public diplomacy. Some points received more positive treatment than others, but that would also be expected. The talking point receiving the most positive treatment by all radio services affirmed the importance of strategic arms reduction at the Moscow summit (NSC point 8); the second most affirmed talking point was related: Agreement on strategic weapons reduction was a feasible goal provided the Soviet Union approached the negotiations constructively (NSC point 9). Related to these talking points and also affirmed were points 7 (arms reductions were a means to secure the security of the United States and its allies) and 11 (conventional forces reduction and the elimination of chemical arms were issues requiring agreement). Talking point 10 (SDI should not be curtailed) received a more tepid endorsement.

More controversial talking points (receiving both support and significant denial) were those more critical of the Soviet Union. Point 1 claimed that the U.S. agenda for its relations with the Soviet Union (an agenda repeatedly stated during the buildup to the summit and used as the basis for organizing reports during the summit, particularly by VOA) provided the basis for progress if the Soviet Union were realistic. Point

3 (actually denied more than affirmed) criticized the Soviet Union for using rhetoric at variance with its actions. Point 4 claimed that the Soviets continued to deny basic human rights; 5 claimed that the Soviets were not being helpful in ending regional conflicts; and 2 claimed success for Reagan's "realistic" policies toward the Soviet Union. Point 6, the United States wanted to increase bilateral exchanges with the Soviet Union provided that security and human rights concerns were not violated, was weakly endorsed by those services that included it in their reports (see Appendix 1).[7]

Point 1: The U.S. Agenda. All the socialist services denied the validity of this point, as did Brussels Calling and Radio Cairo. All other services, except VOA and Radio Canada, affirmed the claim weakly or ignored it. VOA and Radio Canada carried strong endorsements of this point.

Point 2: Reagan's Policies. Again, VOA and Radio Canada carried the strongest affirmations of this point, followed by Radio Netherlands, the BBC, and Radio Moscow. Only Radio Prague denied the claim.

Point 3: Soviet Rhetoric. The strongest endorsement of this point came from VOA and Brussels Calling. Weaker endorsements came from the BBC, Radio Netherlands, and Radio Canada. Denials emerged in reports of Radio Moscow, Radio Berlin, Radio Prague, Radio Japan, and Radio South Africa.

Point 4: Human Rights. This point gained the strong endorsement of VOA, the BBC, and Radio Canada and weaker affirmations from Radio Netherlands, Deutsche Welle, and Radio Australia. This was nearly universal Western agreement. Radio Moscow was the only service carrying a negative coefficient on this issue. Otherwise, however, it was a nonissue, with nine services avoiding it altogether.

Point 5: Regional Conflict. This issue, which had been a major source of conflict in Washington six months earlier, was of little interest to most of the radio services analyzed (ten avoided it). Radio Cairo denied the point most strongly; weaker denials came from Radio Moscow and Radio Prague. Weak endorsements emerged from VOA, the BBC, and Deutsche Welle.

Point 6: Bilateral Exchanges. This issue was a tepid one in Moscow. Radio Japan endorsed the claim most strongly by far, followed by Radio Moscow and a variety of services on both sides of the ideological divide.

Point 7: Arms Negotiations and Security. Radio Japan and Brussels Calling carried the strongest endorsements of this talking point, understandable given Japan's pacifist position and Belgium's historic efforts to maintain neutrality in European conflicts (even though a member of NATO in the post–World War II period). A variety of other services, both Western and socialist, endorsed this point at about the same level, with weaker endorsements from Radio Moscow and Radio Berlin.

Point 8: Strategic Weapons Reduction Key to the Moscow Summit. Except for Radio Cairo, Radio South Africa, Radio Havana, and Radio Baghdad, this point received strong endorsements across the spectrum. One curious note was that, among all the services with positive coefficients, VOA's was the weakest.

Point 9: Strategic Weapons Reduction Agreement Possible. Expectations of the Moscow summit were not as strong as the general agreement that strategic arms reduction was a key element of the summit. Although endorsements came from VOA, Radio Moscow, the BBC, Deutsche Welle, Radio Berlin, Radio Prague, Radio Canada, Radio Australia, and Radio Japan, all of their coefficients were lower on this point than on the previous one. Radio Moscow was the lone dissenter of the services that reported on the issue.

Point 10: SDI Cannot Be Limited. Radio Japan endorsed this talking point most strongly, followed by weak endorsements from a variety of European services, including Radio Turkey, and from the central European services. Radio Canada and Radio Australia also agreed, but both VOA and Radio Moscow carried negative coefficients on this point.

Point 11: Balancing Conventional Forces and a Global Ban on Chemical Weapons Necessary. There were no negative coefficients on this claim. Radio Japan, Radio Australia, and Deutsche Welle carried the most positive coefficients.

A variety of countries obviously saw the responsibility for relations between the superpowers as more equal than the U.S.–inspired talking points suggested. If credit were due, it was due to both countries; if blame were to be apportioned, it would go to both. The strong negative coefficients on several points by Radio Cairo, for instance, probably indicate the position of Middle Eastern and other countries on the fringe of the postwar standoff between East and West in central Europe. Radio Cairo apparently saw the roles of the two superpowers as more equivalent than the U.S. claims suggested. The Soviets weren't as obstinate as the United States implied, or the United States was equally guilty. These results suggest, too, that the treatment accorded to the NSC themes was not so much a function of the success of U.S. public diplomacy efforts as of different services using different filters to analyze and report the news. Different interests resulted in different reports.

One particularly telling example of this difference in reporting is useful in attesting to its truth. On May 18 Gorbachev met with a group of journalists from the *Washington Post* and *Newsweek*. Although this interview was outside the actual analysis period, the reports of it did not appear in either publication until May 22. Several of the radio services analyzed carried stories on the interview between May 22 and 24.

Gorbachev began the interview by indicating that he was "convinced that positive trends are unfolding in the world. There is a turn from confrontation to coexistence. The winds of the cold war are being replaced by coexistence" (*USSR–USA Summit*, p. 5). He indicated (p. 6) that the continuation of dialogue between the two countries was important and hoped "that we will be able to rise to a new level of dialogue and mutual understanding. And if an agreement on a 50-percent reduction in strategic offensive weapons comes to be drafted under the present US Administration, I see no reason why President Reagan and I should not sign it. I would certainly welcome that." Later he said (p. 7), "We have clearly formulated our choice: the arms race must be stopped and then reversed." He proposed a 50% cut in strategic weapons, the elimination of chemical weapons, and the reduction of conventional armaments in Europe.

Gorbachev called President Reagan a realist. He defined this (p. 10) as the "ability to adapt one's views to the changing situation, while remaining faithful to one's convictions."

Gorbachev also indicated his willingness to cooperate with the United States and other countries to resolve regional conflicts (p. 11) and said (p. 12), "The world has ample proof that dragged-out conflicts are the result of politics being exposed to pressure from outdated stereotypes."

When discussing *glasnost* Gorbachev also mentioned human rights (p. 13): "While freedom of speech is indispensable for glasnost, we see glasnost as a broader phenomenon. For us it is not just the right of every citizen to openly say what he or she thinks about all social and political questions, but also the duty of the ruling Party and all bodies of authority and administration to ensure openness in decision-making, be accountable for their actions, act on criticism, and consider advice and recommendations from the shopfloor, public organizations and individuals."

Gorbachev continued the Soviet objections to the strategic defense initiative, one of the sticking points in the START negotiations. Although his country favored the 50% reduction in strategic weapons being discussed with the United States, he said (pp. 26–27), "If we sign with one hand a treaty reducing strategic offensive arms in one area and at the same time launch an arms race in space or at sea, what would be the point? That would be senseless." Soviet objections, he continued, were not whimsical. Neither were they "some kind of tactical subterfuge or maneuver from the Soviet side, but rather a carefully thought-out and responsible position. . . . If we just replace one kind of arms race with another, particularly in space, things would take a dramatic turn: we would undermine the trust that has been built; we would depreciate all the experience we have accumulated at the Geneva negotiations." In a pointed reference to Reagan, Gorbachev said (p. 27), "I think he who pushes for an arms race in space is committing a crime against the people—his own people, and others. That must be said with all responsibility, and with clarity."

Although this interview, as Whelan (1990, p. 5) put it, was part of the "pre-summit diplomatic choreography intended to seek negotiating advantages," Gorbachev's success must be judged equivocally, if the reports carried by the international radio services are any indication. Although the interview covered four full pages of the *Washington Post* on May 22 and was therefore available to Reagan and his summit team, as well as the world's press, prior to the U.S. contingent's departure for Helsinki, the reports about it were surprisingly different. The radio services analyzed here chose to emphasize quite different portions of the interview for presentation to their audiences.

The Voice of America carried two stories on May 23. The first, lasting forty-two seconds, claimed that Gorbachev had called a Soviet dissident, Grigoryants, a "parasite who weakens the democratic process." What Gorbachev actually said was:

Our people know that Grigoryants's "organization" is tied not only organizationally but also financially to the West, that his constant visitors and guests are Western correspondents. Therefore people think of it as some kind of alien phenomenon in our society sponging on the democratic process and on *perestroika*. This happens—it happens in nature, too; all kinds of parasites attach themselves to a living organism and try to harm it. (*USSR–USA Summit*, 1988, p. 25)

Not only was this point a minor one insofar as the interview was concerned, but VOA's report arguably distorted Gorbachev's actual statement. Gorbachev criticized not Grigoryants himself but his organization, and the "living organism" weakened by parasites was either the "democratic process" or "perestroika" (or both).

VOA's second story, lasting 3:18, began with Gorbachev's indicating that he would ask Reagan to approve a joint space mission to Mars. It then switched to Reagan's science advisor, who indicated that cooperation "must start smaller" and that Afghanistan was a problem. The report returned to Gorbachev's remark that such new cooperation would replace the winds of the Cold War and then countered this remark with an "American" desire to see a general improvement in

U.S.–Soviet relations first. The report ended with an indication that NASA was ready to support the Soviet Mars mission scheduled for 1994 and suggested possible cooperation in the 1998 NASA mission to collect Martian soil samples.

Relatively few of Gorbachev's own remarks were reported in either story. In both instances, once directly and the other indirectly, VOA chose to emphasize the human rights and regional conflict issues that continued to separate the superpowers. It was as though VOA could not yet relinquish the bipolar Cold War world in reporting the interview. In essence, VOA (at least on this issue) was the mouthpiece of the Cold War hawks in the Reagan administration.

Radio Moscow used the Gorbachev interview and its publication in the Soviet Union as the lead-in to an extensive interview with U.S. ambassador Jack Matlock. The story lasted nearly fourteen minutes, with Matlock remarking that neither the Soviet nor the "American" people want war and that improvement in the Soviet–"American" atmosphere helps the whole world. "Dialogue is the essence of how we manage the relationship. We cannot expect that all tensions will disappear." The character of this interview was startlingly different from VOA's apparently more somber estimate of U.S.–Soviet relations, and Matlock's comments themselves seemed to suggest a far more understanding (or conciliatory) approach to the Soviets than VOA's reporting did. Radio Moscow seemed to have moved further to put the Cold War behind it than had VOA.[8]

Radio Moscow's report on the interview itself (1:08 in length) began with Gorbachev's remark that dialogue between the United States and the Soviet Union had caused a major turn in their relations, from confrontation to coexistence. The story continued by reporting Gorbachev's assessment of the summit agenda: that it would cover "key problems of the modern world"; that he would propose a joint flight to Mars; that he saw no obstacles to signing an agreement with Reagan on a 50% reduction in nuclear arms; and that he saw no reason to cut arms in one sphere while starting an arms race in space.

The BBC carried news of the interview during its press review of May 23. Both the *Telegraph* and the *Financial Times* had carried stories on the interview, which the BBC then summarized. Its story was thus third-hand. The *Telegraph* story, the BBC said, suggested that Gorbachev had "gone out of his way to warm the atmosphere" of the summit by praising Mr. Reagan as a "realist" who could change his mind without changing his convictions. The *Financial Times* had noted the proposal of a joint space mission to Mars.

The Voice of Turkey carried a thirty-six-second story that Gorbachev would propose a joint unmanned space mission to Mars and that he hoped that a strategic weapons treaty would be signed before Reagan left office. Radio Japan carried a 4:18 news commentary on the summit generally that included reference to Gorbachev's interview. His remarks, the commentator said, made it clear that the Soviet Union was aware of her responsibility and noted the necessity of eliminating nuclear and chemical weapons from Europe and the desire for cultural cooperation.

Radio South Africa's report led with Gorbachev's declared willingness to cooperate with the United States and other countries in resolving regional conflicts such as Angola (where South Africa itself was deeply involved). They used Gorbachev's remark that the world has ample proof that dragged-out conflicts are the result of pressure of outdated stereotypes and continued with his claim that political settlements of regional conflicts and the prevention of new ones would gradually become international principles. The reporter then said that Gorbachev expected to discuss regional conflicts with Reagan and that Gorbachev warned that the talks would be productive only if every nation was free to choose its own way to achieve political stability.

Whelan (1990, pp. 17–18) argues that various meanings could be attached to Gorbachev's interview. He summarizes the interview by saying that Gorbachev:

- endorsed the popular belief in the decompression of the Cold War
- restated his faith in a continuing and necessary dialogue with the United States
- restated his faith in Reagan as a realist
- did not doubt that the goal of a nuclear-free world could be accomplished
- invested in the strategic weapons negotiations a positive and appealing content
- laid down anew his opposition to SDI and a loose interpretation of the ABM treaty
- reiterated that the withdrawal from Afghanistan was an indication of Soviet intentions to resolve regional conflicts peacefully
- emphasized the irreconcilable differences between Soviet and "American" views on human rights, while citing Soviet human rights advances under *perestroika*

Given this summation, Gorbachev largely failed to influence the reporting of international radio services. Each service, rather than accurately summarizing his remarks, put a spin on them to emphasize its own view of the world. Predictably Radio Moscow reported more elements of the interview than other services; Gorbachev was a Soviet spokesman. Equally understandable were the choices made by VOA and Radio South Africa: Each concentrated on those elements of the interview that corresponded with their government's respective national interest. VOA's posture is curious, given its claims to be an independent and objective news stance in accordance with the canons of American journalistic practice, except that its judgments reflected a general American view, one that had been nurtured by history itself, as well as Reagan's skillful rhetorical exploitation. It thus provided what has been called an "American optic."

The BBC largely chose to ignore the interview in its news reports, picking it up only as a function of its press review. It largely remained aloof from pre-summit posturing. The Voice of Turkey and VOA both chose to report elements of the interview that were insignificant. Only Radio Japan took the time to assess the significance of Gorbachev's remarks as a whole and to contextualize them to provide overall understanding to its audience. The remainder of the services analyzed ignored the interview altogether.

Judging by this example, it would matter significantly that audiences attend to different radio services. No single service would have provided a complete picture of Gorbachev's remarks; most had axes to grind of one kind or another. None was enlightening to an audience that might have wondered what to expect from the impending summit meeting.

If propaganda were a major element in the radio news reports about the Moscow summit, it would presumably reveal itself most clearly in the reports of Radio Moscow and the Voice of America.[9] To provide a basis of comparison, these two services were examined with two others: the BBC and Radio Prague. Radio Moscow filed 126 stories on the summit, VOA 116, BBC 80, and Radio Prague 65. These were the four most prolific services examined. This approach also allowed comparisons to be made across the ideological divide, as the BBC broadcasts from a NATO country and Radio Prague from a Warsaw Pact one.[10]

Using the NSC talking points as a reference point, the differences in the treatment of the summit across these four services is apparent. Using the Im[1] coefficient, VOA strongly affirmed points 1, 4, and 8. It weakly affirmed points 2, 3, 5, 6, 7, 9, and 11 and weakly denied point 10 (that SDI could not be limited). Talking points 1 and 2 were affirmations of the Reagan administration's position vis-à-vis the Soviet Union; points 3 and 4 were critical of the Soviets on the issues of trust and human rights. VOA's strong affirmations of three of these four points did serve to legitimize those aspects of the NSC agenda. Talking points 6 through

9 and 11 were actually claims of both the United States and the Soviet Union; they were thus "uncontroversial" insofar as U.S. interests were concerned. The only oddity here, then, is VOA's weak denial of SDI. This denial, along with the weak affirmations of most talking points, does suggest an independent posture.

Radio Moscow, in contrast, denied points 1, 3, 4, 5, and 10. It weakly affirmed claims 2, 6, 7, 9, and 11 and strongly affirmed point 8. Though not a perfect opposition to VOA, clearly the Soviet service was defining the terms of discourse and thus the political contours of the world fundamentally differently. At least insofar as points critical of the Soviet Union are concerned (1–5), only claim 2 (that Reagan's policies toward the Soviet Union had been successful) received any affirmation from Radio Moscow. That positive note may itself indicate a willingness of Radio Moscow to "go easy" on Reagan, who had reversed field and agreed to visit the "evil empire." Affirmations of points 6, 8, 9, and 11 are no surprise. The denial of 10 (SDI) was a clear affirmation of the official position of the Soviet state and was reiterated by Gorbachev in his pre-summit *Washington Post* interview.

The BBC affirmed talking points 1, 2, 3, 5, 7, 10, and 11 weakly and 4, 8, and 9 strongly. It did not cover point 6 (United States favoring bilateral exchanges). The BBC's weak affirmation of most of the contentious points (1–3) and its strong affirmation of the "noncontroversial" claims (7–9 and 11) indicate an independent stance vis-à-vis U.S. foreign policy goals. Its affirmations of points 8 through 10 were actually stronger than those of the VOA itself, and its portrayal of SDI (point 10) indicates a solid preference for Reagan's arms control stance. Affirmations of points 4 and 5 could be construed as indicating a compatibility of interests on the part of Western democracies generally: opposing denials of human rights and the desire to resolve regional conflicts, with the Soviet threats on Afghanistan resulting in strong affirmations of the U.S. position.

Radio Prague weakly denied points 1, 2, 3, and 5. It did not deal with points 3 and 4. It affirmed points 4, 6, 7, 9, and 10 (weakly) and 8 and 11 more strongly. Its positions, in other words, were the most complex of all four of these services. Radio Prague's choices suggest, based on its denials of the Reagan agenda (claims 1 and 2) and its refusal to condemn Soviet rhetoric (point 3) or to endorse the U.S. stand on regional conflicts, that it was the most propagandistic service of all. Its positions, in fact, were all arguably in Czechoslovakia's interest. It was perhaps struggling to make sense of the developing post–Cold War environment. In one sense, it was following the Soviet line even more closely than Radio Moscow itself. In another, it seemed to be representing Czechoslovakia's own independent interests.

These generalizations do not capture the nuance of radio reports on the summit by these four services, of course. On a variety of policy themes, one service or another achieved near or actual neutrality in its reports or affirmed those that were in the interests of all countries. Using Ellul's argument, however, even the affirmation of noncontroversy itself can be propaganda, as it confirms the prevailing wisdom that has somehow gripped the interests of all countries. This wisdom could change, of course, as it has done over the course of the nearly fifty years of postwar history.

These conclusions suggest that, for an audience to receive a wholly balanced view of the Moscow summit, it would have to attend to a variety of radio services. Beyond these four, most others (with the exception of Radio Netherlands) largely provided secondhand or short summary reports on the summit. Of these four, the BBC was arguably the most independent of superpower interests, but even then the common wisdom of the West strongly influenced the reports presented. The mix of reports available via all four of these services together, however, might have allowed an audience enough information for them to come to independent decisions about what was occurring and how closely rhetoric matched reality at this event.

One indicator of potential propaganda is the significance placed by various radio services on U.S.–Soviet relations. In the pre-summit period (days 1–7) emphasis on such relations would indicate an effort to contextualize the upcoming but unpredictable events of the summit. The Soviet Union's long-standing desire to be seen as an equal of the United States in world affairs suggests that significant time would be spent prior to the summit "puffing up" its significance to U.S.–Soviet relations and commenting on the turn in relations signified by Reagan's visit to the "evil empire." In the post-summit period, stories on this issue should be expected to concentrate on the outcomes of the summit for U.S.–Soviet relations: the end of the previously unpredictable events and the assessment of significance. Stories during the summit would be reported "on the fly," attempting to make sense unreflectively (or reactively) to events as they unfolded. Examining the number of stories filed, then, by different radio services across the eighteen-day analysis period would indicate which of these three approaches was used by each one.

Radio Prague and the BBC were nearly mirror opposites of each other on this score. Radio Prague concentrated its U.S.–Soviet relations stories in the pre-summit period, with only one post-summit assessment story filed. The BBC, however, filed only one pre-summit story on this issue, while concentrating on post-summit assessments. Neither service, however, devoted significant time to this issue, particularly when compared to Radio Moscow.

Radio Moscow and the Voice of America both engaged in pre-summit contextualizing of their relations and in-summit reacting to the unfolding events. To a lesser degree they both used post-summit assessment as well, although Radio Moscow was apparently more concerned to do so than was VOA. Generally speaking, the two superpower services were more concerned about the state of their relations and the way that other countries saw their posturing than was either the BBC or Radio Prague. This, however, is not surprising, particularly in the public diplomacy–conscious administrations of Reagan and Gorbachev. Radio Moscow overshadowed VOA's attention to this issue, devoting over two hours of its pre-summit newscasts to it, compared to VOA's less than fourteen minutes. During the summit Radio Moscow spent nearly another fifty-two additional minutes (to VOA's nine), and still another twenty-two minutes after the summit (to VOA's three).

Although drawing conclusions based on only one measurement is problematic, these differences do suggest that the different radio services placed different values on efforts to contextualize the summit. Because contextualization is crucial to propaganda, the differences exposed here imply that Radio Moscow was the most propagandistic service during this period, and the BBC the least so. Although VOA and Radio Moscow both reported events and provided an interpretive "patina" for them, it was Radio Moscow that contextualized and assessed to the greatest degree. Such efforts could lead to the conclusion that Radio Moscow was most concerned to manipulate its audience's understanding of the summit and therefore most likely to propagandize.

Such activities are not necessarily condemnatory. All services, to one extent or another, selectively reported the summit and explained it to audiences differently. Examining the coverage provided by Radio Moscow and VOA more carefully indicates additional similarities and differences in their choices. First, there were differences in the choices they made about the aspects of the summit to emphasize in the pre-summit, in-summit, and post-summit periods.

VOA's treatment of the various aspects of the summit was generally lower-key and more comprehensive than Radio Moscow's. In the pre-summit period VOA reported equal numbers of stories on the summit itself (particularly its agenda that had been pushed hard by the Reagan administration), human rights, arms reduction, and regional disputes. During the summit VOA concentrated on arms reduction stories and summit reports until the last day, when it shifted its emphasis to human rights (the result of Reagan's speeches and meetings with dissidents and students). The number of VOA stories rapidly fell off after the summit. Its summit stories peaked on day 14 and then disappeared. Its stories on regional disputes (with a summit peg) peaked on the eighteenth day. Most other subjects were dropped as major concerns on day 12. In terms of time devoted to various subjects, VOA's primary concern was with conflict questions—human rights and regional conflicts. This preference, resulting from Reagan's highlighting of human rights in Helsinki and his confrontational agenda in Moscow, upstaged VOA's coverage of the actual progress of the summit talks, the INF treaty ratification and exchange of instruments, and SDI.

Before the summit Radio Moscow preferred stories about personalities, principally Reagan and Gorbachev, and their respective countries. It also emphasized certain aspects of the Soviet Union's domestic policies, including emigration. These concerns receded over the analysis period and eventually were overtaken (in the post-summit reports) by concern for summit outcomes and the INF treaty. Neither of these choices was surprising. The INF emphasis emerged from the last-minute U.S. Senate debate and fear that ratification delay might strip even the low-key centerpiece of the Moscow summit away. The emigration emphasis was the result of U.S. pressure on the summit agenda itself and probably of fear of what might result from that emphasis during the actual summit events. Concern for conflict issues also rose over the analysis period.

The situation with the BBC and Radio Prague differed in most respects from the superpower services. The BBC emphasized the summit itself in all three time-based analysis periods. Of greatest interest to the BBC beyond these "nuts and bolts" issues were long-range political issues: peace, NATO and the defense of Europe, the relations between the United States and its allies and the Soviet Union and its allies, disarmament, and general East and West European relations. Radio Prague was also interested in these issues, particularly in the pre-summit period, and also reported extensively on the summit and conflict issues.

Both VOA's and Radio Moscow's coverage of the summit came primarily from news stories themselves, rather than from commentaries, editorials, interviews, and the like. VOA's news coverage clearly peaked on day 11 (the last day of the summit), while Radio Moscow's news coverage did not build to a true climax but peaked several times at equal levels. Both used "non-news" approaches to the summit sparingly, perhaps avoiding the more obvious approaches that might be seen as propagandistic.

The two services did use the two forms of reporting, however, to respond to selective issues at the summit. Compared to all non-news stories filed by all services, for instance, VOA's non-news treatment of the two superpowers (as captured in NSC talking points 1 through 5) was enormously more affirmative (using the Im^1 coefficient). Its non-news treatment of these points was also significantly more positive than was its news treatment. Only on the less controversial issues (6 through 9) did VOA's non-news stories match the treatments provided by its own non-news or by news/non-news stories generally. On claim 10 (SDI) VOA's non-news stories provided one of the highest affirmations, while its news stories contributed by far the most significant denial. In other words, the approaches of the two types of stories were directly antagonistic to one another.

Radio Moscow's treatment of the talking points also provided some curious results. While both its news and non-news stories denied points 3, 4, and 10 at significant levels, on other claims its coverage was also more equivocal. Its news stories denied point 5 (thus claiming that the Soviet Union was helpful in solving regional conflicts), but its non-news stories had a zero Im^1 coefficient on that issue. Its non-news stories denied talking point 1 (thus denying that Reagan's policies toward the Soviet Union had been successful), but its news stories again had a zero Im^1 coefficient. On point 7 (that arms negotiations were a means to assure the security of the United States and its allies), Radio Moscow's news stories affirmed it even more strongly than news stories generally, while its non-news stories denied the NSC claim. On themes 6, 8, and 9, Radio Moscow joined VOA and news/non-news stories generally in affirming the NSC. On theme 11, Radio Moscow news stories also affirmed strongly the NSC position (that the balancing of conventional forces and chemical weapons reduction were significant issues requiring agreement), while its non-news stories provided a zero Im^1 coefficient.

It is difficult to generalize about these results, but it does appear that both services used non-news stories more obviously to contextualize the summit than they did "straight" news. In cases where the service affirmed the NSC position, the affirmations provided by non-news stories were generally significantly higher than that achieved by the news stories; in some cases the non-news stories denied what the news stories affirmed. In sum, the non-news stories appear to have been more volatile than news stories. Again, however, there were a few exceptions.

As in the case of the Washington summit, it mattered what radio service audiences attended to for news of Moscow. It did not matter in the same way, however. Apparently the nature of news as defined by the international radio services was changing or the nature of the summit itself demanded a different sort of coverage. One indicator was the difference in mean story length and standard deviations for each of the services. During the Washington summit, the differences in these two statistics were sometimes quite large. During the Moscow summit coverage, most of these differences were reduced. The services that were evaluated during both summits were VOA, Radio Moscow, the BBC, Deutsche Welle, Radio Netherlands, and Radio Japan. VOA, the BBC, Deutsche Welle, and Radio Japan, all of which had standard deviations larger than their mean story length for Washington (indicating looser editorial control over story length across news broadcasts), reversed that for Moscow. Radio Netherlands and Radio Moscow remained consistent, with the Dutch service retaining its higher mean story length, and the Soviet one continuing its tradition of great variations in story length on summit-related stories.

VOA's coverage was less actuality-based than it had been for Washington. That was partially the result of functioning in a distant place. Radio Moscow failed to continue the wider coverage it had achieved in Washington. That was undoubtedly the result of uncertainty within Radio Moscow: Its place in the world was being altered by *glasnost*. It was also the result of the more highly focused Reagan administration's approach to the summit. Reagan's own agenda, established prior to his departure from Washington, confirmed in his address and comments in Helsinki, and pursued single-mindedly in Moscow, focused the summit in a way that made it difficult to be eclectic in the choice of topics.

The treatment of the NSC's claims about both the United States and the Soviet Union during the Moscow summit also changed from Washington. Some of the talking points were apparently so innocuous that anyone could agree with them. Others were more pointedly critical, leading to clear discrepancies of treatment depending on the ideological posture of the service.

As significant were the choices made by various services concerning how to explain the significance of events at the summit to their audiences. They chose to cast the events in ways that allowed them to pursue distinctive agendas and thus provided audiences with significantly different choices of information. All the people would not be provided with all the information all of the time, by any service.

As in Washington different levels of responsiveness to government expectations existed and for the same basic reasons. Because each service was selective in the news it reported and the ways it reported the news, it could slant information. This was most obvious in the use of press reviews, but it was not confined to these reports. Western services preferred the American claims during the summit (particularly on the sensitive issue of human rights), while socialist services preferred Moscow's approach.

The Western services retained the event-centered approach of Washington, too, even while exploring some topics with other approaches. Both the United States and the Soviet Union tried to exploit public relations opportunities afforded (and engineered) to take the initiative in the summit, which provided the grist for Western-style news. The nature of the agenda, however, with emphasis on such matters as human rights and regional conflicts, also provided ample opportunity for more contextual and assessment coverage than had Washington with its single focal point.

The centerpiece of the Washington summit (the INF treaty) provided an easy hook for news services to use in claiming that the event was a significant news event. The very lack of hook in Moscow meant that the reporters had to watch the unfolding events carefully to create substance and provided the openings for various public relations gambits on the part of the summit participants. Although the lack of focus was worrisome to the Soviets, it may have been a blessing in disguise. Gorbachev received Reagan's endorsement for the changes he had made and was able to speak candidly and critically about Reagan's "preaching." The Soviets were also able to direct attention toward U.S. human rights problems, notably with native Americans and Soviet immigrants to the United States. Because the summit was unfocused, the news stories that emerged from it were more interesting and more amenable to services choosing the aspects that they would concentrate on.

The Moscow summit news coverage made as much use of the "mythic mode" of seeing the world as had Washington. Even as the Cold War was winding down, the news coverage continued to stress the "eternal and recurring features" of both the human condition and of U.S.–Soviet or East-West relations (see Dahlgren & Chakrapani, 1982, p. 61). Although the historical view, with its emphasis on process, was also present, the "event" of Moscow itself and the need to explain its significance to the world, apparently suggested to the news services that their approach should continue to revolve around notions of the apocalyptic. Was nuclear holocaust nearing or receding? Would the poorer nations of the world see their concerns raised or lowered in world consciousness as the superpowers began to accommodate one another—even to cooperate in some areas of the world? Would the "new thinking" of the Soviet Union, or of Reagan himself as he recanted his "evil empire" metaphor, result in new initiatives to solve the world's problems? What would be the future of the world if the two superpowers actually called off the Cold War?

Such questions went unanswered. Reagan left office prior to the anticipated fifth summit, the Berlin Wall came down, the Velvet Revolution unfolded in central and eastern Europe. The world changed, and it was up to Gorbachev and his new counterpart, George Bush, to make a new beginning.

NOTES

1. This term indicates the European political reality of 1988, prior to the opening of borders between East and West, the destruction of the Berlin Wall, and the reunification of Germany into a single nation. The reunification resulted in the closing down of Radio Berlin.

2. Certainly not all reports for all languages would be identical. At VOA, for instance, reports about the summit in various languages of the Soviet Union, such as Ukrainian, Uzbek, Armenian, Azerbaijani, and Georgian, would vary from the Russian- or English-language reports to the extent that they would emphasize "regional" material. The basics of stories about the summit, however, would be largely alike.

3. The total amount of time available is not absolute in international broadcasting, as the time is often stretched for important events. The measure is thus merely an indication of relative significance, not an absolute measure. In Table 5.2, the total number of minutes available has been adjusted to reflect the fact that some broadcasts could not be coded, because of interference or unintelligibility or because they were inadvertently left unrecorded.

4. The U.S. diplomatic establishment had long sought to give prominence to the human rights issue in the U.S.–Soviet context. Arguably, the delay allowed the issue finally to achieve its due. However, the suspense of delayed ratification may have made that a more interesting story journalistically.

5. The White House clearly was preoccupied with Reagan's image vis-à-vis Gorbachev. They were preparing for history's judgments of Reagan's presidency. Other members of the government, however, especially the Conference on Security and Cooperation in Europe (CSCE) members, were more seriously interested in human rights as a publicity vehicle to promote solutions to security issues in the European context.

6. For this portion of the analysis the services were grouped into five inclusive classes: VOA, Radio Moscow, Western, socialist, and other.

7. All these points are clearly issues that journalists themselves could define as newsworthy, although many of them were not so defined by various radio services. They are not designed to create news, but to focus the reports of such newsworthy subjects in a manner compatible with U.S. interests. Examining the entire grid of coefficients suggests, however, that the United States was only partially successful. Of the 176 possible coefficients, 74 cells are blank (42%). Radio Baghdad and Radio Havana were not interested in the summit at all, and Radio South Africa and Radio Cairo had little interest. As would be expected, the keenest interest in the summit and thus in its newsworthy issues was shown by the two superpower services, European services, and the services of Canada and Japan. It was only this subset of services, then, that the U.S. public diplomacy apparatus could influence, insofar as international radio operations were concerned.

8. This may have been the result of questions in Moscow about what the role of the changing Soviet Union would be on the world stage. With the Soviet Union having abandoned many of the long-standing characteristics of Soviet activity (secrecy, denial, confrontation, defensive posturing, etc.), the question was, what now? As the White House had not yet shifted dramatically, VOA was left to report the summit using all the traditional (and wrong) categories.

9. VOA's news operation is independent of its editorial activities. VOA news is not to be "propaganda," but comprehensive and truthful. As indicated in Chapter 2, however, propaganda can be judged from differing perspectives. It is worth examining VOA's stance vis-à-vis Radio Moscow, even if the term "propaganda" itself is anath-

ema to VOA or its parent, USIA, and might not be an accurate descriptor from some points of view.

10. The Warsaw Pact is now defunct.

Chapter 6

The 1989 Summits

The Moscow summit of 1988 was Ronald Reagan's "swan song," insofar as U.S.–Soviet relations were concerned. In one sense the change in U.S. administrations in January 1989 did not change the tenor of those relations. George Bush's primary love was foreign policy, and he apparently intended to continue U.S. policies to contain the Soviet Union, planning both to deter potential aggression and to reduce nuclear, chemical-biological, and conventional arsenals, particularly in Europe. Bush was also committed to the strategic defense initiative (SDI). Not much had changed.

In another sense, however, the focus of U.S. foreign policy did shift. There was less direction of Bush's activities by the foreign policy establishment than of Reagan's, both because of his own experience as ambassador to the People's Republic of China and director of the CIA and because of the style of his presidency. As Campbell and Rockman put it (1991, p. viii), Reagan had been "goal focused. Certainly, Reagan never backed away from an opportunity for confrontation when he believed there was a matter worth confronting." George Bush, they said, is "a more typical case than not ["nondescript and less susceptible to personal stereotyping"]. His leadership style therefore tends to blend into a set of political circumstances that offer him slim pickings. He is a pastel political personality serving in a mostly pastel time that offers him a range of shades from which to choose." As Rockman explained (1991, p. 3), "George Bush was elected as a Republican essentially to continue the Reagan agenda in a somewhat more tempered way." His choice of a "pragmatist," James Baker, to be secretary of state epitomized the less ideological character of his new presidency (the description is Berman & Jentleson's, 1991, p. 101). Although less ideological, Baker had been a part of the foreign policy discussions of the Reagan administration, often condensing abstract and complicated discussions into prose that Reagan felt comfortable reading, although he was often uninterested in the actual options or considerations presented by the discussions themselves.

Despite the momentum established in the Reagan–Gorbachev meetings of 1987–1988 and the new "detente" between the superpowers, Bush did not meet Gorbachev until December of 1989.[1] Part of the reason for the delay was the rapidly changing complexion of the world itself. Gorbachev's avowed commitment to change led the Soviet Union to disengage from Afghanistan, to withdraw aid from Nicaragua, and to stand aside while its empire in central and eastern Europe crumbled (see Berman & Jentleson, 1991, p. 93). Within the space of the first few months of Bush's presidency, it seemed possible to begin to think of a post–Cold War world.[2] What sort of world would it be? What would be the respective positions of the two superpowers in that world? How would they characterize one another to the world after seventy years of sparring and vilification? Was the change the result of one man alone, Mikhail Gorbachev, or of an actual change in the Soviet system, one that would bring demilitarization or destabilization?

THE BEIJING AND BRUSSELS SUMMITS, MAY 1989

Before Bush's and Gorbachev's first face-to-face meeting in the Malta harbor in November, two "precursor" summits were held, both in May 1989. The first of these was a summit between Gorbachev and Deng Xiao Peng, which occurred between May 15 and May 18, just before the massacre at Tiananmen Square. Gorbachev's visit to Beijing was his first with the Chinese leadership and, despite the economic and political differences of the two countries, could have signaled a new rapprochement between the two communist superpowers. The second summit, a brief affair on May 29 and 30, involved George Bush. It was held on the fortieth anniversary of the NATO alliance. Bush traveled to Brussels to commemorate the event and to meet with European leaders.

The analysis period for these two summits was from May 1 to May 31. The period began a full two weeks prior to the Beijing summit, but extended only a day after the conclusion of the Brussels summit. Although different in kind from the other analysis periods, this approach allowed two distinctive issues to be addressed. First, a longer baseline was available prior to the initiation of the first summit. This allowed more precise conclusions to be drawn about the inauguration of summit coverage than could be made with the one-week pre-summit analysis period. Second, the shifting emphasis of different radio services from one summit to the next could be evaluated. Interest in the Beijing summit might have been reduced prematurely by attention given to the Brussels summit, which began only eleven days after the conclusion of Gorbachev's and Deng's discussions. It also allowed analysis to be conducted when only one of the two superpowers was present. In one case the Soviet Union was a participant, and in the other, the United States.

The radio services analyzed included Radio Austria, the BBC, Brussels Calling (the Flemish broadcaster from Belgium), Radio Canada, Christian Science Monitor World Radio (a nongovernmental broadcaster referred to hereafter as CSM), Radio Moscow, and VOA. These seven services filed a total of 367 stories over the thirty-one-day analysis period. These included eight stories as early as May 1 and fifteen as late as May 31. The days with the most stories filed were May 23 (twenty-five stories), May 18 (twenty-four stories), and May 12 (twenty-two stories). Of these days, only May 18 coincided with one of the two summits.

Over the month-long analysis period, the BBC filed the most coded stories, followed by Radio Moscow, VOA, CSM, Radio Canada, Brussels Calling, and Radio Austria (see Table 6.1). This result was, in itself, unusual compared to the other summits analyzed, where the number of stories filed was dominated by the two superpowers. BBC's dominance here may be indicative of either its long-term approach to news reporting (thus having a less reactive posture than other Western news services) or the greater attention paid by the BBC to areas of the world outside the obvious superpower orbit (North America and Europe). The BBC had filed seventeen stories prior to the usual analysis period (i.e., more than one week before the inauguration of the Beijing summit), compared to eight for Radio Moscow and eleven for VOA. It is difficult to determine whether these differences are significant, however.

The BBC's coverage (based on the number of stories filed per day) during the month had six distinct peaks. These occurred on May 3–4, 12, 15, 18–19, 24, and 29, when it reached a plateau matched on the next two days. These peaks occurred within the flow of coverage over the month and obviously stand out compared to stories filed on surrounding days. The three middle peaks, on May 15, 18–19, and 24, are obviously associated with the Beijing summit, while the last peak (May 29–31) is clearly the result of the Brussels summit (see Table 6.2).

VOA's most obvious peak coverage occurred on May 15, 24, and 29. The fifteenth was during the Beijing summit, and the twenty-ninth was during the Brussels summit. Radio Moscow filed more stories than any

Table 6.1
Basic Quantitative Measures of Summit Coverage, May 1989

	Beijing Summit			Brussels Summit		
Service	Stories	Minutes	Days	Stories	Minutes	Days
BBC	57	69.63	17	29	35.71	9
VOA	35	74.19	13	21	45.71	8
Radio Moscow	49	154.85	17	32	50.91	9
CSM	20	25.82	8	20	37.91	8
Radio Canada	25	36.10	17	12	17.47	6
Brussels Calling	14	9.63	16	11	18.59	6
Radio Austria	6	10.03	12	6	.95	6

other service on any single day on May 11, and its coverage also peaked on May 21 and 23. Although it also provided a significant number of stories during May 12–14, it is notable that none of its heaviest filing dates coincided with actual summit meeting days. Analysis based on each day's summit stories as a percentage of total stories filed by each of these services over the month of May results in the same peaks of coverage as does simple number of stories filed.

The other four services' coverage peaked at lower levels than that of the three major services, and there was a good deal of congruence in their choices. The standout dates for number and percentage of stories filed were May 3 (Radio Canada), May 17 and 19 (CSM), May 23 (CSM, Brussels Calling, and Radio Canada), and May 26 (CSM). Only CSM's coverage on May 17 and 19 actually coincided with one of the two summits.

One might expect, given CSM's independent status and its grounding in the canons of "American" journalism, that it would be the most reactive of all services. This, however, does not appear to be the case, at least over this month of analysis. CSM did clearly react to the end of the Beijing summit, filing 15% of its month's summit-related stories on May 19, but its pattern of coverage does not otherwise appear to be reactive. Neither does its coverage coincide directly (except for May 29) with the coverage of either the BBC or VOA, both of which depend on a similar news value orientation.

There were several aspects to the Beijing summit that could serve as the focus of news stories. One was the nature of the meeting itself.

Table 6.2
Radio Service Coverage of the Beijing and Brussels Summits, May 1989: Number of Stories and Percentage of News Hole Used, by Service and Date

Date	BBC No.	BBC %	VOA No.	VOA %	Radio Moscow No.	Radio Moscow %	Radio Austria No.	Radio Austria %	Brussels Calling No.	Brussels Calling %	Radio Canada No.	Radio Canada %	CSM No.	CSM %
May 1	NA	NA	4	14.17	1	1.24	NA	NA	NA	NA	2	8.60	NA	NA
May 2	4	16.57	2	8.67	2	3.68	NA	NA	2	6.40	1	15.87	NA	NA
May 3	6	18.83	NA	NA	1	1.11	NA	NA	1	2.93	3	30.53	NA	NA
May 4	5	8.07	2	5.83	1	2.11	1	4.40	NA	NA	NA	NA	NA	NA
May 5	1	8.33	3	13.67	2	40.38	2	75.60	NA	NA	NA	NA	NA	NA
May 6	NA	NA	NA	NA	NA	NA	NA	NA	NA	NA	NA	NA	NA	NA
May 7	NA	NA	NA	NA	1	2.51	NA	NA	NA	NA	1	6.67	NA	NA
May 8	1	0.90	3	13.87	NA	NA	NA	NA	1	NA	2	16.33	NA	NA
May 9	NA	NA	3	71.47	NA	NA	NA	NA	1	6.13	NA	NA	NA	NA
May 10	1	1.20	1	1.87	2	6.13	NA	NA	1	2.93	1	7.53	NA	NA
May 11	3	15.47	3	12.57	8	46.44	NA	NA	NA	NA	1	6.67	NA	NA
May 12	7	36.13	NA	NA	6	56.00	1	31.70	1	3.33	2	18.60	3	29.00
May 13	4	21.80	NA	NA	5	12.84	NA	NA	NA	NA	NA	NA	2	2.40
May 14	4	19.17	NA	NA	5	19.16	NA	NA	NA	NA	NA	NA	NA	NA
May 15	6	32.43	5	25.70	2	5.51	NA	NA	NA	NA	1	6.87	1	3.73
May 16	4	15.53	3	76.57	1	89.49	NA	NA	1	28.53	2	20.53	2	4.16
May 17	3	18.07	4	13.87	3	7.09	2	2.20	NA	NA	1	8.13	4	26.87
May 18	7	27.70	3	7.33	6	26.89	NA	NA	3	8.33	2	25.47	2	22.20
May 19	6	28.17	NA	NA	4	48.64	NA	NA	2	19.33	2	29.93	7	12.83
May 20	NA	NA	NA	NA	NA	NA	NA	NA	NA	NA	NA	NA	NA	NA
May 21	2	9.17	NA	NA	6	30.24	NA	NA	NA	NA	NA	NA	NA	NA
May 22	2	13.00	NA	NA	4	21.36	NA	NA	3	20.20	2	20.87	3	25.90
May 23	3	30.63	4	NA	6	50.04	NA	NA	4	8.93	4	45.20	4	51.77
May 24	5	17.07	5	19.20	5	5.69	1	6.40	NA	NA	NA	NA	1	2.93
May 25	1	3.27	3	76.03	3	4.89	1	1.70	1	24.27	NA	NA	1	3.00
May 26	2	7.57	2	16.33	3	6.91	2	5.20	NA	NA	2	12.27	5	25.87
May 27	NA	NA	NA	NA	NA	NA	NA	NA	NA	NA	NA	NA	NA	NA
May 28	NA	NA	NA	NA	NA	NA	NA	NA	NA	NA	NA	NA	NA	NA
May 29	4	26.20	NA	NA	3	10.36	NA	NA	1	7.87	3	37.60	3	26.10
May 30	4	19.73	4	29.23	NA	NA	2	1.00	NA	NA	NA	NA	1	2.77
May 31	4	13.93	4	17.03	1	0.76	1	1.70	3	74.07	1	7.13	2	3.33

Second was the ongoing student protests that were apparently organized to take advantage of the news media in Beijing to cover the summit, as well as the specific demands of students and the issue of democratization in China. Third was the issue of superpower relations: a possible rapprochement between China and the Soviet Union, the East-West axis in the light of changing Sino-Soviet relations, and the focus of future relations, Asia or Europe. Fourth were a variety of portrayals—of Deng, Gorbachev, or even President Bush, of the deescalating Cold War, of the INF treaty. The analysis examined all these issues both from the aspect of treatment by the seven services and in terms of U.S. foreign policy objectives.

The treatment of the leaders of these three superpowers, as well as those of their respective countries and allies, was calculated over the entire month-long analysis period. These will be dealt with separately from the two summits themselves. Certain other aspects of the month's coverage, however, can be discussed in relation to specific summits. First, for instance, are the portrayals of Chinese government actions, the Chinese leadership, Chinese policies toward the United States and the Soviet Union, and the relationship between official Chinese rhetoric and its actions. Also at issue is the treatment accorded to the Chinese student protests, which continued after the conclusion of the Deng–Gorbachev summit. Finally, there is the larger issue of Chinese-Soviet and Chinese–U.S. relations and the degree of congruence between radio coverage and American foreign policy objectives. These issues will be discussed in the first section of this chapter.

All the services that reported about Chinese foreign policy generally agreed that the policies were realistic and had resulted in improved foreign relations. All services except Radio Canada, which had no stories on this issue, agreed that better relations existed between China and the Soviet Union as a result of Chinese policies. Only Radio Moscow suggested that Chinese policies had also resulted in better relations with the West. None of the services, however, reported extensively on this issue, with the number of stories dealing with it varying from one to five over the thirty-one-day period.

The BBC, CSM, and VOA also carried stories implying that Chinese rhetoric remained distinct from its behavior, but, again, this issue arose in only a few instances. None of the other services carried stories that dealt with this issue.

The issue that resulted in the largest number of stories filed over the month was that of the student protests in Beijing and the response of the government. The coverage of the protests resulted eventually in the Chinese government's decision to jam the incoming signals of both the BBC and VOA (beginning on May 21). The Tiananmen Square massacre, however, occurred after the end of the analysis period. Already in May, before the major confrontations between the students and government troops occurred, these international radio services were staking out their coverage patterns. Chinese actions, for instance, were described by VOA, Radio Canada, CSM, and the BBC in significantly negative terms and by Radio Moscow in less negative ways. Radio Austria carried no stories about Chinese government behavior over this period, and the coverage of Brussels Calling was too brief to determine an overall coverage pattern. The Chinese leadership, too, was the focus of significant negative coverage, with Radio Canada having the most negative portrayals, followed by CSM, Brussels Calling, BBC, VOA, and Radio Moscow (see Table 6.3).

These patterns themselves do not explain the decision of the Chinese government to jam the BBC and VOA. It is useful to remember, however, that the BBC and VOA had far larger audiences for their Mandarin services than either Radio Canada or CSM, making them more likely targets for jamming. Arguably, too, their reports would be seen by audiences as more credible, as they are representative of more "powerful" countries. Unfortunately the end of the analysis period prior to Tiananmen Square prevents any discussion of whether the Chinese government's decision was based in reality or merely political expediency. Clearly, however, neither the BBC nor VOA, at least prior to June 1, was alone in discussing the student–government confrontation in terms that were unflattering to Chinese authorities. It is useful to compare these negative portrayals, however, with those of the students, as carried by these services. Radio Moscow, as might be expected, carried the most negative portrayals of the students' activities, but the BBC and CSM also carried significantly negative portrayals of them. Radio Austria and Radio Canada were less negative concerning the students, and Brussels Calling was neutral. Only VOA carried positive portrayals of the students over this thirty-one-day analysis period.

Insofar as the summit was concerned, the various services generally agreed that it had resulted in better relations between China and the Soviet Union. Again, however, this judgment was based on very few stories (surprisingly) that reported about these relations. Only Brussels Calling and VOA reported on the state of Chinese–U.S. relations. Brussels Calling carried one story saying that relations between China and the United States were satisfactory or improving (a story the news editor may have regretted the next month), and VOA carried one story saying that the Chinese were to blame for the state of China's relations with the United States. Otherwise, this was a nonissue to all the services.

If it had not been for Tiananmen Square, the summit between Gorbachev and Deng might have been almost a nonevent. CSM, for in-

Table 6.3
Im[1] Coefficients for Radio Service Coverage of Chinese Government Actions,
the Chinese Leadership, and Chinese Student Leadership in May 1989

Service	Gov't. Actions	Leadership	Student Leaders
CSM	-0.65	-0.77	-0.56
VOA	-0.78	-0.50	0.04
BBC	-0.53	-0.53	-0.62
Radio Moscow	-0.13	-0.08	-0.70
Brussels Calling	0.0	-0.67	0.0
Radio Canada	-0.69	-0.94	-0.22
Radio Austria	No stories	No stories	No stories

stance, filed eighteen stories that focused on the Chinese students over the analysis period, compared to only two on the Beijing summit (and three on the NATO summit). Other services were similar. VOA filed fourteen of its sixty summit-related stories in May on the Chinese students, and six apiece on the Beijing and NATO summits. The BBC filed thirty-six of eighty-six total stories on the Chinese students, five on the Beijing summit, and seven on the NATO summit. Brussels Calling filed only three stories on the students, the same as on the Beijing summit, but eight on the NATO summit held in Brussels. Likewise, Radio Austria filed only three stories on the students, but none on the Beijing summit and only one on the NATO summit. Radio Canada filed nine student stories, four Beijing summit stories, and three NATO summit stories; it also reported one story (using 2.9% of its summit-related coverage) on political reform in China. Besides Belgium's service, only Radio Moscow was significantly different from the overall pattern: it filed six stories focused on the Chinese students, nine on the Beijing summit, and five on the NATO summit.

The reasons for the coverage of the Tiananmen Square events are apparent in hindsight. Perhaps the focus on the students also decreased the coverage of the Deng–Gorbachev discussions.[3] But the significance of the NATO summit—while small in comparison to full-blown superpower meetings—has another reason. The focus of the world's attention had been drawn, largely because of the initiatives of President Gorbachev in eastern and central Europe and improving U.S.–Soviet relations, to the European continent.[4] The Cold War had been fought in Europe and was ending in Europe as well. The treaties signed had dealt with European defense; the Soviet empire in Europe was beginning to crumble. Asia, despite its size, population, and resources, did not capture these radio services' attention. This reality meant that the radio services would shift their focus to the NATO summit in Brussels, meeting on May 29 and 30.

It is instructive to examine the focus of the stories filed by these various services on issues related to the two summits. The tilt in interest toward the NATO summit and its attendant issues is apparent, as is the upstaging of the Beijing summit by student protests in Tiananmen Square (see Table 6.4).

Each service's agenda for the two summits can be seen rather easily in this table. Although all seven services reported about both the Beijing and Brussels summits, the percentage of stories on all summit issues reported by each service varied widely. The CSM's focus was on the Chinese student protests and regional conflicts. VOA, while filing nearly a quarter of its stories on the student protests, was more focused, overall, on Europe, with over half of its stories focusing on the Brussels summit, the INF treaty, the Soviet Union, strategic and conventional weapons reduction in Europe, NATO and European defense, U.S. relations with its allies, the progress of *glasnost* and *perestroika*, and U.S.–Soviet relations. Except for the student protests, it filed less than 17% of its stories that month on China. The BBC was also preoccupied with European issues, with over 39% of stories on Europe and over 13% on China.[5] It did have the second highest percentage of stories (behind CSM) devoted to the student protests, however. Radio Moscow, as had traditionally been the case, was concerned about the Soviet Union's place in the world. Of its summit stories in May, 21% concerned its relations with the United States, with over 11% devoted to its relations with its European allies and with China. It was far less interested in reporting on the student protests than were the major Western radio services, filing only 7.4% of its stories in May on the protests. Besides its relations with other countries, over 27% of its other summit-related stories concerned Europe, compared to 12.3% on China. Radio Austria was also Europe-centered, devoting over 18% of its stories to the issue of conventional weapons reduction and an equal number to President Bush. It filed no stories focused on the Beijing summit, although over a quarter of its summit-related output dealt with the student protests. Likewise, Brussels Calling devoted one third of its stories to the NATO summit and over 37% to European defense and U.S.–allies relations, contrasted to 12.5% each on the Beijing summit and the student protests. Finally, Radio Canada filed nearly 50% of its stories on European issues, over one quarter on the student protests, and the remainder on China.

Unlike the similar treatments used to report on China and the Beijing summit (with the exception of Radio Moscow), the various radio services

Table 6.4
Stories Filed, by Service, on Summit Issues as a Percentage of Total Summit-Related Stories in May 1989

Issue	CSM	VOA	BBC	Radio Moscow	Radio Austria	Brussels Calling	Radio Canada
Brussels Summit	4.9	10.0	8.1	6.2	9.1	33.3	8.6
USA	0	0	0	1.2	0	0	0
Pres. Bush	2.4	3.3	1.2	0	18.2	0	0
INF Treaty	0	1.7	0	0	0	0	0
Soviet Union	0	1.7	0	4.9	0	0	2.9
Regional Conflict	12.2	5.0	2.3	13.6	0	0	0
Strategic Weapon Reduction	0	1.7	0	0	0	0	2.9
NATO/ Europe Defense	2.4	11.7	14.0	11.1	9.1	29.2	14.3
Conven. Weapon Reduction	0	1.7	5.8	1.2	18.2	0	0
Treaty Adhere.	0	0	1.2	0	0	0	0
U.S.–Ally Relations	7.3	6.7	3.5	2.5	0	8.3	5.7
Soviet-Ally Relations	2.4	0	1.2	6.2	0	0	0
Trade Issues	0	0	0	1.2	0	0	0
U.S.–Soviet Relations	2.4	8.3	5.8	21.0	9.1	0	11.4
Glasnost/ *Perestroika*	0	6.7	0	2.5	0	0	2.9
Human Rights	0	1.7	2.3	1.2	0	0	0
China-Soviet Relations	4.9	0	1.7	4.9	0	0	0
Chinese Leaders	7.3	3.3	3.5	1.2	9.1	0	5.7
Student Protests	43.9	23.3	41.9	7.4	27.3	12.5	25.7
Beijing Summit	7.3	10.0	8.1	11.1	0	12.5	11.4
China	2.4	3.3	0	0	0	0	2.9

often accorded significantly different treatments to the issues that surrounded the Brussels NATO summit. The political posture of the different countries represented in the analysis seemed directly to influence how they reported about the summit and its related issues. Radio Austria, sitting on the edge of Eastern Europe, was extraordinarily positive in its treatment of NATO actions, with the alliance moving quickly by mid-1989 to defuse tensions in Europe. Both VOA and Radio Moscow, along with Brussels Calling, were also positive in their treatments, but to a significantly lesser degree. The other three services, BBC, Radio Canada, and CSM, were all negative, almost reverse-imaging the position of VOA, Radio Moscow, and Brussels Calling (see Appendix 2).

U.S. and Soviet actions also received different responses. Only VOA accorded positive treatment to U.S. actions, with the other services all reporting negatively to varying degrees. Of those services that reported on Soviet actions, only Radio Moscow saw them in a positive light, with the three North American–based services, CSM, Radio Canada, and VOA, all reporting negatively about them. It appears that the two superpowers may have been seen by the independent services as being more willing to continue their own rivalry than to assure stability in Europe. Only the services representing the two superpowers were willing to see the actions of their own government more positively.

The two superpower presidents' policies were seen somewhat differently, perhaps reflecting the difficulty in implementing rhetoric and policy in action. Although the policies were often seen positively, the actions still were treated negatively. Gorbachev's policies were seen positively both by Radio Moscow, which was to be expected, and by Radio Canada, with CSM and Radio Austria both achieving a neutral Im^1 coefficient. Only Brussels Calling provided a significantly negative coefficient, with BBC and VOA being slightly negative (see Appendix 2). Similarly, only the BBC and Radio Moscow saw Bush's policies somewhat negatively, with all other services except CSM (which carried no stories on this issue) being significantly positive.

The United States also failed, by and large, to have its political or rhetorical positions mirrored in reports about the NATO summit, particularly by foreign radio services. Most of the traditional U.S. rhetorical postures went unreported by foreign radios. Only the BBC, CSM, and VOA, for instance, carried stories that suggested that what the Soviets said was distinct from what they did. Only VOA treated such U.S. claims positively, with the other two services casting doubt on them (see Appendix 1). Likewise, the claim that the Soviet Union continued to deny basic human rights was treated positively only by VOA, but doubted or denied by both the BBC and Radio Moscow. CSM was neutral on this issue.

The Christian Science Monitor World Radio affirmed most obviously the claim that Soviet behavior had not assisted in the resolution of regional conflicts, with lesser affirmation coming from VOA and the BBC. Both Radio Moscow and Radio Canada denied the claim, with the most robust denials coming from the stories of Radio Canada.

All services agreed that arms negotiations were a means to ensure security, but they disagreed about which country needed to be more constructive in its approach to strategic arms talks. The Western services all agreed that when the Soviets were more constructive the talks could lead to agreement. VOA and Radio Moscow agreed that the Chinese needed to be more constructive. Radio Moscow, along with VOA, BBC, and Radio Canada, claimed that agreement was possible if the West were constructive. Radio Moscow's coverage on this point clearly pointed the finger at the West, with Western services pointing back, although less strongly (see Appendix 1). All the services agreed, too, that SDI should not impede a strategic weapons reduction agreement; Radio Moscow thus reversed its position during the Reagan years.

In addition to the problem of strategic weapons, all the services (except Radio Austria, which carried no stories on this issue) agreed that balancing conventional forces and reaching a global ban on chemical weapons were issues that required agreement. The strongest affirmations came from stations representing the superpowers.

Finally, Gorbachev's popularity seemed to continue in the West. Although CSM and Brussels Calling were slightly negative in describing the Soviet president, VOA was neutral; and the remainder of the Western services were all positive in their treatment of him (see Appendix 2).

Although neither of these summits qualified as a true U.S.–Soviet superpower summit, they are nevertheless instructive about the nature of decision-making by international radio services. Both the People's Republic of China and the Soviet Union, for instance, wanted their discussions to be widely reported by the international press. However, the Chinese students were successful, at least among these services (with the exception of Radio Moscow), in upstaging this event. This may be indicative either of the independence of these services or (ironically) of their lack of independence. If they were merely responding to the students' activities based on their own assessments of the significance, then we would judge them independent. The problem is that Western governments, especially the United States, were also eager to provide encouragement for democratization in China. The success of citizen rebellion in the Philippines was still fresh, and the winds of change were blowing in Europe as well. Gorbachev seemed to be encouraging gradual change in the communist bloc. Perhaps another dictatorship might be toppled if given some encouragement. We do not know how much encouragement or assistance (if any) any of these services received from their respective governments to report about the student protests, or whether the wishes of these governments were merely coincidental with the independent judgments of the news organizations. At any rate, the plans of the Soviet and Chinese leadership were disrupted.

As suggested earlier, too, it was also easy for these services to abandon lingering attention to the Beijing meeting in favor of coverage of the upcoming NATO summit, at least in English-language coverage throughout the North Atlantic community. As the focus of arms control negotiations, the impending end of the Cold War, and the decreasing tensions between the superpowers had all been centered largely in Europe, it was easy for them to refocus resources on Brussels, despite the fact that little of substance occurred at the summit and the Soviet Union was not present.

THE MALTA SUMMIT, NOVEMBER AND DECEMBER 1989

By the time Presidents Bush and Gorbachev did meet aboard warships in a harbor of Malta, it was possible to speak of the end of the Cold War.[6] Yet Malta was billed, not as the first post–Cold War summit, but as a get-acquainted meeting or a "pre-summit" between the two men. Caution seemed to be the order of the day, with Bush particularly reluctant to announce prematurely any new modus vivendi with the "evil empire" (see Berman & Jentleson, 1991, p. 112). As Rockman put it (1991, p. 15), "Being more addicted to cold-war orthodoxies when he began his administration than Ronald Reagan was when he ended his, Bush's reaction to the powerful events around him was slow and cautious until it became clear that the old orthodoxy was crumbling."

Within the first two years of his presidency Bush met with Gorbachev three times. Shortly after their third meeting, the Soviet coup effectively ended Gorbachev's presidency, despite his brief return to power. During these summits, as well as in meetings between Baker and his Soviet counterpart, Eduard Shevardnadze, until his resignation in December 1990, the United States and the Soviets progressed toward treaties on conventional force reductions in Europe (CFE) and a START treaty, as well as understandings on several regional issues, including the Middle East, the Iraqi invasion of Kuwait and the subsequent Persian Gulf war, German reunification, Angola, Cambodia, and Afghanistan. "Perhaps the highest compliment is that U.S.–Soviet diplomatic relations were normalized" (Berman & Jentleson, 1991, p. 112).

Clearly, by December 1989, the political symbols that had defined U.S.–Soviet relations had significantly changed from what had been true only eighteen months before.[7] The two superpowers were looking for ways to cooperate, accommodate, and relate with one another. They sought new symbols to refer and give meaning to the emerging redefinition of "superpower."

Another part of the context for this summit was the diminished role of the National Security Council in setting forth the rhetorical structure for U.S. participation. The NSC prepared no talking points for the president or other spokespersons, who were on their own. Bush, however, did ask the Heritage Foundation, a Washington "think tank," to prepare some pre-summit recommendations for his use (see "Nation," 1989, 27 November, p. 20).

The venue for the summit was to be U.S. and Soviet warships anchored in a Malta harbor. The press was largely "stuck" on-shore. After the weather changed for the worse, the two presidents were also stuck— on the larger Soviet warship. It was thus difficult for the press to cover the summit in the detail to which it had become accustomed during the preceding two summits. This was perhaps a deliberate effort (at least partially) on the part of the two men to become better acquainted outside the spotlight and to avoid raising the hopes of people through the press for some dramatic announcement from Malta. The intervention of poor weather just made matters worse. The result was a much-diminished quantity of radio news reports by international services.

Gorbachev met with the pope in the Vatican on his way to Malta, coming prepared to "atone" for the Soviet Union's "mistake in treating religion superficially" (Sheehy, 1990, p. 220). At Malta, Sheehy wrote (p. 221), George Bush stepped forward "as a full booster of perestroika and the personal leadership cult of Mikhail Gorbachev." He also arrived with several specific proposals for concluding arms control deals and integrating the Soviet Union into the West's economic system. Such effort, although it—along with the Vatican visit—provided the "pinnacle of Mikhail Gorbachev's life" (Sheehy, 1990, p. 219), did not culminate in extensive Malta summit coverage.

Eight radio services' coverage of the Malta summit were analyzed: VOA, Radio Moscow, the BBC, Radio Prague, Radio Bucharest, Radio Budapest, Radio Sofia, and Radio Beijing. Altogether, over the fourteen-day analysis period, these services filed 121 stories, for an average of a little more than one story per day per service. More stories were filed by these radio organizations before the summit began than during or after it. Altogether these eight services filed sixty-seven stories between November 27 and December 1 (five days), thirty-five stories from December 2 to December 5 (four days), and nineteen stories between

December 6 and 10 (five days).[8] This imbalance is the result, I think, both of disappointment among the press about the lack of concrete outcomes from the summit and of the poor weather conditions that restricted their access to the presidents or their spokespersons. It is undoubtedly also true that, because of the neutral location for the summit (in neither the United States or the Soviet Union), neither country had undertaken the elaborate preparations to accommodate the press that would have been the case in Washington or Moscow.

While both VOA and Radio Moscow did post-summit stories, Radio Moscow, as usual, reported more stories after the conclusion of the meetings. Its former ideological allies, represented by services based in Bulgaria, Czechoslovakia, Hungary, and Romania, dropped the summit as an issue for news coverage almost immediately after its conclusion. It was far less significant to them than other issues associated with the changes in Europe than had been the case during the period of a more obviously bipolar world. Like VOA, the BBC also did some post-summit reporting, but both were more content to allow the summit discussion to end with the conclusion of the formal meetings than was Radio Moscow (see Table 6.5). One of the major peaks in the Soviet service's coverage occurred on December 10, well after the summit's conclusion. The focus of all its stories that day was U.S.–Soviet relations, a topic that the Soviet Union struggled to make sense of during the rapid dissipation of superpower rivalry during that year.

Although Radio Moscow filed a significant percentage of all stories on the summit during each day of the analysis period, during the summit itself (December 2–4) the other services' larger degree of attention had the effect of reducing its dominance.[9] Both the BBC and VOA provided significant percentages of the total coverage provided by these eight services on December 1, preparing for the summit to begin, and coverage was well distributed over all the services on the summit's first day. By December 4, however, several of the services had lost interest in the summit, leaving the coverage to the BBC, VOA, Radio Moscow, Radio Prague, and Radio Beijing. After December 5, only the BBC and the two superpowers had anything left to say about the summit. Compared to the earlier Reagan–Gorbachev meetings, this summit meeting was apparently judged as having little to offer to the world.[10]

The relatively light coverage accorded to the Malta meeting also meant that most services had relatively little opportunity to characterize Bush or Gorbachev, their countries' actions, or even what had become generally a major topic of discussion: the end of the Cold War. The services that characterized Bush, for instance, generally saw him in a positive light—perhaps not surprisingly, as he had been in office for only a few months. The portrayals provided by VOA, Radio Moscow, and

Table 6.5
Radio Service Coverage of the Malta Summit, Nov.–Dec. 1989: Number of Stories
and Percentage of News Hole Used, by Service and Date

Date	Radio Sofia No.	%	Radio Beijing No.	%	Radio Prague No.	%	Radio Bucharest No.	%
Nov. 27	0	0	1	10	1	7.69	2	66.67
Nov. 28	1	16.67	1	10	2	15.38	0	0
Nov. 29	1	16.67	2	20	3	20.08	0	0
Nov. 30	1	16.67	2	20	2	15.38	0	0
Dec. 1	0	0	1	10	1	7.69	1	33.33
Dec. 2	1	16.67	1	10	1	7.69	0	0
Dec. 3	1	16.67	2	20	1	7.69	0	0
Dec. 4	0	0	0	0	1	7.69	0	0
Dec. 5	1	16.67	0	0	1	7.69	0	0
Dec. 6	0	0	0	0	0	0	0	0
Dec. 7	0	0	0	0	0	0	0	0
Dec. 8	0	0	0	0	0	0	0	0
Dec. 9	0	0	0	0	0	0	0	0
Dec. 10	0	0	0	0	0	0	0	0

Date	Radio Budapest No.	%	VOA No.	%	Radio Moscow No.	%	BBC No.	%
Nov. 27	1	10	1	4.17	4	11.76	1	4.76
Nov. 28	2	20	3	12.50	2	5.88	3	14.29
Nov. 29	1	10	3	12.50	3	8.82	2	9.52
Nov. 30	2	20	2	8.33	3	8.82	2	9.52
Dec. 1	1	10	3	12.50	2	5.88	4	19.05
Dec. 2	1	10	1	4.17	1	2.94	1	4.76
Dec. 3	1	10	2	8.33	3	8.82	1	4.76
Dec. 4	1	10	3	12.50	4	11.76	2	9.52
Dec. 5	0	0	2	8.33	1	2.94	1	4.76
Dec. 6	0	0	1	4.17	2	5.88	1	4.76
Dec. 7	0	0	0	0	2	5.88	0	0
Dec. 8	0	0	1	4.17	2	5.88	1	4.76
Dec. 9	0	0	1	4.17	1	2.94	1	4.76
Dec. 10	0	0	1	4.17	4	11.76	1	4.76

the BBC were similar (with Im^1 coefficients between .57 and .68). Radio Sofia provided the most positive portrayal (at 1.0). Gorbachev likewise had generally positive portrayals. VOA's coverage coefficients for the two men were nearly identical, BBC's were somewhat lower for Gorbachev, and Radio Moscow's were considerably higher for Gorbachev. The biggest difference was the coverage provided by Radio Sofia, which had nothing to say about Gorbachev, thus giving him a coefficient of zero.

There were few surprises in the portrayals of the actions of the two superpowers, either. VOA portrayed U.S. actions positively, and Radio Moscow portrayed Soviet actions positively. VOA's coverage of Soviet actions was more equivocal, with an Im^1 coefficient of zero. Radio Moscow's Im^1 coefficient for U.S. actions was significantly negative (-0.73), as was Radio Sofia's (an interesting result, given its positive portrayal of President Bush). The BBC's coefficients for U.S. actions were positive, but for Soviet actions were negative. Radio Prague was neutral respecting the U.S. and positive for the Soviet Union. Radio Budapest was positive regarding both superpowers, while Radio Bucharest's Im^1 coefficient on Soviet actions was significantly negative, and for U.S. actions neutral. Radio Beijing had nothing to say about the actions of either country.

The various services generally described NATO in positive terms, too. Although Radio Moscow's portrayals were slightly less positive than those of VOA, its Im^1 coefficient was actually higher than that of the BBC. Radio Prague's coefficient was positive, and the highest coefficient for portrayal was that of Radio Bucharest. On the negative side, Radio Sofia's Im^1 coefficient was the lowest of all services, but its opinion was shared by both Radio Budapest and Radio Beijing.

These results, I think, are reflective of the confusion attending the changing political complexion of Europe during 1989. The East European services appeared to be confused about their roles. They had achieved a certain measure of independence from the "party line," but they may have been unsure how long their leashes were, just how bold they could afford to be. Radio Beijing may have been worried about the impending dominance of NATO in Europe with the crumbling of the socialist bloc and unsure what such superiority might mean to their own relationship with the Soviet Union, the Europeans, or the United States. VOA's posture seems somewhat mellow, still standoffish in respect to Soviet intentions but supportive of the changes represented by Gorbachev (essentially a mirror image of Bush's attitude toward the changes—positive and cautious). Radio Moscow was likewise ameliorated, less ideological in its willingness to see positive elements in U.S. positions and in its new president, yet unsure about NATO.

The Malta summit was the first meeting between the leaders of the superpowers where the question of whether the Cold War might be ending could be addressed. Few of the services provided explicit descriptions of the end of this war, however, indicating the uncertainty about whether it was in fact over. Only four services provided descriptions of the "end of the Cold War." These were VOA, Radio Moscow, the BBC, and Radio Beijing. The BBC's positive descriptions were twice as favorable as those of Radio Moscow. This may reflect the European desire for the end of the Cold War, one that made the continent uniquely vulnerable in the contention of the superpowers, while Radio Moscow's somewhat lower—yet still positive—portrayal may again reflect its uncertainty about what the future would mean if the postwar bipolar world were redefined. Radio Beijing and VOA each provided only one description, with both thus being equally negative.

Whatever the positions of these services was on whether the Cold War was or was not over, they all had the opportunity to portray others' claims of that fact. All of them included statements from various people who claimed that the Cold War was over. They thus had opportunities to put these claims into contexts that could be either positive or negative. There was remarkable symmetry in their treatments of such claims. All coefficients for all services were positive, with coefficients ranging from 0.3 to 1.0. This result reflects the wish that the Cold War could end, even when the results of its closure could not be clearly anticipated (see Appendix 2).

The services examined could focus their stories on any aspect of the summit that they chose. Collapsing the various foci of the stories coded into five categories allows some comparison to be made of the choices they made. The five categories used were (1) reports about the summit itself, on the INF treaty or the strategic defense initiative; (2) reports on personality—Bush, Gorbachev, or their respective countries, or on the relations between the two presidents; (3) reports on matters of conflict between the two countries—human rights and regional disputes; (4) reports on weapons reductions—strategic weapons, conventional weapons, or adherence to previous treaties; and (5) reports on long-range political issues—U.S.–ally, Soviet-ally, East-West, or U.S.–Soviet relations, trade issues, *glasnost*, *perestroika*, and the end of the Cold War. Each of the services had a slightly different mix of stories on these issues. Only the four most important services will be discussed here: VOA, BBC, Radio Moscow, and Radio Prague.

VOA's principal concerns were personality and long-range political issues. It had little interest in the summit itself, indicating the lower-key nature of the summit—and perhaps the difficulty of covering it. Radio Moscow was more interested in the progress of the summit than was

VOA, but its principal concerns were conflict issues with the United States and the personalities of the two presidents. This may have been the result of curiosity about the new U.S. president. It was also significantly interested in long-range political issues. All three of these major foci fell within the tradition of Radio Moscow reporting: making sure that the Soviet Union's place in the world was acknowledged by playing up the significance of its relations with the United States. The BBC's overriding concern was in weapons reduction, indicative of the general interest of the Western European countries. It also reported on long-range political issues and, to a lesser degree, on the personalities and progress of the summit itself. Radio Prague, which filed fewer total stories, focused primarily on the summit and on personality issues. It reported no stories on conflicts or weapons.

By the time of the Malta summit, it might have been possible for international radio services to suggest that the world had embarked on a new path, what George Bush would eventually come to call the "new world order" and what Mikhail Gorbachev had referred to as "new thinking." The stories reported were examined to determine whether these terms were used or if the concept they embodied was even referred to by the services. Ten of the ninety-six stories coded for Malta included some reference to "new thinking." Radio Moscow used the term or provided an indirect reference to it in five stories, the BBC in three, and Radio Prague in two. Each of these three services used the term directly in only one story. The notion of a "new world order" received even less attention, with only two stories making some reference to it, and both denying that any such new world order had yet come into being. VOA reported one of these stories, and Radio Beijing the other.

Several issues that had become flashpoints in U.S.–Soviet relations had not been resolved by the time Ronald Reagan left office. These included such issues as the Soviet policies on human rights questions—freedom of speech, travel, and emigration—SDI, and Soviet "adventurism" in developing countries, leading to regional conflicts. Despite their central status during the Reagan years and the fact that the two countries had reached consensus on none of them, they largely had become nonissues by the time of the Malta summit. Human rights figured in only one VOA story and was ignored by all other services. SDI disappeared altogether. VOA reported on Soviet adventurism in three stories, with one of these backpedaling on the issue. Radio Moscow carried five stories that denied any Soviet culpability in regional conflict, and five additional stories that implied U.S. or Western complicity in aggravating regional tensions. These contentious issues essentially disappeared from the public arena represented by these services.

Even arms control issues themselves took a back seat at Malta. Although the various services carried a total of twenty-one stories on the role of arms negotiations in ensuring security, none of them tackled the issue directly, but were content to deal with it only indirectly. The BBC and Radio Moscow carried the most stories on this issue (at six and five stories respectively). Only VOA, BBC, and Radio Moscow carried stories on the issue of whether the Soviet Union was taking, or had taken, a constructive approach to arms control negotiations. All agreed that when that happened, an agreement would be forthcoming. Radio Moscow emphasized that arms control agreements required that both sides approach them constructively, with both the BBC and Radio Prague taking a similar posture in only one story apiece.

With these old issues dormant in 1989, there were other issues to explore. What predominated in the services' coverage of Malta was U.S.–Soviet relations. Perhaps it was indeed a get-acquainted meeting more than a summit. Forty-four of the ninety-six stories coded for the Malta summit (45.8%) included some reference to U.S.–Soviet relations. Most of these (thirty-three) reported on the generally satisfactory or improving nature of these relations. VOA carried nine stories with this claim, Radio Moscow fourteen, the BBC six, Radio Prague two, and Radio Budapest and Radio Beijing one apiece. Three other stories (one each by Radio Moscow, BBC, and Radio Budapest) gave credit equally to the two superpowers for their improving relations, but Radio Moscow claimed in two other stories that the Soviets should get the credit for the improvements and in three others that the Americans should get the blame for any tensions in those relations. Only Radio Beijing saw fit to urge caution in judging the U.S.–Soviet relationship since, it said, tensions continued.

The three 1989 summits were perhaps no more than a respite in the increasingly quick-paced changes affecting East-West relations. The Beijing Soviet-Chinese summit was overshadowed by the events occurring in that city's streets. The Brussels summit was little more than an opportunity for the NATO allies to regroup and think together about the changes overtaking Europe. The Malta summit was but a brief opportunity for Mikhail Gorbachev to meet his new counterpart in the United States, and for George Bush to begin his watch with the man that Gail Sheehy said (1990) had "changed the world."

NOTES

1. Bush did not offer to meet with Gorbachev until mid-July, awaiting the result of a policy review that, because of its delayed conclusion, worried Margaret Thatcher, Gorbachev, and the U.S. foreign policy establishment.

2. As Gaddis put it (1992, p. 130), when Bush entered the White House, "the point at issue no longer seemed to be 'how to fight the Cold War' at all, but rather 'is the Cold War over?' "

3. It may be, too, that both VOA and the BBC saw the summit as merely a sideshow to the important story in Beijing: the pro-democracy movement.

4. Daniel Benjamin wrote in *Time* (1989, May 29, p. 36) that, despite Gorbachev's and Deng's plans to take the world spotlight, it was the 3,000 students on a hunger strike in Tiananmen Square that transfixed the eye. The students eventually became the most serious challenge that the Chinese leadership had ever faced (see also Birnbaum & Chua-Eoan, 1989, p. 24).

5. BBC and VOA Asian-language services, particularly Mandarin, would have carried a far greater proportion of Asian- and Chinese-related news, but such services were not part of this analysis.

6. A *Time*-CNN poll conducted on November 15, 1989, asked Americans whether they thought the Cold War had ended. While 73% responded "no," 27% were already inclined to draw such a conclusion.

7. Hinckley (1990, p. 7) defines a political symbol as "The communication by political actors to others for a purpose, in which the specific object referred to conveys a larger range of meaning, typically with emotional, moral, or psychological impact. This larger meaning need not be independently or factually true, but will tap ideas people want to believe as true."

8. I divide the fourteen-day period up this way, rather than following the actual summit dates, because of the differences in time zones. What is an evening report from one country arrives the next morning in another country; in the case of Radio Beijing, it arrives the preceding day, as it broadcasts across the international date line into North America.

9. The summit actually occurred on December 2 and 3, but due to the differences in time zones, much of the coverage was actually broadcast December 4.

10. Both Bush and Gorbachev had actually been reluctant to call their two-day meeting a summit at all. *Time* magazine said on November 13 (p. 32) that neither Bush nor Gorbachev would call their scheduled first meeting a summit. It had no scheduled agenda, and the two men planned no communique to end the meeting. By November 27, however, *Time* was referring to the upcoming meeting (p. 20) as a summit.

Chapter 7

The 1990 Washington
Superpower Summit

Mikhail Gorbachev returned to Washington, D.C., on May 30, 1990, to spend five days (through June 3) participating in an official summit with George Bush. This was almost exactly three years after he had first visited the city to meet with Ronald Reagan. The context of this second visit was significantly different, however, than that of his Washington debut. As George J. Church (1990, June 11, p. 12) put it, "The electricity generated at past superpower summits by the prospect of mortal enemies edging toward peace was blessedly missing. This time the meetings were between two world leaders whose nations are fully at peace but have conflicting interests and needs. The grand gesture was replaced by haggling over money and politics."

Gorbachev's tenure as president of the Soviet Union was already slowly beginning to unravel. Increasingly his policies were under attack by Boris Yeltsin, the president of Russia. George Bush, too, was facing new strains in the NATO alliance created by Chancellor Helmut Kohl's insistence on a united German state. Both superpower economies were in serious difficulties, the Soviet Union struggling with *perestroika* and the United States with a ballooning deficit. The meeting was to be the last U.S.–Soviet superpower summit. In August 1990 a coup by Soviet "hardliners" temporarily deposed Gorbachev from power, trapping him in his dacha for several days while resistance led by Boris Yeltsin's defiant response from the Moscow White House mounted. Eventually the junta that seized control of the federal government gave up, probably because of Soviet troops' refusal to fire on their own citizens; and

Gorbachev was briefly returned to power until the Soviet Union broke apart on January 1, 1991.

Analysis of the 1990 Washington summit included five services: from the West, VOA, the BBC, and Radio Netherlands, and from the East, Radio Moscow and Radio Berlin. The analysis period extended from May 23 to June 8, thus beginning seven days before Gorbachev's arrival in Washington and extending for five days following his departure. The analysis is based on a total of 166 stories.

The peak day for stories filed by all five services was May 29, the day preceding the initiation of the summit. Lesser peaks occurred halfway through the summit (on June 1) and on the two days following the summit, June 4 and 5. VOA's story total led all services, and it filed at least six stories on the summit on five separate days: May 28, 30, and 31 and June 3 and 4. The BBC's peaks occurred on May 29 and 31 and June 1 and 4. Radio Netherlands had no major peaks; Radio Berlin peaked on May 23 and 29 and on June 6. Radio Moscow filed far fewer stories on this summit than on previous ones, and its coverage peaked signifi-cantly only on June 4.

Over 10% of all stories filed by the five services were aired on May 29. Nearly 10% were also aired on June 1, and nearly 9% on June 4. The BBC filed over 12% of its summit story total on both June 1 and 4, matching the overall percentage peaks. Radio Netherlands filed over 12% of its summit story total on May 27 and 31, while Radio Berlin peaked at nearly 12% of its total on three occasions: May 23 and 29 and June 6. Like these services, VOA's and Radio Moscow's coverage using percentage of total stories filed mirrored the number of stories filed.

As was the case with previous summits, stories were coded to deter-mine the primary foci of coverage. For the Washington summit, thirty-six separate focus codes were used. These were grouped into a five-part typology: (1) summit issues, which included all stories that reported on the day-to-day events of the summit, discussions of the INF treaty, and the strategic defense initiative (SDI); (2) personalities, including stories on the two presidents and their countries, on the theme of interdepend-ence in world affairs, and the domestic concerns of the two nations; (3) conflict, which emphasized human rights, involvement in regional disputes, the situation of the Baltic republics, and German reunification; (4) weapons issues, including reduction of all types of weapons, adher-ence to treaties and arms control agreements, and the START treaty; and (5) long-range political issues, including the defense of Europe, U.S.–ally and Soviet-ally relationships, the importance of the Third World, trade, the progress of *glasnost* and *perestroika*, the end of the Cold War and the achievement of a new world order, Soviet-Korean relations, achieving peace, and the development of the Soviet economy.

For the BBC, the greatest focus of stories was the summit itself (33%), with lesser attention given to personalities (27.8%), long-range political issues (16.7%), regional conflict (11%), and weapons reduction (5.6%). Clearly, the major focus of previous postwar summits, weapons reduction, had been reduced in significance by the time of this 1990 summit for the BBC. The relatively large percentage of stories (nearly 17%) devoted to long-range political issues suggests that the BBC was looking for a new paradigm to explain the relations between the superpowers.

The other services did not focus their stories on these five story categories in the same fashion. Radio Berlin, for instance, focused nearly half its stories on long-range political issues and a third on the summit. It downplayed conflict, weapons, and personality issues. Of course, the long-range political issues were probably the most salient to the tottering East German government just before what would become a rush to reunification. With this impending momentous change in central Europe, weapons reduction was no longer a major issue. The service, too, may have had enough of personality cults to devote many stories to such issues. (Helmut Kohl was probably of more interest than either Bush or Gorbachev.) Radio Berlin seems to have at last achieved a measure of independence just before its own demise.

Radio Moscow was even more single-minded in its coverage. Nearly half of its stories were devoted to summit issues (not unexpected), and another 39% to long-range political issues. It reported no stories focused on personality: the summit proceeded almost without important persons. The spotlight that had shown so brightly on the public relations of Reagan and Gorbachev had been switched off. It focused only 10% of its stories on conflict issues: it was as though such disputes—which had been major bones of contention during the Reagan years—had been made irrelevant in the thawing Cold War.

VOA continued to spread its stories across the various story categories, achieving the most even spread of the five services. The two major categories of Radio Moscow and Radio Berlin stories—the summit and long-range political issues—were VOA's focus in only 56% of stories. It continued to report on personality (an American specialty), with another 20% of stories focused there. In addition, 17% of VOA stories focused on conflict (perhaps the Cold War still raged, at least regarding such issues as human rights and "adventurism"), and the remaining 7% on weapons issues.

None of Radio Netherlands's stories focused on any of these categories of issues. It focused on "other."

As with previous summits a variety of statements and issues were tested using a modified Im coefficient technique. Since Mikhail Gorbachev had been developing his theme of "new thinking," the first issue tested was the treatment of this concept. It referred to the necessity for both superpowers and their European allies (and former allies) to begin to think about their relations using new categories. He had expressed hope, for instance, that both the Soviet Union and the United States could be considered part of Europe for purposes of reaching security arrangements that would guarantee peaceful relations across the continent. All five services were disposed to describe such ideas positively. The most positive in their portrayal were the BBC (2.0) and Radio Berlin (1.5). Surprisingly, Radio Moscow was less positive than these two services (1.14) and nearly even with Radio Netherlands (1.0) and VOA (1.0) in portraying "new thinking."

The lack of attention given to the old categories of discourse about the Soviet Union can be seen in the portrayals of the Soviet Union as an adventuristic predator in the developing world. The theme of Soviet meddling in regional conflicts had been promulgated as part of the original talking points preceding the 1987 Washington summit. Only three years later, only Radio Moscow and VOA bothered to report stories where this theme was explored. Both of them denied that the Soviet Union continued to be adventuristic! Radio Moscow's denials were stronger than were those of VOA (-1.5 to -0.5).

By 1990, too, the radio services were agreed that balancing conventional forces in Europe and achieving a worldwide ban on chemical weapons were significant issues requiring agreement. Four of the five services agreed on this point equally (with 1.0s); only Radio Netherlands lagged (at 0.5) in its affirmation of this point. Less and less seemed to divide the approach taken to East-West relations by these five radio news operations.

On one last issue, the issue of Soviet human rights, which had been a focal point of Reagan's visit to Moscow in 1988, there did continue to be some disagreement, but the "bedfellows" were indeed a bit strange. The BBC did not report stories that took a position on the question of whether or not the Soviets continued to deny basic human rights of speech, religion, travel, and emigration. Only Radio Moscow denied this proposition, and it continued to do so strongly (-2.0). The VOA's coefficient on this issue was significantly reduced from earlier summits (at 1.4), however, while both Radio Netherlands and Radio Berlin made the claim most strongly (and identically at 2.0). In Radio Berlin's case, this portrayal may have been the result of its increasing independence from the "party line," even while the Berlin Wall remained intact. Radio Netherlands, which had historically focused on some difficult human rights issues and had been critical of both superpowers on this score in earlier summits, continued its tradition.

Also of interest, given the public relations contest between the superpowers that had been set off by Mikhail Gorbachev in 1985 with his *glasnost* initiative, is the portrayal of the two presidents. Radio Berlin and VOA both portrayed President Bush more positively than President Gorbachev. VOA's portrayal of Bush was about twice as positive as its portrayal of Gorbachev. This was to be expected. Radio Berlin's somewhat more positive portrayal of Bush than Gorbachev, however, was less predictable and, as were other matters already discussed, likely the result of growing independence. There may also have been some sense of betrayal by the East Germans on this point in 1990. The BBC and Radio Netherlands both portrayed President Gorbachev significantly more positively than President Bush. This perhaps indicates the European position that Gorbachev had done more, conceded more, and been responsible for more reductions of tension in Europe than had the United States. By this measure we might say that the Soviet Union had won the public relations battle, at least insofar as Western European opinion was concerned. Radio Moscow was also more positive in its portrayals of Gorbachev than Bush, but not by a wide margin. Both men received high positive modified Im coefficients (see Appendix 2).

Europe in 1990 was still affected by four major players: the two superpowers, NATO, and the Warsaw Pact. The stories reported by these four services were also analyzed to determine how the actions of these four players were portrayed by the radio services. The most positive portrayals of all four actors came from Radio Moscow, with a stair-step portrayal of Soviet actions (most positive), followed by Warsaw Pact, U.S., and NATO actions. Of all the services, these portrayals seem most coincident with what we might expect.

VOA, by contrast, portrayed the actions of the Warsaw Pact most favorably, followed by U.S. and NATO actions. It portrayed Soviet actions negatively, but only slightly so. Radio Berlin also portrayed the Warsaw Pact's actions most positively, followed by Soviet actions and U.S. actions. It portrayed NATO actions negatively, the only service to do so. These portrayals were also generally in character with what we might expect from the "old" Radio Berlin, but not consistent with the independence that it seemed to be exhibiting on other issues. Perhaps it was indicative of turmoil within the news operation.

Radio Netherlands was the most negative service in its portrayals. It portrayed the actions of both the Soviet Union and the United States in equally negative ways and did not portray Warsaw Pact actions at all. Only NATO actions received positive portrayals from the service, but these were tepid by comparison with the other services. The BBC was the most conservative of the five services in its portrayals of the major players' actions. It did give the highest positive portrayal of NATO actions of all services, but its second highest positive modified Im coefficient went to the Soviet Union. Third was the United States. It provided no portrayals of Warsaw Pact actions (see Appendix 2).

It was perhaps easy for the BBC and Radio Netherlands to see positive moves by NATO, since the two services function in NATO countries. This would also be true of Radio Berlin and Radio Moscow portrayals of Warsaw Pact actions. Some of the other portrayals—such as VOA's positive portrayals of the Warsaw Pact, and Radio Netherlands's equally negative portrayals of both American and Soviet actions—are less easy to explain. Perhaps VOA was being encouraging and Radio Netherlands evenhanded, even if negative.

These portrayals are largely consistent, too, with the last set examined. They involved portrayals of Gorbachev's policies toward NATO and on two statements: that the world had embarked on a new world order (President Bush's counterpoint to Gorbachev's "new thinking") and that the Cold War was over. All the services agreed, based on their portrayals of statements made, that the Cold War had ended. All provided significantly positive Im^1 coefficients (between 1.5 [Radio Netherlands] and 2.0 [Radio Berlin]). All except Radio Netherlands also endorsed the idea that the world had embarked on a new world order. (Radio Netherlands did not carry any stories including reports or commentary on this issue.) The two superpower services had the highest Im^1 coefficients on this statement (VOA at 1.71 and Radio Moscow at 2.0), but the BBC was not far behind (at 1.5). Radio Berlin provided the least positive assessment, probably fretting about the future (1.14). All agreed, too, that Gorbachev's policies toward NATO were positive ones. The BBC portrayed statements to that effect most positively (2.0), followed by Radio Moscow (1.73), VOA (1.33), Radio Berlin (0.83), and Radio Netherlands (0.67). Overall, Radio Berlin and Radio Netherlands seemed somewhat more pessimistic about the state of Europe in 1990 than did the other three services.

Three other issues raised in the research were not sufficiently interesting to warrant detailed reports. The SDI debate, which had been such a flashpoint between the United States and the Soviet Union only two years earlier, was irrelevant by 1990, judging by the lack of coverage it received. The question of whether the Soviet Union had been constructive in achieving a strategic arms limitation treaty was also little discussed, but all services—to the extent that they mentioned the issue at all—were positive in their treatment of the Soviet role. Finally, on the claim (originally proposed by the NSC prior to the 1987 Washington summit) that arms negotiations are not an end in themselves, but a means to ensure security, all services also agreed by nearly the same margin of 2:1, thus achieving modified Im coefficients of 2 in nearly all cases.

The 1990 Washington summit was the least interesting of the six summits analyzed. The radio services on both sides of the teetering Iron Curtain were moving toward consensus in their coverage of superpower relations, and the issues that had for so long divided East and West were resolved, forgotten, or replaced by other concerns about which there was more agreement. The ideological divide had narrowed.

Various political commentators have argued that it was Soviet initiative that was crucial in narrowing the gap between East and West. Sheehy has described Gorbachev as "the man who changed the world," and Haslam has commented (1990, p. 177) that Gorbachev broke with previous Soviet policies "in redefining security as a political problem requiring a political rather than a military solution." The various radio services, particularly those not directly representing the two superpowers, appear to have agreed with such assessments. The services had tempered their earlier largely negative portrayals of the Soviet Union by 1990; they also had recognized the historic opportunity that Gorbachev's "new thinking" seemed to offer the West. Even in the East, if Radio Berlin can be taken as representative, the winds of change seemed clearly to be blowing in representations of political and military concerns.

Chapter 8

Conclusions: Trends in News Coverage and Propaganda, 1987–1990

This book analyzes international radio news coverage of summit meetings during five separate periods over approximately four years. Four of these periods bracket superpower summit meetings held in Washington (1987), Moscow (1988), Malta (1989), and Washington (1990). The fifth brackets two summits, each of which involved one of the two superpowers, occurring within days of each other in 1989. The analysis also includes two summits attended by President Ronald Reagan and two by President George Bush.

This chapter will concentrate on only the four superpower summits and on the coverage of some of the services whose coverage was tracked over several (or all) of the summits. The three radio services whose coverage was included in all four summits were the BBC, Radio Moscow, and the Voice of America. Radio Netherlands was analyzed for three summits, and Deutsche Welle, Radio Prague, Radio Berlin, and Radio Budapest for two summits. This chapter will report on some comparative measures concerning these services.

Conventional wisdom about journalistic priorities suggests that news organizations pay more attention to events that are closer by, because they are presumably easier to cover and have more immediate impact on audiences. This is somewhat hard to judge in the case of international radio services, as by definition they are broadcasting to audiences often far outside their own borders. It did seem useful, however, to judge whether services altered the time devoted to summit stories as the summits moved from one side of the Atlantic to the other or occurred in "hostile," "friendly," or "neutral" territory. These characterizations of place would vary according to the service analyzed. Washington is friendly to VOA, Moscow hostile, and Malta neutral. The opposite case applies to Radio Moscow. The other Western and socialist services might not define such places as equally salient, however, merely because of alliance structures. It is more appropriate to examine the changes in their coverage according to distance. Thus, Malta would be the closest, Moscow next, and Washington the most distant location for western European services, while for socialist services, the order would be Moscow, Malta, and Washington.

This logic is not supported by the evidence, based on the mean story length reported by each service over the four summits. The mean story length of BBC coverage, for instance, gradually declines over the four summits, from over two minutes per story in 1987 to less than one minute in 1990, regardless of the summit site. VOA's also declines from the 1987 Washington summit through the 1989 Malta summit, but then jumps back up to a level above that of the 1988 Moscow summit. This provides some support to the hypothesis that "friendly" locations gain more coverage. VOA's two highest mean summit lengths were for the two summits occurring in Washington where its production facilities are located. Radio Moscow's mean story length also consistently declines over the four-summit series, regardless of site, thus offsetting the VOA confirmation.

Further confusion on this score is offered by the remainder of the services. Deutsche Welle's mean story lengths were higher in Washington, where it too has production facilities (as does the BBC, although this same pattern does not apply to its coverage) than in Moscow. Radio Prague's was higher in Moscow than in Malta. Radio Berlin's was higher in Washington (1990) than in Moscow, while Radio Budapest's was nearly identical in Washington (1987) and Malta.

There is thus no consistent confirmation of the hypothesis that coverage intensity is affected by either distance from the country broadcasting or by its characterization as "friendly," "hostile," or "neutral," at least insofar as international radio services are concerned (see Table 8.1).

The patterns followed by the various services can also be seen easily in figures. For both the BBC and Radio Moscow the summit of most significance was the breakthrough 1987 Washington summit. After that, arguably, the Cold War began to wind down (perhaps beginning as early as 1985 with Gorbachev's initiatives), and so each summit became subsequently less interesting. The same pattern affected VOA, with the exception of the 1990 Washington summit, when its mean story length jumped back up, reflecting the ease of coverage it had being back on home turf (see Figure 8.1).

Table 8.1
Mean Story Lengths by Service and Summit

Service	Washington 87	Moscow 88	Malta 89	Washington 90
BBC	2.15	1.59	1.51	0.93
VOA	3.42	2.36	1.06	2.50
Radio Moscow	4.18	3.50	2.34	1.21
Radio Netherlands	2.92	1.44	NA	1.08
Deutsche Welle	2.17	1.28	NA	NA
Radio Berlin	NA	0.81	NA	2.11
Radio Prague	NA	1.56	0.85	NA
Radio Budapest	0.78	NA	0.73	NA

The same general trends affected the remaining services tested here as well. The general trend in stories was reduced length and detail. The only exception to this trend was Radio Berlin, from the 1988 Moscow to the 1990 Washington summit. Again, domestic circumstances (as with VOA) drove Radio Berlin to longer stories in 1990 (see Figure 8.2).

Another telling statistic is the percentage of deviation in mean story length from the mean story length for all services coded for each summit. If one examines the three major world news services (BBC, VOA, and Radio Moscow), for instance, the burden of superpower status clearly shows. VOA and Radio Moscow both reported the summits through the 1989 Malta summit with story lengths significantly in excess of the mean, while the BBC, with greater independence from superpower rivalry, reported these occasions with story lengths under the mean. Radio Moscow's deviation from the mean story length peaked with the Moscow summit, and VOA's with the second Washington summit. Its better than 40% deviation from the mean in 1990, compared to only 11% in 1987, is probably indicative of the difficulties of casting a summit without a centerpiece (thus reporting on an unfocused event), as well as the relative lack of direction from the Bush White House, leading to potentially less well-defined (and thus longer) news stories (see Figure 8.3).

The remaining services all reported stories with mean story lengths significantly under the all-summit mean story length—with one exception, Radio Berlin in 1990. This is yet another indication of the revitalization of Radio Berlin in the midst of the Velvet Revolution, particularly when its -60% deviation in mean story length for the 1988 Moscow summit is considered. Presumably, as Moscow's showpiece socialist ally in 1988, Radio Berlin could have been expected to have easy access to summit principals (at least on the Soviet side) and could have chosen to

Figure 8.1
Means of Story Length by Summit

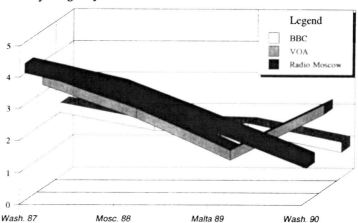

| Wash. 87 | Mosc. 88 | Malta 89 | Wash. 90 |

Figure 8.2
Means of Story Length by Summit for Selected Services

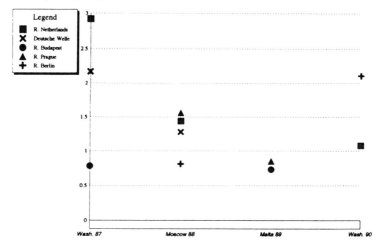

make the most of it in the Soviet capital. It chose not to do so, but came alive before the 1990 summit (see Figure 8.4).

As the four superpower summits occurred, the various radio services had opportunities either to establish a pattern of coverage and stick to it or to alter it to take advantage of changing circumstances. This choice was complicated, however, by the access that reporters had to the actual summit participants or their spokespersons, by the weather (in Malta), and by the changing world context that made some issues irrelevant over the three-year period or elevated new issues to prominence. In

Figure 8.3
Percentage of Story Length Deviation from Mean Story Length by Summit

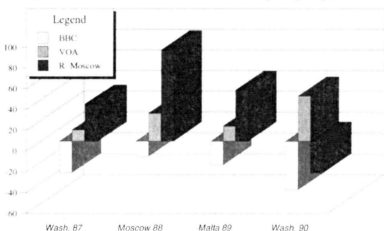

Figure 8.4
Percentage of Story Length Deviation from Mean by Summit for Selected Services

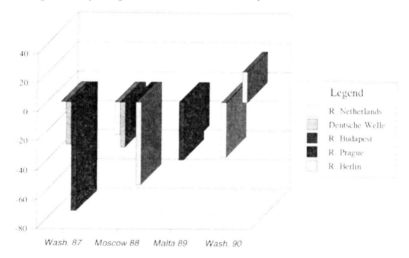

other words, although the news organizations might have had some agenda to follow in reporting summits, their ability to stick to an agenda was compromised both by conditions outside their control and by the efforts of the two countries to direct news coverage in particular directions.

The willingness of news services to seek out information can be seen by examining the primary information sources that news organizations used to report the various summits. Most organizations, as already noted in earlier chapters, seemed to depend on wire services to provide information for their rather brief reports of summit events and decisions. The three principal worldwide news organizations that covered the events, however, VOA, BBC, and Radio Moscow, depended largely on their own news staffs to determine the focus of summit coverage and what information to use to report their stories.

INFORMATION SOURCES FOR THE VOICE OF AMERICA

In 1987 VOA's primary source of information was its own news staff (56% of all stories reported). This means that the reporters cited no external sources of information in their stories, although they may have used them. Twenty percent of stories were based on sound bites, usually statements from Reagan and Gorbachev, and 16% on actualities, that is, on-site live reports of events such as Gorbachev's arrival ceremony at Andrews Air Force Base (see Figure 8.5).

For the remainder of the summits, the coding scheme used was more complex, allowing for more differentiation in sources of information. Reporters cited no source of information in 14% of Moscow summit stories, 21% of Malta stories, and 15% of Washington 1990 stories. In each of these three summits VOA reporters used somewhat different primary sources on which to base their stories. In Moscow (1988), for instance, the most used sources were actualities and sound bites (20% of all summit-related stories), U.S. spokespersons (18%), and Soviet spokespersons and multiple sources (both 11%). News briefings accounted for only 2% of primary sources, and interviews and discussions only 6% (see Figure 8.6).

In Malta, however, the situation was significantly different. Of all stories, 38% were based on news briefings, followed by U.S. spokespersons (16%), and other news media (10%). Actualities and sound bites, Soviet spokespersons, and multiple sources each accounted for only 5% of all sources (see Figure 8.7). This apparent sudden change was the result of reduced access to alternative sources of information at this summit, occasioned both by the weather that "trapped" Presidents Bush and Gorbachev on board ship and by the neutrality of the location, which meant that no special provisions had been made for the press, as was done for all three of the other summits.

In 1990 at the second Washington summit, VOA returned to its previous coverage, depending on actualities and sound bites for 37% of prime sources in stories reported, followed by news briefings (13%) and other news media and multiple sources (10% each). It used U.S. spokespersons as primary sources in 8% of stories, Soviet spokespersons in 2%, and personal observations for 5% (see Figure 8.8).

Figure 8.5
Primary Information Sources, VOA, Washington Summit 1987

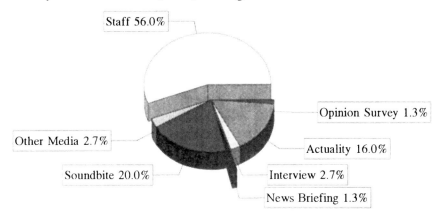

Staff 56.0%
Opinion Survey 1.3%
Other Media 2.7%
Actuality 16.0%
Soundbite 20.0%
Interview 2.7%
News Briefing 1.3%

Figure 8.6
Primary Information Sources, VOA, Moscow Summit 1988

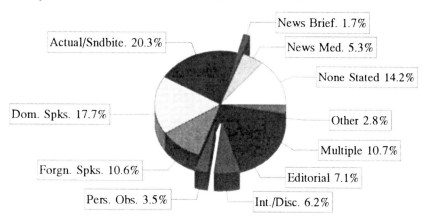

News Brief. 1.7%
News Med. 5.3%
Actual/Sndbite. 20.3%
None Stated 14.2%
Dom. Spks. 17.7%
Other 2.8%
Multiple 10.7%
Forgn. Spks. 10.6%
Editorial 7.1%
Pers. Obs. 3.5%
Int./Disc. 6.2%

Figure 8.7
Primary Information Sources, VOA, Malta Summit 1989

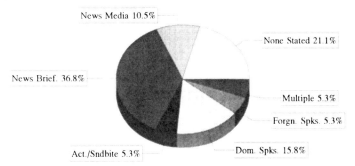

News Media 10.5%
None Stated 21.1%
News Brief. 36.8%
Multiple 5.3%
Forgn. Spks. 5.3%
Act./Sndbite 5.3%
Dom. Spks. 15.8%

Figure 8.8
Primary Information Sources, VOA, Washington Summit 1990

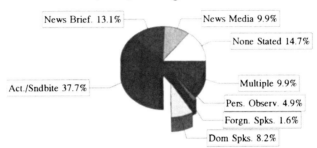

INFORMATION SOURCES FOR THE BBC

For the BBC, the calculations of dependence are made difficult by the nature of the BBC broadcasts. Unlike the VOA, which handled each story as an independent stand-alone report, providing only brief headlines to inaugurate its newscasts, the BBC condensed its correspondents' reports into shorter versions to begin each broadcast. The earlier stories were not merely headlines, however, but were reported as stories, carrying some detail that would be covered more fully later. The result is that, for Washington 1987, 44% of BBC stories were coded as provided by staff, that is, without another cited source. Thirty percent of stories were based on actuality reports (these were the lengthier correspondents' reports), and 26% on other news media. This last result is also occasioned by a BBC peculiarity in its broadcasts—reports of what British newspapers were reporting on important international issues. (Deutsche Welle also carries extensive coverage of newspaper reports, and some smaller services do as well.) The reports from the British press were summit-related, however, if the reports concerned the business of the summit.

Reporting the stories of the British press puts the BBC in a curious position. It cultivates its reputation as an objective, impartial news organization and yet reports on the coverage of British newspapers, which are notoriously partisan. The two-party system that dominates British politics and the nature of parliamentary democracy result in various newspapers being labeled as pro-Tory (Conservative Party) or pro-Labour (Party). Statements of the British prime minister, then, often result in partisan reaction in the press. This reaction is then carried by the BBC, without disclaimer, which arguably compromises its own stance of impartiality.

In Moscow only 13% of stories carried no cited source (the BBC had changed its news approach by then). The newscasts still based over one quarter of stories on other news media (primarily press summaries) and based the same percentage on U.S. and Soviet spokespersons. British spokespersons accounted for 7% of prime sources, and actualities and sound bites for 11%. No stories were based primarily on news briefings.

Like the VOA, the BBC at Malta had to be more dependent on news briefings (44%). Somewhat fewer stories used no cited source (25%), 13% used non-British spokespersons (i. e., U.S. and Soviet), and 12% used multiple sources. Only 6% of stories used actualities and sound bites, the result of the situation at Malta.

By 1990 the BBC had arguably begun to lose some interest in the superpower summits. The Malta summit (the first meeting of Bush and Gorbachev since the inauguration of Bush's presidency) had resulted in little substantive change, and the two presidents had begun to speak in conciliatory tones about East-West relations. A "new world order" and "new thinking" had become the watchwords of change. As the 1990 summit had no centerpiece and no substantial crises had erupted (except arguably the situation in Lithuania), there was little of major interest to independent news organizations. Over one-third of BBC reports for this Washington summit carried no cited source, with 19% citing multiple sources, and 15% each news briefings, actualities and sound bites, and U.S./Soviet spokespersons.

INFORMATION SOURCES FOR RADIO MOSCOW

Radio Moscow, as the most obviously propagandistically organized news organization during this period, used more varied sources to report about the summits. The reports often used man-on-the-street interviews to get reactions to the summit and on U.S.–Soviet relations, usually with an overlay of the Soviet Union's place in the world or its desire for peaceful relations. Using such a technique (unusual in international news coverage) meant that it could show what the "plain folks" in the Soviet Union thought about world events and their country's role in international affairs.[1] It also mixed commentary, editorializing, news analysis, and reporting together into single, often complex, reports. This required that some judgment be exercised to determine what the primary information source was for each story.

For Washington 1987 Radio Moscow staff accounted for one third of all primary information sources (i.e., no other source cited in the report). Other principal sources include U.S. spokespersons (20%), actualities and sound bites (13%), personal opinion or editorializing (10%), other media (usually Soviet newspapers, 9%), and other radio services (7%). Man-on-the-street interviews provided 3% of primary sources, as did press briefings.

At the Moscow summit Soviet spokespersons (who were not used as primary information sources at all in Washington) were relied on in 21%

of stories, followed by multiple sources (18%), U.S. spokespersons and no cited source (14% each), and actualities and sound bites, man-on-the-street interviews, and other media (6% each). Personal opinion and editorializing provided primary sources in only 2% of stories, and interviews and discussions provided sources for 4% of stories.

At Malta press briefings provided primary information for 21% of stories, followed by Soviet spokespersons (19%), other media and multiple sources (13% each), other (9%), and personal observation (6%). As with the other services, actualities and sound bites were infrequently available and provided primary information in only 3% of stories; U.S. spokespersons provided primary information for the same number of stories.

After Malta Radio Moscow began to suffer significant reductions in its budget, and its ability to cover foreign stories was significantly reduced. The problem is clearly evident in the information sources that Radio Moscow used in Washington 1990. It largely had to abandon its own peculiar type of reporting to stretch its available funds. The result: 36% of all stories reported were based on press briefings, and another 19% on press releases. When these two "pseudo-events" are added to the stories in which no cited source was used, nearly three quarters of sources for Radio Moscow reports from the Washington summit are accounted for. In addition, Soviet and American spokespersons each supplied primary information for 10% of stories, and multiple sources informed 6% of stories.

Over the period of this analysis, then, the propaganda content (at least as defined by source selection) of Radio Moscow's news reports declined. This was not necessarily the result, however, of an ideological shift (although the rapprochement of the superpowers probably played a role), but of circumstances beyond its control: first, the oddity of venue and weather in Malta that clearly affected the nature of coverage provided by all the news services, and second, the deteriorating economic conditions of the Soviet Union in the months leading up to the August coup (conditions that have continued to deteriorate since).

COMPARATIVE APPROACHES TO SUMMIT REPORTING

There are a variety of other measures that might have suggested shifting emphases in the coverage of these three radio news services: placement of stories in each newscast, importance attached to the summit (based on position of summit stories in newscast segments), or patterns of reporting over the four analysis periods. However, none of these measures changed significantly for any of these services over the summits studied and thus do not reveal any such shifts.

There are, however, two other principal indicators that suggest changes in these services' approach to summit reporting. The first is the treatment accorded to the summit principals and their countries, and the second is the change in treatment of declared contentious issues between the superpowers, specifically human rights and involvement in regional conflicts.

Two U.S. presidents served during this three-year period: Ronald Reagan and George Bush. Collapsing portrayals into a more general one of treatment of U.S. presidents indicates several interesting (if not startling) trends. Both the BBC and VOA, for instance, followed the same basic pattern in reporting the two summits in which each president participated: the president's participation in his initial summit was reported more favorably than his second. One difference, however, in the two services' approach is that the BBC thought more highly of Bush's initial summit than of Reagan's, while the VOA reversed this pattern.

By the 1987 Washington summit the BBC (along with much of Western Europe) had already formed clear impressions of Reagan and his leadership of the "free world." It is thus not surprising that Bush's handling of the Malta summit (his first) would result in more positive press (assuming no major blunders are committed) than Reagan's fourth summit. (I should note, however, that Radio Netherlands actually reported Reagan's performance in Moscow more positively than it did in Washington, perhaps the result of Reagan going on the offensive on issues clearly of interest to the Dutch, such as human rights.)

VOA's treatment is also explainable. By the 1987 Washington summit the Reagan administration had its rhetoric and expectations well tuned. It had focused the National Security Council on the problem of Reagan's public performance in Reykjavik, a performance that had led to relief in Western Europe that Reagan had failed to strike a deal with Gorbachev (one they considered to be detrimental to their own security interests), and to claims that the summit itself had been a failure (which Gorbachev tried unsuccessfully to counteract).[2]

In Moscow, however, Reagan seemed to want to pick a fight. He had stopped in Helsinki to commemorate the human rights accords signed there, as though to tweak the Soviet nose. He met with dissidents and visited a newly reopened Russian church. Although he gave some praise to the reforms that Gorbachev had spearheaded, his actions might have made his comments—even those at Moscow University where he "explained at length the virtues of democracy in the political, economic, cultural and legal spheres, pointing out the value of freedom as a liberating and creative force for mankind"—seem contradictory (Whelan, 1990, p. 45).[3] His ideological posturing never had gone down well with the American foreign policy establishment, nor with independently minded journalists (including those at VOA). What was the point, particularly since the Soviet Union was changing so rapidly? Who wanted the instability that might accompany demands for even more concessions or refusals to recognize the momentous changes that had already occurred? Reagan's penchant for phraseology without sustained strategic thinking must have worried those who were responsible for presenting America's case to the world. Thus VOA's coverage—reacting to the larger questions that underlay Reagan's new posture—declined as the focus itself began to blur.[4]

George Bush also suffered from blurred focus. Almost the antithesis of Reagan, he was the prisoner of events, rather than someone who seemed to be able to resist them when it suited his purpose. Although his treatment was better at the Malta summit, by the time of Washington 1990 little forward momentum had developed. There was simply less to say.

Radio Moscow's treatment of the two U.S. presidents followed a different path. First, it was less volatile, with coefficients remaining in the same basic range for all four summits. This is itself perhaps a function of being less reactive to events: ideology tends to put things in perspective, as the big picture is always more important than particular events. Predictably, Reagan's conduct at the Moscow summit was treated less charitably than in Washington: He was seen as actively and unfairly provocative. Radio Moscow liked George Bush's performance at both his summits more than either of Reagan's, but he also saw a slight decline in treatment from Malta to Washington.

Radio Netherlands's increased positive treatment of Reagan has already been noted. Radio Netherlands was included in the analysis for only one of Bush's summits (Washington 1990), and he was seen somewhat less favorably there than Reagan had been in either of his summits.

Radio Berlin shows the most startling change of these five services. Only one summit for each president was included, but the coefficient accorded to Bush for Washington 1990 was on the order of six times that of Reagan in Moscow. This is another indicator of the momentous change that Eastern Europe and Radio Berlin itself had undergone in the relaxation of hostilities between East and West in Europe between 1988 and 1990 (see Figure 8.9).

Descriptions of Mikhail Gorbachev also varied, but not necessarily in a direction that would be predicted. Accounts of Gorbachev by the BBC, Radio Netherlands, and Radio Berlin all improved over the time frame of the four summits. Descriptions by VOA and Radio Moscow mirrored each other, improving from Washington 1987 through Malta 1989, but both declining for Washington 1990 (see Figure 8.10).

Figure 8.9
Im[1] Coefficients for Treatment of U.S. Presidents, Selected Services

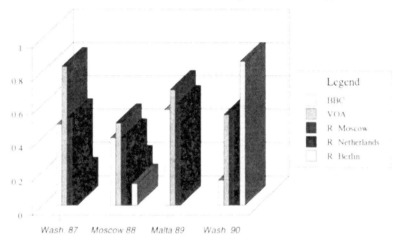

Figure 8.10
Im[1] Coefficients for Treatment of Mikhail Gorbachev, Selected Services

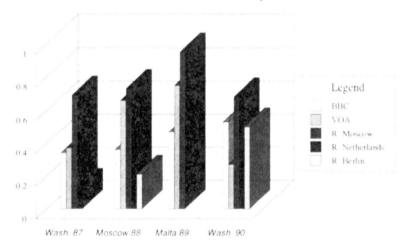

The BBC's coefficients of the two U.S. presidents were consistently higher than those for Gorbachev until the 1990 Washington summit, when its treatment of Gorbachev (still ascending) overtook that of President Bush, whose portrayal by the BBC dropped significantly. VOA's description of Reagan at Washington in 1987 exceeded that for Gorbachev; the presidents' respective depictions were reversed in Moscow. VOA treated Gorbachev at Malta slightly more positively than President Bush, although it reversed its treatments of the two men in Washington 1990. This pattern may be the result of the location of VOA.

Operating in its hometown may have resulted in more positive statements by people who were close to the U.S. administrations and available for interviews. Once outside the country, VOA may have reflected
official statements and press releases as much as other services.[5]

Despite Radio Moscow's pattern—again mirroring VOA's—its portrayals of Gorbachev were consistently higher than those accorded to
the two U.S. presidents. Radio Netherlands described Reagan in 1987
and 1988 more positively than Gorbachev, but Gorbachev more positively, compared to President Bush in 1990. Radio Berlin portrayed
Gorbachev more positively than Reagan in 1988, but Bush more positively than Gorbachev in 1990. Generally speaking, then, these three
services were more positive in their treatment of Reagan than of Bush.
This may have been the result of the fact that, by 1987, the world was
clear about where Reagan stood on East-West issues, while Bush was
never as sharply defined. He may thus have suffered in comparison to
Gorbachev, who by 1989 clearly intended to follow a path of reform
(even if there were retrenchment and equivocation in response to domestic political realities) and thus was held in high esteem by those who
evaluated him as a clear contrast to former Soviet leaders. Gorbachev
suffered somewhat—at least in the eyes of some of the services—during
the second Washington summit, but by then many in the world saw him
as the leader of a decaying superpower on the brink of beggar status.[6]

The three presidents represented countries that were active in the
world. Each of the radio news organizations thus had the opportunity
to portray the actions of their countries as well as their leaders. The
portrayals of action, like those of the presidents, differed, and not in
necessarily predictable ways.

VOA described U.S. actions consistently positively, with only the
portrayal of the Moscow summit dipping slightly under the norm for
its reports. The BBC was also consistently positive, but at a lower
level—except for Malta, when its reports exceeded even those of VOA.
The two summits analyzed for Radio Berlin also resulted in positive
portrayals for U.S. actions, with the Washington 1990 summit levels
doubling those of Moscow 1988.

The two most interesting situations were those of Radio Moscow and
Radio Netherlands. The two Reagan–Gorbachev summits found Radio
Moscow portraying U.S. actions at slightly positive, and then negative,
levels. The portrayal of Malta, however, dropped precipitously, but it
was followed by the most positive portrayal from any of these radio
services during the second Washington summit. Radio Netherlands's
were the reverse mirror image of Radio Moscow's. Whatever one service
saw the United States doing positively, the other saw in precisely
opposite terms (see Figure 8.11).

Figure 8.11
Im^1 Coefficients for Treatment of U.S. Actions, Selected Services

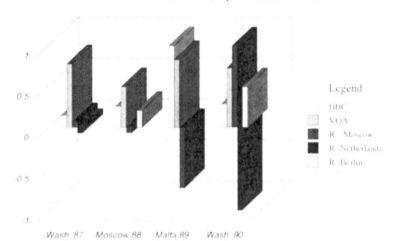

The portrayals of Soviet actions largely reversed those of the United States. VOA portrayed Soviet actions negatively for three of the four summits—with only Malta gaining a zero Im^1 coefficient, although the negativity was at a modest level and improved from Washington 1987 to Washington 1990. The BBC was negative in its depictions through the first three summits (with the level of negativity actually growing for each summit), but it reversed its assessment for the 1990 summit.

Radio Moscow was consistent with what we would expect. All of its portrayals were positive, with the level of positive portrayal rising as each summit occurred. It was almost as though it tried to hold back the collapse of the Soviet Union by rhetoric alone. This statement may be seen as aggrandizing; but judging from the close level of portrayal for the first two summits and then the upward jumps of portrayals for Malta and Washington 1990, it does not seem out of order. The positivity of the portrayals actually increased as the fortunes of the Soviet Union itself declined, with the decline becoming obvious after the end of the Moscow summit.

Radio Netherlands portrayed Soviet actions negatively in coverage of both Washington summits and slightly positively in Moscow. Its negative evaluation of Soviet actions nearly matched in each case its portrayals of U.S. actions. It was either equally objective or equally cynical in all three summits. Similarly, Radio Berlin was positive in its evaluations of Soviet actions at both the Moscow and Washington 1990 summits. Although it had seen U.S. actions highly positively in 1990, it was even more positive about Soviet actions. Perhaps it was responding with relief to the decreased tension and to the role of both countries in relieving the stress in central Europe (see Figure 8.12).

Figure 8.12
Im¹ Coefficients for Treatment of Soviet Actions, Selected Services

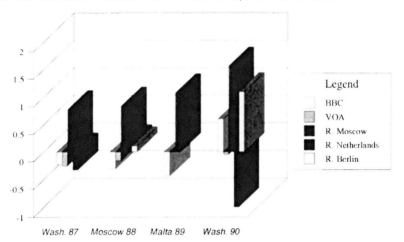

The final comparisons here will concern two clearly contentious issues between the two superpowers—issues that the U.S. National Security Council stated in unequivocal terms. The first was human rights and the role of the Soviet state in denying basic rights to its own citizens. The second was the alleged Soviet role in fomenting regional conflict in one form or another, sometimes referred to as "adventurism."

Although the specific human rights issues were framed differently by the parties to the summits, there is enough similarity to make a level of comparison useful. This analysis will concentrate on the degree to which service reports agreed with the declared U.S. position—that is, the degree to which U.S. efforts to engage in public diplomacy on these issues succeeded.

In 1987 the efforts on human rights were largely successful, with the four services covering that summit (including Radio Moscow) agreeing that human rights were a matter of significance that required agreements to be reached. Of course, as discussed in an earlier chapter, this claim was vague enough to allow Soviet agreement, even if they would disagree on the specifics of what human rights were and what obligations they were under in terms of meeting Western expectations on such issues as free speech and dissent and Jewish emigration. At the Moscow summit the U.S. position was framed more contentiously, as was U.S. rhetoric in Moscow itself. The result: agreement with the U.S. position declined to near zero status among the services analyzed, with VOA registering nearly twice the agreement with the U.S. position as the BBC, and Radio Moscow providing a slightly negative portrayal.

This contentious position was also coded for the two subsequent summits. The result was that, in Malta, both the BBC and Radio Moscow assessed this position in a clearly negative fashion, and the VOA at a neutral level. Then in 1990, Radio Moscow's portrayal dropped to the lowest level for any service at any summit (perhaps the Soviets were tiring of the criticism), and the portrayals of VOA, Radio Netherlands, and Radio Berlin jumped to new highs. The BBC achieved a neutral coefficient for its portrayals.

Why the sudden change in 1990? Even the BBC's neutral portrayal suggested a higher degree of agreement than had its negative portrayal of the U.S. position in 1989, and these changes came after developments in central and eastern Europe indicated a withdrawal of Soviet hegemony and the beginning of the destruction of the Iron Curtain. One clear problem for the Soviets was the crackdown in the Baltic republics. This was of clear concern to European services on both sides of the old ideological divide and undoubtedly resulted in their turnaround to endorse the U.S. condemnation of Soviet human rights violations. Second, the crackdown played to a strong suit in Radio Netherlands's coverage on human rights, which would result in heightened concern in that service. Third, the new freedom apparent in Radio Berlin's coverage allowed it to be more critical than it could have been in earlier years. The overall result: clearly negative coverage of the Soviet position on human rights even in the face of a general move toward liberalized emigration and the increasingly tolerant attitude toward dissent, at least in the Russian Republic itself (see Figure 8.13).

Figure 8.13
Agreement with the U.S. Position on Human Rights, Selected Services

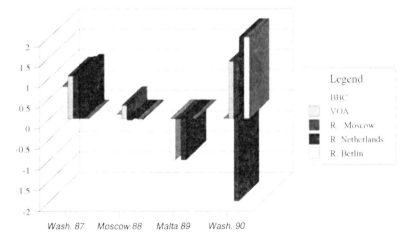

Wash. 87   Moscow 88   Malta 89   Wash. 90

The American claims about Soviet adventurism were also less pointed in 1987. All three Western services were thus able to provide strong endorsements of the U.S. position. Only Radio Moscow demurred, achieving a neutral coefficient. Despite the more pointed American claim in 1988 that the Soviets continued to exacerbate regional conflicts, all services achieved nearly neutral coefficients, with the BBC and VOA slightly positive (endorsing the claim of involvement) and Radio Moscow slightly negative (denying it).

During the last two summits all the services, except VOA and Radio Moscow, were uninterested in the issue of Soviet involvement in regional conflict. Either they considered the point moot as a result of the rapprochement, considering that whatever hot spots remained would quickly achieve resolution (after all, the Soviets were out of Afghanistan), or they were more concerned with the rapidly changing European situation. In Malta VOA was the only service to portray the Soviets as continuing to interfere in regional conflicts, and Radio Moscow the only service to deny it. Six months later in Washington both VOA and Radio Moscow were denying that the Soviets were continuing to be adventuristic in regional conflicts. This claim had truly become a nonissue (see Figure 8.14).

On a variety of levels, then, the various radio services appear to have begun the process of seeing the relations between East and West in less ideological terms. Whatever the particular commitment of these services to journalistic forms, their coverage of issues was more convergent than divergent over this four-year period. Clearly, the domestic political situation of the various countries affected how these services portrayed superpower relations, not necessarily because of interference in, or direction to, the services, but because of the types of statements made by the old adversaries (which were themselves converging) and the actions that backed up these statements. In some cases, new freedom—as in the case of Radio Berlin—allowed it to take a more objective posture.[7] In other cases, the news values of the news organizations, and especially the reactive reporting posture of the West, resulted in convergence simply because the "stuff" of their reporting—claims, statements, press releases, articulated policies, and actions—became less pointed. Lack of criticism by sources led thus to more neutral portrayals by the news organizations.

The evidence from this study does not suggest, then, that efforts to practice public diplomacy by influencing international radio coverage were particularly effective. A variety of mitigating factors influenced the decision-making within the international radio services, many of which were not under their control. The changing historical and rhetorical circumstances that were, in sum, more crucial in defining coverage of the summits are the subjects of the last chapter.

Figure 8.14
Agreement with U.S. Position that Soviets Interfere in Regional Conflicts

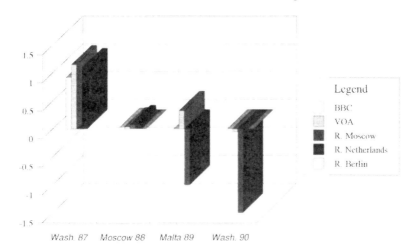

Legend

BBC
VOA
R. Moscow
R. Netherlands
R. Berlin

Wash. 87   Moscow 88   Malta 89   Wash. 90

NOTES

1. "Plain folks" is one of the seven classic propaganda devices originally discussed by Lee and Lee (1939). See Severin and Tankard, 1992, pp. 92, 93.

2. Haslam (1990, p. 168) says that Gorbachev was "somewhat defensive about the results of the Reykjavic summit: 'It was not a failure; it was a breakthrough,' he insisted." The Soviets were surprised, he says (p. 167), that "the collapse of the talks came as welcome news to Western Europe. There the news that the Americans were interested in abolishing nuclear weapons induced the same kind of trauma that Carter's statements on the subject had produced."

3. Whelan (1990, p. 44) calls Reagan's address "A Lesson in American Civics" and notes that it was "in marked contrast to his discourse on the 'evil empire.' " But he did warn in the speech (p. 45) against putting trust in reform that was not "institutionalized, and against seeing peace as merely a 'tactical stage in an enduring conflict,' a cardinal principle in Soviet foreign policy during the days before Gorbachev." His audience was largely impressed, Whelan says (pp. 46–47), and Reagan shed his image as a superficial old-fashioned cold warrior.

4. Gaddis (1992, p. 123) says that Reagan "combined militancy with a surprising degree of operational pragmatism and a shrewd sense of timing." He mixed warnings about Soviet military strength with a strong self-confidence. But,

> while complexity, sophistication, and nuance may be prerequisites for intellectual leadership, they are not necessarily so for political leadership, and can at times actually get in the way. President Reagan generally meant precisely what he said: when he came out in favor of negotiations from strength, or for strategic arms reductions as opposed to limitations, or even for making nuclear weapons ultimately irrelevant and obsolete, he did not do so in the "killer amendment" spirit favored by geopolitical sophisticates on the right; the President may have been conservative but he was never devious. (p. 131)

That may have been what confused the issue insofar as reporters were concerned.

5. These alterations in depiction are reflective of the sort of information available to the services to use in their reports: press releases, statements, interviews, speeches,

briefings, and documents. Although what is reported is necessarily selected, the slant that occurs in the depictions is not necessarily the result of conscious bias (although it can be so), but also of the type of information made available. There were clearly differences in the degree of control that governments exerted over the radio services that reported on these summits during the analysis period.

6. Beschloss and Talbott (1993, p. 220) say that, at the 1990 summit, "Robert Blackwill [of the National Security Council] noted how much less controlled, exacting, and commanding Gorbachev seemed than he had at Malta." Shevardnadze, they say (p. 218), made it clear that Gorbachev's domestic difficulties "made him . . . desperate for the benefits of good relations with the United States." When I visited Moscow in May 1992 the people often described themselves as the beggars of the world, despite the well-publicized problems of other areas of the world. Their perceptions were colored, I think, by recognition of how far they had fallen, not only in material terms but also in terms of stature in the world.

7. What I mean by objective here is not necessarily the Western news value of objectivity, but rather the ability to report free of the ideological control previously exercised by Moscow.

Chapter 9

Symbolic Constructs and Historical Circumstances: Effects on the Global Information Order

Between 1987 and 1990 the world witnessed some of the most remarkable postwar political transformations imaginable, none of which were anticipated by the foreign policy establishments in either East or West. As one participant in a 1985 foreign policy institute meeting, called to draft recommendations for U.S. policy toward the Soviet Union through the next decade, put it,

> After listening to several hours of discussion, . . . I tentatively raised my hand and asked whether we should not be looking ahead to the possibility that the Cold War might someday end: should we not give at least some thought to how we would like it to do so, and to what might then replace it? An embarrassed silence ensued, broken finally by the observation from a highly-respected senior diplomat: "Oh, it hadn't occurred to any of us that it would ever end." (Gaddis, 1992, p. vii)

As another observer remarked (Mason, 1992, p. 44), "neither Western nor Soviet observers expected [Gorbachev] to be a radical reformer," but the changes he introduced, principally *perestroika*, *glasnost*, and radical reform in the Soviet Union, "became impossible to control. . . . Almost imperceptibly, the Soviet system evolved to a point at which the clock could not be turned back" (p. 48). These changes were accompanied by "new thinking" in foreign policy, and the "organic link" between domestic and foreign policy was emphasized (p. 49), resulting in a radical reorientation of Soviet policy toward its East European allies, the West, and developing countries. These changes, in turn, resulted in new proposals for arms control, withdrawal from active participation in "progressive" causes in Nicaragua, Cuba, Angola, and Afghanistan, and the decision to allow the Velvet Revolution to take place in Eastern Europe without intervention.[1]

There is no single date that can be identified as the one when the Cold War ended. Its demise, like its beginning, was evolutionary and resulted from a decision or series of decisions simply to think about adversaries in different linguistic terms than had been used before. The end of the Cold War was, at root, a transformation in symbolic constructs, out of which could spin the more concrete manifestations that would allow old antagonists to claim that change had occurred.

For over forty years both the American and Soviet peoples had been taught to think of one another—or at least of one another's governments—using particular linguistic categories. Even Reagan's decision to characterize the Soviet Union as an "evil empire" was not a truly new departure in American thinking. Although some members of his administration objected to the characterization prior to his use of it in a speech to the National Association of Evangelicals, and he himself retreated from the characterization only a few months later (and claimed not to believe it any more during the 1988 Moscow summit), he was surprised at the strong negative reactions it prompted within the United States (see Oberdorfer, 1991, pp. 22–24; Gaddis, 1992, p. 125; Goldfarb, 1989, p. 186).

This period of history provided a rich ground for dealing with some of the accepted conventions for understanding global journalism practice precisely because of the changing linguistic (and thus symbolic) context within which it functioned. As conceptions of the Cold War were not abandoned on one identifiable date, it was possible to examine reporting during the different analytic time frames to determine how and when linguistic frames shifted in reporting about superpower relations. It was important, as the frames shifted, to determine their effect on the way that reporters characterized the summits, their participants, and respective countries. For instance, Pearce, Johnson, and Branham (1992, p. 169) suggest that the relations between the United States and the Soviet Union were characterized by "moral attenuation," a situation

> when each party in a dispute defines its own position as the embodiment of moral virtue, which is to be perceived or rejected by the other. Both Reagan and Gorbachev located their respective countries' history in a sacred story that showed them as acting with

high moral standards to accomplish historically important purposes in ways that deserve respect. However, each also portrayed the other as not deserving respect. The other's actions were taken as sufficient "proof" of the perfidies of the other's social and political system and history. As a result, each found himself living in a moral order that afforded himself the opportunity for a life of dignity, honor, even valor, but found that this moral quality was disqualified in conversation with the other.

This, of course, is exactly what Reagan suggested in his characterization of the Soviet Union as an evil empire.

The degree of moral attenuation over the course of this four-year period shifted. One obvious shift occurred when Reagan left office and George Bush became the new U.S. president. Bush's rhetorical abilities were fundamentally different from Reagan's (and largely inferior), but even more important than that was the fact that Reagan had actually altered the linguistic frame such that it limited how Bush could characterize Gorbachev and the Soviet Union. Further limits were introduced, of course, by the actual historical conditions that Bush inherited coming into office. The Soviet Union, and particularly Gorbachev, had a new moral mantle that it was necessary to account for: Emigration rules had been eased, more expression was being allowed, involvement in regional conflicts had been reduced, and some liberalization in Eastern Europe had already occurred.

This analysis suggests that it was the shifting of linguistic frames that is most important in understanding news judgments over this period, at least insofar as international radio news about the summits is concerned, and not explanations based on proximity, news traditions, or judgments about the significance of events, or even funding or direction of news organizations by governments wishing to spin stories to their advantage. Certainly, reporters were making judgments, and governments were seeking sympathetic stories. In the final analysis, however, reporters wrote stories within legitimized symbolic contexts and linguistic frames; they wrote for audiences that were cultivated to see the world in particular ways and had to remain within the shifting dimensions of that understanding if these audiences were going to attend to their stories.

To make this point more concrete, take the issue of Mikhail Gorbachev. Who was he? How should Americans see him? Could he be trusted? Was he truly different? Gorbachev said in a television address to the Soviet people in 1987 that "the Soviet leadership is ready for transferring our relations [with the United States] into a channel of mutual understanding, into a channel of constructive interaction in the interests of our countries and the entire world" (Gorbachev, 1990, pp. 88, 89). Margaret Thatcher had said of Gorbachev in 1984, even before he became general secretary, "I like Mr. Gorbachev. We can do business together" (quoted by Oberdorfer, 1991, p. 154). In 1983, on an official visit to Canada as a member of the Politburo, Gorbachev had "more than passed his test as a potential statesman, although there was almost no U.S. newspaper coverage of his visit. The Soviet ambassador to Canada, Alexander Yakovlev, later remarked frostily that it was interesting that Americans didn't want to know anything about a future Soviet leader, since by 1983 Gorbachev was already an obvious potential successor." Geoffrey Pearson, the Canadian ambassador to the Soviet Union, assessing Gorbachev, concluded: "The guy, by all accounts, seems to be extraordinarily capable—well educated, bright, hardworking, and to the extent you can be in these things, personable" (Sheehy, 1990, p. 148).

The American political establishment, however, did not see Gorbachev in such glowing terms. In 1988 George Bush "warned reporters, 'The Cold War isn't over.' . . . [H]e cautioned against a 'euphoric, naively optimistic view about what comes next.' Privately he was disturbed by Reagan's 'sentimentality' about Gorbachev." (Beschloss & Talbott, 1993, p. 9). On January 22, 1989, Brent Scowcroft said, "Gorbachev's foreign policy might be secretly intended to throw the West off its guard and give the Soviet Union time to restore its economy and build new military power before a world Communist offensive" (Beschloss & Talbott, 1993, p. 17). And on February 12, 1989, Bush asked in Kennebunkport, "Suppose, God forbid, that [Gorbachev's] heart stops tomorrow. Is there *perestroika* after Gorbachev?" (Beschloss & Talbott, 1993, p. 22).

The point here is not that Bush was shortsighted in recognizing the changes undertaken by Gorbachev (although arguably that is true), but that he was reflecting a historical predilection among American statesmen to be cautious in the face of momentous change. Other periods of détente had come and gone, and relations with the Soviet Union had returned to the old pattern of Cold War hostility. That Bush was cautious, given the American reading of the history of superpower relations, is no surprise.

Meanwhile, however, other countries, such as Britain and Canada, did see reason to reassess relations with the Soviet Union. Gorbachev, too, was busy attempting to redefine relations with Western Europe.

Given the differing assessments of Gorbachev's leadership or Soviet intentions, then, we should expect that the linguistic frames would shift at different times and to different degrees from one country to another—and that the news product of each country's international radio service would reflect that difference. The changes seen, too, should reflect not only such symbolic shifts, but also the degree of independence from government direction, the a priori news traditions of a given service (including the importance of news to a service's operations and the length of the newscast), and the news budgets and technical capability available to services.

The result of considering such factors is a complex matrix, not all of which is testable. If we limit the discussion here to four services, BBC, VOA, Radio Moscow, and Radio Prague, the differences during the analytic period would be defined as follows. The BBC had (1) a high degree of independence from government direction; (2) long-standing news traditions, definitions of news significant to the success of its World Service, and attention to lengthy and detailed news reports; (3) an adequate news budget (defined by the existence of significant numbers of field reporters or stringers); and (4) a high degree of technical capability as evidenced by live reports from the field. VOA had (1) a degree of independence from government direction (not as high as the BBC, as evidenced by history[2]); (2) long-standing news traditions (including editorials), somewhat less dependence on news than the BBC as the basis for success, and attention to lengthy and detailed news reports; (3) an adequate news budget; and (4) a high degree of technical capability. Radio Moscow had (1) little to no independence from government direction at first, but gradually developed a degree of it; (2) no news traditions (defined as news seen as independent of ideology), and thus no dependence on news as the basis of success, but it did provide long and detailed reports and commentary on events; (3) an inadequate news budget; and (4) limited technical capability. Radio Prague had (1) little to no independence from government direction at first, but rapidly developing independence after the Velvet Revolution; (2) no news traditions or dependence on news, and usually only brief reports and commentary; (3) an inadequate news budget; and (4) very limited technical capability.

As these characterizations suggest, changes were occurring (particularly in the case of Radio Moscow and the Eastern European services) in the matrix itself over this period. In addition to the notations here, the technical capability for collecting and reporting on-site news was increasing for some services (notably BBC and VOA) with the application of satellites to news operations, even while financial constraints prevented their competition (notably Radio Moscow) from following their lead. Even as Radio Moscow began to develop an independent posture over the period of this study, the expense of operationalizing that posture (coupled with the economic difficulties of the Soviet Union) prevented it from fully forming.

When this matrix is superimposed on the shifting linguistic frames already discussed, the result defies easy characterization. Clearly, if we examine the issue of reactive versus contextual stories, however, we can imagine why it would be easier to shift from one of these categories to the other under this schema than to shift from propaganda to objectivity in news reports. Using the Im^1 coefficient as the basis for judging propaganda suggests that, if a service were to seek to become less propagandistic, it would require some new technical capability to be added to its operations so that it could provide different types of reporting. Financial stress could prevent that from occurring; so could the intervention of events themselves, or confusion about what new symbolic constructs are appropriate or how to apply them in a rapidly changing environment, such as the one experienced over the course of this study.

It seems clear, based on studying these summits, that ideology became less important as a linguistic frame to understand the nature of super-power relations. But the intervention of other uncontrollable factors prevented a clear demonstration of that reduced significance. What we are left with is a recognition that summitry per se declined in signifi-cance both because of the decline in Soviet power and the related phenomenon of reduction in superpower rivalries. This alteration was compounded by the difficulties of covering the Malta summit and by the reduced financial capabilities of the East Europeans and Soviets.

The difficulty in shifting symbolic frames can be seen in the choices made about what to emphasize at the summit meetings. If the foci of all the stories filed by all services for each superpower summit meeting are rank ordered by total number of stories filed on each issue, for instance, the result is an amazingly consistent portrayal over the four-year analy-sis period (see Appendix 4). It is no surprise that the events of each summit itself are the primary focus over the period. Neither is it sur-prising that the INF treaty and SDI were the issues of most salience to reporters, given the historic nature of U.S.–Soviet relations in which confrontation over spheres of influence has been the central issue of relations, and arms control the central issue of summits (see, for in-stance, Bialer & Mandelbaum, 1989, p. 93; Haslam, 1990, p. 1; Hough, 1990, p. 235; Paterson, 1992, p. 229; Trofimenko, 1989, pp. 167–180; and White, 1991, pp. 191–197). What is more surprising is the stability of a host of other issues, from the personalities of Soviet and American presidents, the characterizations of the countries they represent and the conflict issues that separate them, to significant weapons issues, encom-passing both nuclear and conventional forces, treaty adherence and verification, and long-range political issues involving the nature of alliances and the ultimate achievement of peace. Few "new" issues interrupted the general focus of the world's radio services. Notable exceptions included the sudden emphasis on the interdependence of states, a major result of Gorbachev's "new thinking" about foreign relations (see, for instance, Lukin, 1989, pp. 163–165), and the issue of the relationship between Nancy Reagan and Raisa Gorbachev during the 1987 Washington and 1988 Moscow summits. Despite the changes in the political complexion of Europe, then, the overall focus of international radio services remained remarkably consistent.

Western services as a group also changed very little over the period. They maintained their basic approach to reporting the news, allowing historical developments to influence their activities but largely maintaining their independence from the dictates of government. None of the services seemed keen to report the summits as the American government wanted it reported. To the extent that U.S. foreign policy objectives, particularly as they were articulated in the talking points, were of "universal" interest, they were usually reported sympathetically; to the extent that they were more parochial (or ideocentric) they were ignored or denied. Most services were content, however, to ignore egregious ideocentric doctrines rather than confront them, for to do so would have appeared nonobjective. Despite the long-standing criticisms of this notion about news reporting, it retains its power as a myth within Western news organizations, one they are loath to repudiate too cavalierly.

Despite such similarities, attending to the news provided by the different news organizations did allow listeners to get distinctive perspectives on these summits. Although listening to VOA would not guarantee a focus on the official American point of view or policy, it would mean opportunity to hear both countries' presidents speak, to follow the day-to-day unfolding of summit events (scheduled and unscheduled), and to hear relatively tightly edited news copy concentrated on subjects whose significance was judged each day. Listening to BBC added a different perspective, press commentary, and extensive correspondents' "eyewitness" reactions to the events as they unfolded. Listening to other European services resulted in slightly different spins, more often than not the result of including domestic press reactions rather than independent broadcast commentary. Listening to Radio Moscow provided more attention to domestic Soviet man-on-the-street reactions, as well as opinions from academics and other U.S.–Soviet experts. Eastern European services likewise provided the same sort of information, but often from a slightly different angle. Once the focus shifts away from major international radio news organizations, the result is largely a rip-and-read approach to the news. Occasionally there are extensive commentaries on these events, but these seem to be more likely the result of having strong ties to one of the two superpowers—and thus having a stake in their relationship—than to a desire to propagandize (even when strong opinions exist).

Perhaps most interesting of all is the extent to which the radio services, either through commentaries, selections from domestic opinion in the press, inclusion of interview guests, or editorials, tried to make sense of the changing relations as they unfolded. As reported in earlier chapters, the various radio services struggled to make sense out of this mutating environment where all of the old categories seemed insufficient to capture reality. Whether they expressed fear, as did the Voice of Free China, hope, as did VOA and Radio Moscow, or even skepticism, as did Radio Netherlands or the press commentaries carried by several different services, each tested the symbolic waters, looking for linguistic categories with which they could express the nature of East-West, capitalist-socialist, or U.S.–Soviet relations.

This analysis suggests that the role of international radio should be more prominent in the debate over the new world information and communication order (NWICO). Surprisingly, given the long history of international radio communication, it is not generally considered in this debate, which has focused on international wire service and domestic news reporting or on the domination of developing countries by Western television, film, and popular recordings. If international radio broadcasting is considered (and now satellite-delivered television news on an international scale), the data suggest that the variety of perspectives available on major international events is substantial. Although the two most prominent international broadcasters operating currently are VOA and the BBC, they are by no means the only services available globally. Radio Moscow still operates globally, albeit on a more limited scale than before; Radio Beijing has increased its operational hours; and several Middle Eastern, European, African, and international commercial and religious broadcasters provide a wealth of perspective on the events of the day. Their existence does not, of course, eliminate reason for concern about news domination, but attention to their activities should either mitigate it to an extent or provide models for increasing involvement by developing countries in such news endeavors.

By 1990 U.S.–Soviet summit meetings had become old hat. This, too, was ironic, given the pressure that Ronald Reagan was under at the end of his second term for being the first U.S. president not to have met with his Soviet counterpart face-to-face. He quickly remedied that situation and became the president who met most frequently with the Soviets. The momentum that he and Mikhail Gorbachev established during Reagan's second term then became the standard for George Bush. His discomfort with the high expectations that came with the winding down of superpower rivalry reintroduced the exasperation that had accompanied Reagan's first term. It seemed that the United States, at least, was uncomfortable with the end of the Cold War. Its conclusion exploded the linguistic categories that had defined the postwar period and left the United States, the Soviet Union, the Soviet Eastern European empire, NATO, and even developing countries scrambling to understand the world without bipolar ideologies.

The new world we now inhabit will eventually develop symbolic constructs sufficient to make sense of it. That will not happen quickly, however, if the time spent birthing this new world is any indication. Although the Berlin Wall came down nearly overnight and its largely peaceful revolution occurred in a matter of months, Eastern Europe still struggles to define itself in the post-Soviet period. And the linguistic categories and symbolic constructs available to assist that endeavor do not yet seem adequate to the task.

NOTES

1. Even as late as 1989 (or at least in a book published in 1989), it made perfect sense to claim that "Gorbachev was not elected to the position of the General Secretary to preside over the dissolution of the Soviet East European empire" (Bialer, 1989, p. 412). George Kennan, one of America's premier foreign policy scholar-diplomats, "told a television interviewer that he was mystified how the Soviet system had produced such a leader" (Oberdorfer, 1991, p. 108).

2. Beschloss and Talbott (1993, p. 51) claim that the Bush White House ordered VOA "to avoid any broadcasts that would inflame the situation" in the Soviet state of Georgia in 1989, but this may have actually been an order to USIA that was never delivered. There is no record of such an order reaching the VOA newsroom. See also Fortner, 1993, p. 221, concerning VOA's "disinformation" broadcast to Libya in 1986.

Treatment Coefficients
for NSC Themes

Im[1] Coefficients, by Service, 1987 Washington Summit

Service	NSC 1	NSC 2	NSC 3	NSC 4	NSC 5
BBC	.37	.79	.92	1.33	1.50
VOA	.90	1.05	1.15	1.00	1.36
Radio Moscow	1.33	1.07	0.00	-0.29	1.40
Radio Netherlands	-0.10	1.13	1.10	2.00	1.55
Deutsche Welle	-0.07	1.00	1.00	NA	1.21
Radio Spain	1.00	1.00	1.00	NA	1.44
Radio Budapest	NA	NA	NA	NA	1.00
Radio Japan	1.22	1.00	1.00	NA	1.75
Voice of Free China	-1.00	NA	NA	NA	-2.00

Im[1] Coefficients, by Service, 1988 Moscow Summit

Service	NSC 1	NSC 2	NSC 3	NSC 4	NSC 5	NSC 6	NSC 7	NSC 8	NSC 9	NSC 10	NSC 11
BBC	0.11	0.03	0.03	0.19	0.03		0.09	0.56	0.29	0.10	0.03
VOA	0.33	0.09	0.12	0.23	0.04	0.07	0.10	0.31	0.10	-0.02	0.04
Radio Moscow	-0.04	0.02	-0.15	-0.20	-0.08	0.14	0.02	0.64	0.10	-0.04	0.07
Radio Nether.		0.05	0.05	0.09			0.09	0.45	-0.05	0.09	0.05
Deutsche Welle	0.06			0.09	0.03	0.03	0.12	0.61	0.09	0.03	0.21
Brussels Calling	-0.11		0.11				0.22	0.33			0.11
Radio Canada	0.17	0.13	0.04	0.22		0.04	0.09	0.43	0.04	0.04	0.08
Voice of Turkey	0.07					0.07	0.07	0.67		0.07	
Radio Cairo	-0.50				-0.50						
Radio Baghdad											
Radio Berlin	-0.03		-0.06			0.03	0.03	0.53	0.06	0.03	0.09
Radio Prague	-0.08	-0.05	-0.03		-0.05	0.06	0.09	0.70	0.09	0.03	0.16
Radio Australia	0.11			0.11				0.75	0.13	0.13	
Radio Japan			-0.33			0.67	0.67	0.67	0.33	0.67	0.67
Radio S. Africa			-0.33								
Radio Havana											

Treatment Coefficients for Summit Principals and Their Countries

Im[1] Coefficients, by Service, 1987 Washington Summit

Service	Gorbachev	Soviet Union	Reagan	United States
BBC	0.34	-0.23	0.48	0.15
VOA	0.37	-0.26	0.83	0.78
Radio Moscow	0.68	0.77	0.52	0.07
Radio Netherlands	0.13	-0.33	0.17	-0.07
Deutsche Welle	0.18	-0.18	0.13	0.00
Radio Spain	NA	0.57	0.00	0.29
Radio Budapest	0.00	0.00	0.00	0.00
Radio Japan	0.00	0.45	0.13	0.29
Voice of Free China	-0.50	-0.67	0.67	0.00

Im[1] Coefficients, by Service, 1988 Moscow Summit

Service	Gorbachev	Soviet Union	Reagan	United States
BBC	0.36	-0.32	0.40	0.26
VOA	0.65	-0.16	0.48	0.50
Radio Moscow	0.73	0.84	0.39	-0.07
Radio Netherlands	0.00	0.15	0.23	0.08
Deutsche Welle	0.32	-0.57	0.09	-0.12
Brussels Calling	0.00	-1.00	-0.50	-0.80
Radio Canada	0.50	0.00	0.53	0.08
Voice of Turkey	0.21	0.14	0.28	0.10
Radio Cairo	0.50	0.50	0.00	NA
Radio Baghdad	0.00	NA	0.00	NA
Radio Berlin	0.20	0.11	0.13	0.21
Radio Prague	0.39	0.75	0.18	-0.23
Radio Australia	0.50	0.00	0.42	NA
Radio Japan	0.50	-0.67	0.00	NA
Radio South Africa	0.50	0.67	0.00	NA
Radio Havana	NA	NA	NA	NA

*NA = not applicable. No stories mentioned the principal tested.

Im[1] Coefficients, by Service, Beijing and Brussels Summits, 1989

Service	Gorbachev	Bush's Policies toward U.S.S.R.	Gorbachev's Policies	NATO	U.S. Actions	Soviet Actions
CSM	-0.09	No stories	0.00	-0.13	0.36	-1.00
VOA	0.00	1.29	-0.50	0.29	0.13	-1.37
BBC	0.41	-0.25	-0.29	-0.20	0.14	0.00
Radio Moscow	0.52	-0.08	1.37	0.09	-0.74	0.25
Radio Austria	1.00	1.00	0.00	1.00	0.00	-0.33
Brussels Calling	-0.14	1.00	-2.00	0.07	-0.86	No stories
Radio Canada	0.18	2.00	1.00	-0.09	-0.25	No stories

Im[1] Coefficients, by Service, 1989 Malta Summit

Service	Gorbachev	Bush	Soviet Actions	U.S. Actions	NATO	The Cold War	End of the Cold War
VOA	.75	.69	0.00	.83	.14	.89	-1.00
BBC	.47	.57	-.44	1.00	0.00	.69	1.33
Radio Moscow	.96	.60	1.07	-.73	.11	.66	.38
Radio Prague	.71	.33	1.50	0.00	.20	.69	0.00
Radio Sofia	0.00	1.00	0.00	-1.00	-2.00	.33	0.00
Radio Budapest	.33	.29	.67	.50	-.33	.50	0.00
Radio Beijing	0.00	.17	0.00	0.00	-1.00	.75	-1.00
Radio Bucharest	.33	0.00	-2.00	0.00	2.00	.43	0.00

Im[1] Coefficients, by Service, 1990 Washington Summit

Subject	VOA	BBC	Radio Moscow	Radio Netherlands	Radio Berlin
New Thinking	1.00	2.00	1.14	1.00	1.50
Soviet Adventurism	-0.50	None	-1.50	None	None
Conventional Weapons Reduction	1.00	1.00	1.00	.50	1.00
NATO Actions	.57	1.00	.80	.50	-0.44
U.S. Actions	.73	.29	1.00	-1.00	.50
Warsaw Pact Actions	1.00	None	1.25	None	1.40
Soviet Actions	-0.05	.60	1.56	-1.00	1.09
Gorbachev's Policies	1.33	2.00	1.73	.67	.83
Gorbachev	.27	.53	.68	.43	.69
Bush	.54	.15	.57	.14	.86
New World Order	1.71	1.50	1.67	None	1.14
End of Cold War	1.75	1.75	1.67	1.50	2.00
Soviets Violate Human Rights	1.40	None	-2.00	2.00	-2.00

Percentage of Stories Devoted to Selected Summit Issues, by Summit and Service

Washington, 1987

Service	Summit Events	INF Issues	INF Ratification	SDI
VOA	20.00	26.67	Not applicable	2.67
BBC	43.47	26.09	Not applicable	4.35
Radio Moscow	20.00	25.71	Not applicable	0.00
West European Services	29.82	21.05	Not applicable	3.51
East European Services	50.00	0.00	Not applicable	0.00
Middle Eastern Services	None Coded	None Coded	Not applicable	None Coded
Other Services	25.00	25.00	Not applicable	6.25

Moscow, 1988

Service	Summit Events	INF Issues	INF Ratification	SDI
VOA	26.55	0.88	6.19	0.00
BBC	47.14	0.00	4.29	1.43
Radio Moscow	24.60	5.56	7.14	2.38
West European Services	44.64	3.57	10.71	0.00
East European Services	45.59	11.76	16.18	1.47
Middle Eastern Services	55.00	0.00	10.00	0.00
Other Services	68.75	6.25	6.25	0.00

Malta, 1989

Service	Summit Events	INF Issues	INF Ratification	SDI
VOA	4.17	0.00	Not applicable	0.00
BBC	9.52	0.00	Not applicable	4.76
Radio Moscow	8.82	5.88	Not applicable	5.88
East European Services	21.89	0.00	Not applicable	0.00

No West European, Middle Eastern, or "other" services were coded for the Malta summit.

Washington, 1990

Service	Summit Events	INF Issues	INF Ratification	SDI
VOA	24.19	0.00	Not applicable	0.00
BBC	21.43	0.00	Not applicable	0.00
Radio Moscow	41.18	0.00	Not applicable	0.00
West European Services	40.00	0.00	Not applicable	0.00
East European Services	29.63	0.00	Not applicable	0.00

No Middle Eastern or "other" services were coded for the Washington summit.

Rank Order of Principal Superpower Summit Issues, by Summit and Focus, Based on the Total Number of Stories Filed by All Services Coded

Summit Issues	Washington 1987	Moscow 1988	Malta 1989	Washington 1990
Summit Events	1	1	1	1
INF Treaty	2	3	2	2
SDI	3	4	3	3
INF Ratification		2		

Personality	Washington 1987	Moscow 1988	Malta 1989	Washington 1990
Gorbachev	4	5	5	5
Reagan	5	6		
Presidents' Wives	8	9		36
Bush			6	6
United States	6	7	7	7
Soviet Union	7	8	8	8
Soviet Jewish Emigration	9	10		
Soviet Flexibility			9	9
Interdependence of States			4	4
Bush and Gorbachev Relations			22	
U.S. Military-Industrial Complex			23	23
What U.S. Wants from U.S.S.R.			24	24

Conflict Issues	Washington 1987	Moscow 1988	Malta 1989	Washington 1990
Human Rights	10	11	11	11
Arms Control Violations	11			
Regional Conflict	12	12	12	12
German Reunification				32
Baltic Republics				31

Weapons Issues	Washington 1987	Moscow 1988	Malta 1989	Washington 1990
Strategic Weapons Reduction	14	13	13	13
Conventional Forces Reduction	15	14	14	14
Treaty Adherence	16	15	15	15
INF Verification and Inspection		22		
Chemical Weapons				34
START Treaty				22

Long-Term Political Issues	Washington 1987	Moscow 1988	Malta 1989	Washington 1990
Achieving Peace	17	16	16	16
NATO/European Defense	18	17	17	17
U.S.–Allies Relations	19	18	18	18
Soviet-Allies Relations	20	19	19	19
U.S.–Soviet Relations	21	20	20	20
Disarmament		23		
W. Europe– E. Europe Relations		24		
"Third World"			21	21
U.S.–Soviet Trade			25	25
Glasnost			26	26
Perestroika			27	27
End of the Cold War			28	28
The "New World Order"			29	29
"New Thinking"				30
Soviet-Korean Relations				33
Soviet Economy				35

References

Acheson, D. 1969. *Present at the Creation: My Years in the State Department*. New York: W. W. Norton & Company.

Alexandre, L. 1988. *The Voice of America: From Detente to the Reagan Doctrine*. Norwood, NJ: Ablex Publishing Corporation.

Armitage, J. A. 1987. "Commentary." In J. W. McDonald, Jr. (Ed.). *U.S.–Soviet Summitry: Roosevelt through Carter*. Washington, DC: Foreign Service Institute, U.S. Department of State. 46–51.

Article 19. 1988. *Information, Freedom and Censorship*. London: Longman.

Barrington, J. N.d. *Lord Haw Haw of Zeesen*. London: Hutchinson & Co.

BBC. N.d. *Guidelines for Factual Programmes*. London: BBC.

BBC. N.d. *Producers Guidelines*. London: BBC.

Bell, C. 1989. *The Reagan Paradox: U.S. Foreign Policy in the 1980s*. New Brunswick, NJ: Rutgers University Press.

Benjamin, D. 1989. "State of Siege." *Time*. 29 May, 36.

Berman, L. & Jentleson, B. W. 1991. "Bush and the Post-War World: New Challenges for American Leadership." In C. Campbell & B. A. Rockman (Eds.). *The Bush Presidency: First Appraisals*. Chatham, NJ: Chatham House Publishers, Inc. 93–128.

Beschloss, M. R. & Talbott, S. 1993. *At the Highest Levels: The Inside Story of the End of the Cold War*. Boston: Little, Brown and Company.

Bialer, S. 1989. "Central and Eastern Europe, *Perestroika*, and the Future of the Cold War." In W. E. Griffith (Ed.). *Central and Eastern Europe: The Opening Curtain?* Boulder, CO: Westview Press. 401–438.

Bialer, S. & Mandelbaum, M. 1989. *The Global Rivals*. New York: Vintage.

Birnbaum, J. & Chua-Eoan, H. G. 1989. "Despair and Death in a Beijing Square." *Time*. 12 June, 24.

Boorstin, D. 1964. *The Image: A Guide to Pseudo-Events in America*. New York: Harper and Row.

Browne, D. R. 1982. *International Radio Broadcasting: The Limits of the Limitless Medium.* New York: Praeger.

Burlatsky, F. 1987. *From Geneva to Reykjavik.* Moscow: Progress Publishers.

Campbell, C. & Rockman, B. A. 1991. *The Bush Presidency: First Appraisals.* Chatham, NJ: Chatham House Publishers, Inc.

Church, G. J. 1990. "The Last Picture Show." *Time.* 11 June, 12–16.

Churchill, W. S. 1953. *Triumph and Tragedy.* Vol. 6, *The Second World War.* Boston: Houghton Mifflin Company.

Cole, J. A. 1964. *Lord Haw-Haw: The Full Story of William Joyce.* London: Faber and Faber.

Commission on Freedom of the Press. 1947. *A Free and Responsible Press.* Chicago: University of Chicago Press.

Dahlgren, P. & Chakrapani, S. 1982. "The Third World on TV News: Western Ways of Seeing the 'Other.' " In W. C. Adams (Ed.). *Television Coverage of International Affairs.* Norwood, NJ: Ablex Publishing Corporation. 45–65.

Donnelly, D. 1965. *Struggle for the World: The Cold War and Its Causes.* New York: St. Martin's Press.

Duffy, M. & Goodgame, D. 1992. *Marching in Place: The Status Quo Presidency of George Bush.* New York: Simon & Schuster.

Eagleton, T. 1991. *Ideology: An Introduction.* London: Verso.

Edelman, M. 1964. *The Symbolic Uses of Politics.* Urbana, IL: University of Illinois Press.

Elder, C. & Cobb, R. 1983. *The Political Uses of Symbols.* New York: Longman.

Ellul, J. 1965. *Propaganda: The Formation of Men's Attitudes.* Reprint. New York: Vintage Books, 1973.

Erickson, P. D. 1985. *Reagan Speaks: The Making of an American Myth.* New York: New York University Press.

"Evil Empire." 1991. Associated Press Report. 23 November.

Feinsilber, M. 1991. "Cultural Revolution." Associated Press Report. 10 March.

Fejes, F. 1986. *Imperialism, Media and the Good Neighbor: New Deal Foreign Policy and United States Shortwave Broadcasting to Latin America.* Norwood, NJ: Ablex Publishing Corporation.

Fishman, M. 1980. *Manufacturing the News.* Austin, TX: University of Texas Press.

Fontaine, A. 1970. *History of the Cold War: From the October Revolution to the Korean War, 1917–1950.* New York: Vintage Books.

Fortner, R. S. 1978. "Persuasion, Christianity, and Ethics: A Cultural Perspective." *Christian Scholar's Review.* 7. 153–164.

Fortner, R. S. 1991. "Analysis of VOA Broadcasting." In *Analysis of Voice of America Broadcasts to the Middle East during the Persian Gulf Crisis.* Washington, DC: Center for Strategic and International Studies. 3–56.

Fortner, R. S. 1993. *International Communication: History, Conflict, and Control in the Global Metropolis.* Belmont, CA: Wadsworth Publishing Company.

Frederick, H. H. 1986. *Cuban-American Radio Wars: Ideology in International Telecommunications.* Norwood, NJ: Ablex Publishing Corporation.

Gaddis, J. L. 1972. *The United States and the Origins of the Cold War, 1941–1947.* New York: Columbia University Press.

Gaddis, J. L. 1992. *The United States and the End of the Cold War: Implications, Reconsiderations, Provocations.* New York: Oxford University Press.

Gans, H. J. 1979. *Deciding What's News: A Study of CBS Evening News, NBC Nightly News, Newsweek and Time.* New York: Vintage Books.

Gardner, L. C., Schlesinger, A., Jr. & Morgenthau, H. J. 1970. *The Origins of the Cold War.* Waltham, MA: Ginn and Company.

Gergen, D. R. 1991. "Diplomacy in a Television Age." In S. Serfaty (Ed.). *The Media and Foreign Policy*. New York: St. Martin's Press. 47–63.

Gist: US-Soviet Relations. 1991. *US Department of State Dispatch*. 12 August, 599– 606.

Goldfarb, J. 1989. *Beyond Glasnost: The Post-Totalitarian Mind*. Chicago: University of Chicago Press.

Goodnight, G. T. 1992. "Rhetoric, Legitimation, and the End of the Cold War: Ronald Reagan at the Moscow Summit, 1988." In M. Weiler & W. B. Pearce (Eds.). *Reagan and Public Discourse in America*. Tuscaloosa: University of Alabama Press. 43–71.

Gorbachev, M. 1990. *Perestroika and Soviet-American Relations*. Madison, CT: Sphinx Press, Inc.

Great Soviet Encyclopedia. 1973. Third edition (translated). New York: Macmillan.

Green, F. 1988. *American Propaganda Abroad: From Benjamin Franklin to Ronald Reagan*. New York: Hippocrene Books.

Hachten, W. A. 1987. *The World News Prism: Changing Media, Clashing Ideologies*. Second edition. Ames: Iowa State University Press.

Hale, J. 1975. *Radio Power: Propaganda and International Broadcasting*. Philadelphia, PA: Temple University Press.

Harrison, M. 1986. "A Window on the World? Foreign Coverage by a British Radio Current Affairs Program." *Critical Studies in Mass Communication*. 3. 409–428.

Haslam, J. 1990. *The Soviet Union and the Politics of Nuclear Weapons in Europe, 1969–87*. Ithaca, NY: Cornell University Press.

Hawthorn, J. 1987. "Preface." In J. Hawthorn (Ed.). *Propaganda, Persuasion and Polemic*. London: Edward Arnold. vii–xiv.

Hinckley, B. 1990. *The Symbolic Presidency: How Presidents Portray Themselves*. New York: Routledge.

Hough, J. 1990. *Russia and the West: Gorbachev and the Politics of Reform*. Second edition. New York: Touchstone.

Hulteng, J. L. 1979. *The News Media: What Makes Them Tick?* Englewood Cliffs, NJ: Prentice-Hall, Inc.

Hur, K. K. 1984. "A Critical Analysis of International News Flow Research." *Critical Studies in Mass Communication*. 1. 365–378.

Ignatius, D. 1988. "Reagan's Foreign Policy and the Rejection of Diplomacy." In S. Blumenthal & T. B. Edsall (Eds.). *The Reagan Legacy*. New York: Pantheon Books. 173–212.

Iyengar, S. & Kinder, D. R. 1987. *News That Matters: Television and American Opinion*. Chicago: University of Chicago Press.

Janis, J. & Fadner, R. 1949. "The Coefficient of Imbalance." In H. Lasswell, N. Leites & Assoc. (Eds.). *Language of Politics*. Studies in Quantitative Semantics. Cambridge, MA: MIT Press. 153–169.

Jensen, K. M. (Ed.). 1991. *Origins of the Cold War: The Novikov, Kennan, and Roberts "Long Telegrams" of 1946*. Washington, DC: United States Institute of Peace.

Jowett, G. S. & O'Donnell, V. 1986. *Propaganda and Persuasion*. Beverly Hills: Sage Publications.

Kaiser, R. G. 1991. "Gorbachev: Triumph and Failure." *Foreign Affairs*. 70 (Spring). 160–174.

Kennan, G. F. 1947. [Writing as "X"] "The Sources of Soviet Conduct." *Foreign Affairs*. 25 (July). 566–582.

Kennan, G. F. 1967. *Memoirs, 1925–1950*. Boston: Little, Brown & Company.

Korotich, V. & Porter, C. (Eds.). 1990. *The New Soviet Journalism: The Best of the Soviet Weekly Ogonyok*. Boston: Beacon Press.

REFERENCES

LaFeber, W. 1985. *America, Russia, and the Cold War 1945–1984*. New York: Alfred A. Knopf.

Laird, R. F. 1989. "Introduction: The Changing Soviet Environment." In S. L. Clark (Ed.). *Gorbachev's Agenda: Changes in Soviet Domestic and Foreign Policy*. Boulder, CO: Westview Press.

Larson, J. F. 1982. "International Affairs Coverage of US Evening Network News, 1972–1979." In W. C. Adams (Ed.). *Television Coverage of International Affairs*. Norwood, NJ: Ablex Publishing Corporation. 15–41.

Lee, A. M. & Lee, E. B. (Eds.). 1939. *The Fine Art of Propaganda: A Study of Father Coughlin's Speeches*. New York: Harcourt, Brace, and Company.

Lewin, R. 1982. *The Other Ultra: Codes, Ciphers and the Defeat of Japan*. London: Hutchinson.

Lindahl, R. 1978. *Broadcasting across Borders: A Study on the Role of Propaganda in External Broadcasts*. Göteborg Studies in Politics 8. Lund, Sweden: C. W. K. Gleerup.

Lukin, V. P. 1989. "Soviet View." In G. T. Allison & W. L. Ury (Eds.). *Windows of Opportunity: From Cold War to Peaceful Competition in U.S.–Soviet Relations*. Cambridge, MA: Ballinger Publishing Company. 163–165.

MacBride, S. 1984. *Many Voices, One World*. Abridged edition. Paris: Unesco.

Manet, E. G. 1988. *The Hidden War of Information*. Alexandre, L. (Trans.). Norwood, NJ: Ablex Publishing Corporation.

Mansell, G. 1982. *Let Truth Be Told: 50 Years of BBC External Broadcasting*. London: Weidenfeld and Nicolson.

Masmoudi, M. 1981. "The New World Information Order." In J. Richstad & M. H. Anderson (Eds.). *Crisis in International News: Policies and Prospects*. New York: Columbia University Press. 77–96.

Mason, D. S. 1992. *Revolution in East-Central Europe: The Rise and Fall of Communism and the Cold War*. Boulder, CO: Westview Press.

McLeod, D. M., Viswanath, K. & Yoon, Y. 1987. "A Content Analysis of Radio Moscow and the Voice of America: A Test of the 'Sphere of Influence' and the 'Mirror-Image' Hypothesis." Paper presented at the annual conference of the International Communication Association, Montreal, 21–25 May.

Mehta, D. S. 1987. *Mass Media in the USSR*. Moscow: Progress Publishers.

Merrill, J. C. (Ed.). 1991. *Global Journalism: Survey of International Communication*. Second edition. New York: Longman.

Morales, W. Q. 1982. "Revolutions, Earthquakes, and Latin America: The Networks Look at Allende's Chile and Somoza's Nicaragua." In W. C. Adams (Ed.). *Television Coverage of International Affairs*. Norwood, NJ: Ablex Publishing Corporation. 79–113.

Morgenthau, H. J. 1985. Revised by K. W. Thompson. *Politics among Nations: The Struggle for Power and Peace*. Sixth edition. New York: McGraw-Hill, Inc.

Mytton, G. & Forrester, C. 1988. "Audiences for International Radio Broadcasts." *European Journal of Communication*. 3. 457–481.

"Nation." 1989. *Time*. 13 November, 32.

"Nation." 1989. *Time*. 27 November, 20.

Nevitt, B. 1982. *The Communication Ecology: Re-presentation versus Replica*. Toronto: Butterworths.

Oberdorfer, D. 1991. *The Turn: From the Cold War to a New Era*. New York: Poseidon Press.

Paraschos, M. & Rutherford, B. 1985. "Network News Coverage of Invasion of Lebanon by Israeli [sic] in 1982." *Journalism Quarterly*. 62. 457–464.

Paterson, T. G. (Ed.). 1990. *The Origins of the Cold War.* Second edition. Lexington, MA: D. C. Heath.

Paterson, T. G. 1992. *On Every Front: The Making and Unmaking of the Cold War.* Revised edition. New York: W. W. Norton & Company.

Pearce, W. B., Johnson, D. K. & Branham, R. J. 1992. "A Rhetorical Ambush at Reykjavik: A Case Study of the Transformation of Discourse." In M. Weiler & W. B. Pearce (Eds.). *Reagan and Public Discourse in America.* Tuscaloosa, AL: University of Alabama Press. 163–182.

Pratkanis, A. & Aronson, E. 1991. *Age of Propaganda: The Everyday Use and Abuse of Persuasion.* New York: W. H. Freeman and Company.

Robins, K., Webster, F. & Pickering, M. 1987. "Propaganda, Information and Social Control." In J. Hawthorn (Ed.). *Propaganda, Persuasion and Polemic.* London: Edward Arnold. 1–18.

Rockman, B. A. 1991. "The Leadership Style of George Bush." In C. Campbell & B. A. Rockman (Eds.). *The Bush Presidency: First Appraisals.* Chatham, NJ: Chatham House Publishers, Inc. 1–36.

Rolo, C. J. 1942. *Radio Goes to War: The "Fourth Front."* New York: G. P. Putnam's Sons.

Schillinger, E. & Jenswold, J. 1987. "Three Olympiads: A Comparison of *Pravda* and the Washington *Post*." *Journalism Quarterly.* 64. 826–833.

Seabury, P. 1976. *The Rise and Decline of the Cold War.* New York: Basic Books.

Severin, W. J. & Tankard, J. W., Jr. 1992. *Communication Theories: Origins, Methods, and Uses in the Mass Media.* Third edition. New York: Longman.

Sharlet, R. 1989. "Human Rights and Civil Society in Eastern Europe." In W. E. Griffith (Ed.). *Central and Eastern Europe: The Opening Curtain?* Boulder, CO: Westview Press. 156–177.

Sheehy, G. 1990. *The Man Who Changed the World: The Lives of Mikhail S. Gorbachev.* New York: Harper Perennial.

Short, K. R. M. (Ed.). 1983. *Film & Radio Propaganda in World War II.* London: Croom Helm.

Short, K. R. M. (Ed.). 1986. *Western Broadcasting over the Iron Curtain.* New York: St. Martin's Press.

Shulman, H. C. 1990. *The Voice of America: Propaganda and Democracy, 1941–1945.* Madison: University of Wisconsin Press.

Siebert, F. S., Peterson, T. & Schramm, W. 1956. *Four Theories of the Press.* Champaign: University of Illinois Press.

Soley, L. C. 1989. *Radio Warfare: OSS and CIA Subversive Propaganda.* New York: Praeger.

Sussman, L. R. 1988. "Communications: Openness and Censorship." In R. D. Gastil (Ed.). *Freedom in the World: Political Rights & Civil Liberties.* New York: Freedom House. 129–155.

Thompson, K. W. 1981. *Cold War Theories. Volume 1: World Polarization, 1943–1953.* Baton Rouge: University of Louisiana Press.

Trofimenko, H. 1989. "The Emergence of Mutual Security: Its Objective Basis." In G. T. Allison & W. L. Ury (Eds.). *Windows of Opportunity: From Cold War to Peaceful Competition in U.S.–Soviet Relations.* Cambridge, MA: Ballinger Publishing Company. 167–180.

United States Advisory Commission on Public Diplomacy. 1988. *Public Diplomacy: Lessons from the Washington Summit: A Report.* Washington, DC: The Commission.

USSR-USA Summit. 1988. Moscow: no publisher.

van Borcke, A. 1989. "Gorbachev's *Perestroika*: Can the Soviet System Be Reformed?" In S. L. Clark (Ed.). *Gorbachev's Agenda: Changes in Soviet Domestic and Foreign Policy*. Boulder, CO: Westview Press. 13–56.

Van Oudenaren, J. 1989. "The Soviet Union and Eastern Europe: New Prospects and Old Dilemmas." In W. E. Griffith (Ed.). *Central and Eastern Europe: The Opening Curtain?* Boulder, CO: Westview Press. 102–129.

Wasburn, P. C. 1992. *Broadcasting Propaganda: International Radio Broadcasting and the Construction of Political Reality*. Praeger Series in Political Communication. Westport, CT: Praeger.

West, N. 1986. *GCHQ: The Secret Wireless War 1900–86*. London: Weidenfeld and Nicolson.

Whelan, J. G. 1990. *The Moscow Summit, 1988: Reagan and Gorbachev in Negotiation*. Boulder, CO: Westview Press.

White, S. 1991. *Gorbachev and After*. Cambridge: Cambridge University Press.

Whitton, J. B. & Herz, J. H. 1942. "Radio in International Politics." In H. L. Childs & J. B. Whitton (Eds.). *Propaganda by Short Wave*. Princeton: Princeton University Press. 3–48.

"Wick, Worldnet and the War of Ideas." 1986. *Broadcasting*. 111. 3 November, 80.

Wilhelm, D. 1990. *Global Communications and Political Power*. New Brunswick, NJ: Transaction.

Wilson, T. A. 1969. *The First Summit: Roosevelt and Churchill at Placentia Bay 1941*. London: Macdonald.

Winterbotham, F. W. 1974. *The Ultra Secret*. London: Weidenfeld and Nicolson.

Index

About the Author

ROBERT S. FORTNER is professor of Communication Arts and Sciences at Calvin College in Grand Rapids, Michigan. He has also written *International Communication: History, Conflict, and Control of the Global Metropolis* (1993). He has taught at Northwestern University, Drake University, the State University of New York at Plattsburgh, and The George Washington University, where he was founding chair of the Department of Communication. He has done international research for the BBC, VOA, the Center for Strategic and International Studies, and has served as a panel member on VOA satellite broadcasting for the National Research Council.

Lightning Source UK Ltd.
Milton Keynes UK
UKOW051114281012

201311UK00007B/21/P